REV. LEMUEL HAYNES, A.M.

Sincerely yours

Lemuel Haynes

Black Preacher to White America

THE COLLECTED WRITINGS OF LEMUEL HAYNES, 1774-1833

Edited by Richard Newman

INTRODUCTION BY HELEN MACLAM

PREFACE BY MECHAL SOBEL

CARLSON
Publishing Inc

BROOKLYN, NEW YORK 1990

Library of Congress Cataloging-in-Publication Data

Haynes, Lemuel, 1753-1833.
    Black Preacher to white America : the collected writings of Lemuel
Haynes, 1774-1833 / edited by Richard Newman ; introduction by Helen
MacLam ; preface by Mechal Sobel.
        p.   cm.
    Includes bibliographical references.
    ISBN 0-926019-24-4
    1. Theology.   I. Newman, Richard, 1930-   . II. Title.
BR50.H36   1989
230'.58—dc20   89-48246

Typographic design: Julian Waters

Typeface: Bitstream ITC Galliard

Printed on acid-free, 250-year-life paper.

Manufactured in the United States of America.

The frontispiece is from *Sketches of the Life and Character of the Rev. Lemuel
Haynes, A.M.*, by Timothy Mather Cooley, New York: Harper, 1837.

For

Dorothy Porter Wesley

Contents

Foreword

MECHAL SOBEL

Over the last years the work of Richard Newman has rescued the history of Lemuel Haynes from the strange limbo it had fallen into and now his editing of the known writings and reassessment of Haynes' work can well be seen as a landmark—an important recognition of an African-American pioneer.

While this recognition is overdue, it is only within the last decade that we have learned of his extremely important early manuscript essay, "Liberty Further Extended," and I harbor the hope that this publication does not mark the closing of his canon, but that in its wake, other significant works may surface as well. The writing of that extraordinary essay, which maintained "That an African, or, in other terms, that a Negro . . . has an undeniable right to his Liberty . . .," was broken off in mid-sentence, just after a call to "Let the oppressed go free. . . ." In a sense this can be seen as symbolizing Haynes' life: He broke off from his earliest direction, fighting for liberty in the Revolution and in the war of words, and chose to become what he later called "a spiritual watchman." He amply fulfilled the ideal image he had of such a figure, exhibiting "wisdom," "prudence," "patience," "vigilance," but above all "courage and fortitude."

Haynes was a pioneer on the Vermont frontier, a pioneer who broke new ground not in a physical sense nor in a theoretical one, but through the life he led, becoming a teacher, minister, and "father" to generations of white Congregationalists. In this role, he proclaimed highly controversial political and theological positions and did not shirk from very difficult issues facing American society as a whole, such as calling the War of 1812 an "unjust war" that should not be participated in!

There were only some 270 blacks in Vermont in 1790, less than one half of one percent of the population, and while a few were in his immediate area, Haynes lived his life in a mostly white world. But he knew he was perceived as an "African" and he made his views on race and equality known. Moreover, his life's work, his accomplishments, were, I believe, his most important statement, and perhaps they were the proper finish to his early essay. In testing himself and his society he proved his own abilities and expanded previously assumed societal limits. In achieving personal recognition, he achieved recognition for African-American rights and liberties as well.

But his life-work was not without serious conflict, and racial tensions may well have played a role in his dismissal from the West Rutland pulpit he held for thirty years. This turn of events did not embitter him, and he continued to dedicate himself to New England white congregations until his death, concerned, as he always was, with "futurity," and apparently always maintaining his early belief that "It hath pleased god to make of one Blood all nations of men, for to dwell upon the face of the Earth. Acts 17, 26."

University of Haifa

The Paradox of Lemuel Haynes

RICHARD NEWMAN

Lemuel Haynes, as Professor James Melvin Washington has pointed out, defies easy classification. Haynes was the illegitimate child of a black father and white mother. He was a plowboy who composed poetry. He was a foot soldier in a freedom revolution that denied liberty to those most in need of it. He was an intellectual and wit on a rude frontier. He was a Calvinist in the deist and rationalist environment of Vermont. He was a Federalist when the country was turning to Jeffersonian Republicanism. He lived all his life in the white world, but his detractors did not hesitate to call him "nigger."

Professor Washington suggests Haynes' "very duality allowed him to see and experience the double-meanings of 'America.' " While Washington is referring specifically to the ambiguities of Haynes and race, paradox is a concept that goes some distance as a means to understanding much of Haynes' long and unusual life.

The facts of Lemuel Haynes' birth remain obscure. His mother was probably a Scottish servant in West Hartford, Connecticut, named Alice Fitch. But she may have been a woman from a prominent Hartford family named Goodwin. His father was probably a local slave of "unmingled African extraction." But he may have been a black waiter in a Hartford hotel. What is clear is that neither parent wanted anything to do with the unwelcome result of their liaison across racial and class lines.

Brought up as an indentured servant in a pious, loving, and supportive foster home, Haynes learned to be a farmer, but his intellectual curiosity led him to borrow books to read after work by the fireside. "By improving his evenings," as he put it, he became his own teacher of the larger world beyond rural eighteenth-century New England. We cannot know what he thought about what he read but we do know his imaginative mind needed to express itself as well as to absorb. We have the result in early poems and writings which are remarkable not so much for their brilliance as for the fact they were created at all.

Haynes' indenture came to an end as the American Revolution was beginning. He enlisted as a Minuteman, marched out with the local militia at the Lexington alarm, and served with the Continental army at Roxbury and Ticonderoga. By itself this is hardly unusual; his neighbors did the same. What is unusual is that beyond the local patriotism Haynes saw a larger issue. Beyond the provincial impulse for independence he perceived a greater, more philosophically based, a logically and justly expanded idea of freedom.

Haynes painstakingly articulated his thoughts in an essay he called "Liberty Further Extended" in which, essentially, he used a theory of natural rights to argue for an enlargement of the spirit of the Revolution to encompass the millions of black slaves held in bondage. By their very nature revolutionary ideas once released often find their way to places they are not supposed to go. Haynes was neither the first nor the last African American to seize on the notion of natural rights. Only a few years later it would inform part of the thinking of Gabriel in his momentous but unsuccessful slave insurrection aimed at capturing Richmond and setting off a mighty movement of black self liberation.

It would take nearly a century for enough of the rest of the country to catch up with Haynes' vision and actualize his dream. Writing of the Civil War, Bruce Catton said this concept of human freedom "is dangerous; it takes fire, like phosphorus, whenever it is exposed to the air, and the war was exposing it to the winds of heaven." The Revolutionary War may have exposed a freedom "further extended" to Haynes but the new nation's incapacity to see what he saw led to a second, bloodier conflict.

Haynes was not an insurrectionist but his treatise (unpublished until 1983), if not unique in its intellectual content, remains extraordinary given the limitations of its author, the circumstances of its composition, and the fact that the Abolitionist Movement, at least as generally perceived, was years away. Objectively, it may be necessary to re-think the history of anti-slavery protest and understand it was not only a white New England phenomenon but the daily struggle of unnumbered people of color.

Subjectively, there is the question of what was going on in the twenty-three-year-old mind of Lemuel Haynes. He grew up from infancy in a white family whose mother favored him over her own children. He had lived all his life to date in a community, a church, and an army where, as far as we know, he was fully accepted. Yet as the author of a deeply felt poem about the Battle of Lexington he called himself "a young Mollato," and his first sustained intellectual essay had as its central proposition: "That an *African*, or, in other terms, *that a Negro may Justly Chalenge, and has an undeniable right to his Liberty.*"

Lemuel Haynes, who had his liberty, was not questioning the accepted system of indentured servitude which, in fact, saved his life. He was himself a free man in a community of free men in a New England which knew about freedom. He had never seen the cruel chattel slavery system of the South where men and women and children of color were not people but livestock. But Haynes' essay is clearly more than the mental exercise of a developing mind.

He had certainly seen and known black slaves in New England. What did they mean to him? Despite his immediate milieu Haynes defined himself as a person of color, he identified with oppressed African Americans in permanent bondage, and the young soldier imaginatively envisioned the Revolution expanding to include more than his Connecticut friends and neighbors.

Haynes' duality or "twoness," to use Du Bois' familiar term, gave him the ambivalent stance of the participant observer: his involvement, at least psychologically, was restricted by his "otherness" but at the same time his perspective was enhanced. "The double-meanings of 'America'" were clear to him. Haynes lived out his life within the confines of his culture, in the white world which was the only world he knew. But he never forgot, or was allowed to forget, that what he was determined who he was. This is his paradox.

Perhaps Haynes chose the isolation of Vermont for his ministry because on that frontier what restrained New Englanders politely and obliquely called "the peculiarity of his history" made less difference. Perhaps his adulation for George Washington owed as much to the fact that Washington freed his slaves as to the molding of Haynes' life as a soldier in Washington's army. Perhaps the best he could do was to speak out on occasion on behalf of "the poor Africans among us," his father's people, and blame slavery for their abject situation rather than "any distinction that the God of nature hath made in their formation."

At any rate Haynes' intellect and energy and life went at last into his ministry rather than into any involvement with or on behalf of people of

African descent. But even that was no escape from American realities. When he was eased out after his long ministry to the Rutland church he tartly commented that "he lived with the people in Rutland thirty years, and they were so sagacious that at the end of that time they found out that he was *a nigger*, and so turned him away."

Haynes was a faithful pastor and popular preacher and speaker and writer who could turn a memorable phrase. "Lord, we are so selfish we spoil everything we do," he prayed on one occasion. "Zion trembled when he fell," he said at Job Swift's funeral. "To be for him and not for another" sounds like Karl Barth. His ability to create good prose spilled over into his political discourses: "There is counterfeit gold, and counterfeit silver, counterfeit bills, and counterfeit men." There are indeed, but Haynes is not among them.

Haynes wrote in a variety of literary forms. After his youthful attempts at poetry, largely unsuccessful one must say, he seems to have abandoned it. His ministerial career required the constant preparation of sermons—5,500 at Rutland, including 400 funeral sermons. His patriotic political addresses were influenced by the homiletical style. An exception is *Mystery Developed*, his account of the Boorn case. While essentially a piece of reportage it has all the characteristics, as William Robinson points out, of a short story.

Haynes was finally a preacher, however, and his sermons both in form and content are characteristic of his day. We might note his prodigious memorization of Scripture (often slightly misquoted) and the problem of all Calvinist preachers: why call the elect to repentance? *Universal Salvation*, preached in 1805, Haynes' most famous sermon, is remarkable for its satire, its brevity, and the fact that it was reprinted throughout the Northeast in over seventy editions until as late as 1865.

Some contemporary Universalist rebuttals to *Universal Salvation* charged that Haynes' sermon devastating their cause was not the spontaneous reply to Ballou that Haynes claimed it to be, but a carefully and craftily premeditated attack. In either case it is a clever piece. The Haynes sermons we do have are written and formal; unfortunately they reveal little of the extemporaneous gifts of the great preacher Haynes was uniformly held to be. Perhaps, then, *Universal Salvation* is important not only as a successful Calvinist rejoinder to Universalism but also as a clue to Haynes' fluency, wit, and power in the pulpit.

Haynes was respected for his learning and piety, for being a good shepherd, and for his preaching and writing, but he was remembered for his wit. The house of his fellow minister Ashbel Parmlee was destroyed by fire. Haynes asked Parmlee if he had lost his sermon manuscripts, and hearing that he had, commented, "Well, don't you think they gave more light than they ever had done before?" Haynes felt his children were indolent except for his eldest son and namesake. Lemuel, Junior, Haynes explained, was an Arminian believing in the efficacy of works, while his other children were true Calvinists, sure that their faith alone would support them.

Perhaps Haynes' best line came when he inadvertently wandered into a hotel dining room where a group of local supporters were celebrating Andrew Jackson's election to the presidency. At their friendly insistence Haynes joined them in a glass of wine, proposed a toast—"Andrew Jackson, Psalm 109, verse 8"—and went on his way. Only later did someone look up the passage and discover that it read: "Let his days be few, and let another take his office."

Except as a black soldier in the American Revolution Haynes' place in history has never been sure, though over the years he appears from time to time in books and articles. The reason is probably his own decision—if decision it was—to remain in the white world he never made but which was the only one he knew. A number of historic "firsts" can be and have been ascribed to him: M.A. from Middlebury, minister to white congregations, etc. It should be said that while Haynes was probably the first African American ordained by a mainstream Protestant church in this country, the slaves had their own religious leaders, George Liele was preaching to black Baptists in Georgia during Haynes' lifetime, and the Roman Catholic church in Latin America had ordained blacks and men of mixed blood to the priesthood for years.

In some ways Haynes is typically American and his story incorporates elements of American mythology: the Horatio Alger rise from obscurity, the frontier. And there are hints of larger mythic themes: the abandoned child, the permanent exile. But it is Haynes' double-consciousness, as Du Bois calls it, the permanent condition of black Americans, that defines him and provides whatever understanding of this anomalous man we are likely to have. Plural identity is less a contradiction than a paradox, a truth within opposites.

The child deserted by both his black father and white mother was named Lemuel, "Belonging to God." In the Bible that meant so much to him, Lemuel is an unknown king. So Lemuel Haynes remains. In the bringing together of all his known writings he speaks again after a long silence for himself.

Acknowledgments

I am of course indebted to a number of people and institutions for help in preparing this book and I am delighted for the opportunity to express my appreciation.

Alison Ryley of The New York Public Library reawakened my interest in Haynes and this languishing compilation by offering to conduct a computer search for Haynes titles I might have missed in *Lemuel Haynes: A Bio-Bibliography*. The most interesting thing that turned up was his 1774 poem on the death of Asa Burt. It appeared in RLIN because of the careful cataloguing of the American Antiquarian Society where Nancy Burkett and Doris O'Keefe were, as always, interested and helpful. I am grateful, too, to Christopher Bickford of the Connecticut Historical Society and to the staff of the Boston Public Library for sharing their copies of this poem with me.

Two colleagues kindly agreed to contribute introductory material to this book. Mechal Sobel of the University of Haifa wrote the foreword. I admire her scholarship, I am continually impressed by her insight, and I value her friendship. Helen MacLam, an old friend and an early re-discoverer of Haynes, wrote the introduction. Now Social Science Editor at *Choice* magazine, she is formerly librarian at Dartmouth College, the school Haynes presciently "shrunk at the thought" of attending.

We are all indebted to Dorothy Porter Wesley, formerly of the Moorland-Spingarn Research Center at Howard and now at the Du Bois Institute at Harvard, whose pioneering work on Haynes in her "Early American Negro Writings: A Bibliographic Study" (1945) set the highest standards of scholarship and introduced to the world the work of a number of important but neglected African American writers. She is a valued friend and respected mentor, and it is with appreciation and affection that this book is dedicated to her.

We are all indebted, also, to Professor Ruth Bogin whose discovery of Haynes' "Liberty Further Extended" and "The Battle of Lexington" manuscripts in the Houghton Library at Harvard dramatically increased our knowledge of Haynes and our perception of his importance.

Betty Gubert, Diana Lachatanere, Mary Yearwood, and others at the Schomburg Center for Research in Black Culture cheerfully provided access to that great collection, as did Robert Morris and Susan Davis. Other cooperative libraries were the Congregational Library, Boston, the Presbyterian Historical Association, Philadelphia, and the Andover-Harvard Theological Library, Cambridge.

William French of the University Place Bookshop, New York, located an edition of *Universal Salvation* unknown to me at the Library Company of Philadelphia, and James Green kindly verified its existence. Lola Szladits of the Berg Collection at The New York Public Library helped decipher Haynes' handwriting. Randall K. Burkett of the Du Bois Institute at Harvard is always supportive and encouraging.

Finally, thanks to Barbara Bergeron for editing the manuscript and Ralph Carlson for wanting to publish it.

New York City
February 1, 1989

Black Puritan on the Northern Frontier: The Vermont Ministry of Lemuel Haynes

HELEN MacLAM

Pastor of white congregations for more than thirty years, Lemuel Haynes was one of several blacks whose lives made notable contributions to the early history of New England. Haynes' inauspicious beginnings gave little promise of this remarkable man's subsequent career. He was born the illegitimate child of a white mother and a black father in West Hartford, Connecticut, July 18, 1753, and soon afterward his mother deserted him. The identity of Haynes' parents remains a matter of conjecture. Timothy Mather Cooley, Haynes' early biographer, described his mother as "a white woman of respectable New England ancestry," lending credence to the assertion that she was a member of Hartford's prominent Goodwin family.[1] Other researchers have concluded that Haynes' mother was a servant named Alice Fitch, at one time employed by John Haynes of Hartford, and in whose household the child was born.[2]

At five months, the abandoned infant was bound over to David Rose, a pious farmer, one of several emigrants from Durham, Connecticut, who settled, with his family, in Middle Granville, Massachusetts. Although the Roses had several children of their own, Haynes later remarked that Mrs. Rose ". . . had peculiar attachment to me: she treated me as though I were her own child. I remember it was a saying among the neighbours, that she loved Lemuel more than her own children."[3]

As a condition of his indenture Haynes was permitted to attend the district school, but, as a servant in a family of subsistence farmers on the frontier, his opportunities for formal training were meager. The pious nature of the Rose home "where Sabbath was sanctified, daily prayer offered, and the evening preceding the Sabbath sacredly employed in the instruction of the household" was a far more critical factor in his religious and intellectual development than the limited educational offerings of the village school.[4] Haynes was a determined, self-taught student who pored over Scripture until he could repeat from memory most of the texts dealing with the doctrines of grace, a feat that impressed almost everyone who later heard him in the pulpit. He also memorized Watts' psalms and hymns, and many of the writings of Edward Young, Philip Doddridge, and George Whitefield. Throughout his pastoral life, his sermons reflected the perspectives of these early mentors.

Haynes completed his indenture just as revolutionary ferment in America was coming to a head. An ardent patriot, he volunteered in 1774 as a minuteman. Following the battle of Lexington, he and forty-one other men left Granville in April 1775, led by Capt. Lebbeus Ball, to join militia units at Roxbury. On October 21, 1776, Haynes enlisted in the Continental Army, serving in Capt. Aaron Coe's company of the Hampshire County regiment.[5] Under the command of Lt. Col. Timothy Robinson, who eventually became governor of Vermont, Haynes made his first foray into the Vermont wilderness as an army private. He later recalled in a speech at Bennington that "Fifty-four years ago next October I was in this town with troops on their march to Ticonderoga."[6] After less than a month with the Ticonderoga expedition, however, Haynes contracted typhus; he was invalided home on November 17, 1776.

Conditioned by his conservative spiritual and political milieux and reinforced by his experiences in fighting for the Revolution, Haynes developed a lifelong idealization of George Washington and allegiance to the Federalist party. His patriotic fervor was early expressed in a ballad written in 1776, shortly after he served with the minutemen. Entitled "The Battle of Lexington," the work is prefaced by the following statement:

A *Poem* on the inhuman Tragedy perpetrated on the 19th of April 1775 by a Number of the Brittish Troops under the Command of Thomas Gage, which Parricides and Ravages are shocking Displays of ministerial & tyrannic

Vengeance composed by Lemuel a young Mollato who obtained what little knowledge he possesses by his own Application to Letters.[7]

Although unpolished, the work is significant not only because it demonstrates Haynes' religious and political values, but also because it indicates the intelligence and fluency that characterized the mature pastor's sermons and verbal exchanges.

Following his discharge from the army, Haynes returned to Granville to farm, pursuing his study of theology as time permitted. One Saturday night during family worship, an incident occurred that further showed his promising abilities. Haynes was usually designated to read the text chosen for study. On this occasion he substituted a sermon he had written himself, without revealing its authorship. Those present were truly impressed when Haynes admitted that it was not a work of Watts, Whitefield, Doddridge, or Davie but, in fact, his own composition. He began to gain a reputation as "one raised up of God for more than common usefulness,"[8] and was urged to enter the ministry.

Haynes' formal preparation for the pulpit began with instruction in Latin and Greek under the tutelage of Daniel Farrand and William Bradford, two Connecticut clergymen. Bradford also obtained a teaching post for Haynes in Wintonbury (now Bloomfield, Connecticut) to support himself during his course of study. On November 29, 1780, he became licensed to preach. Soon afterward, he was invited to serve as supply pastor to the Middle Granville church, of which he was a charter member.

In 1783 Haynes married Elizabeth Babbit, a young white schoolteacher who was a member of his congregation. At the time of their marriage he was thirty and Elizabeth ten years younger. Ten children were born to the couple between 1785 and 1805.

Haynes had preached in Granville for five years when the church applied to the Association of Ministers in Litchfield County, Connecticut, for his ordination as an evangelist, requesting that the Association ". . . set him apart to the work of the ministry, by the imposition of hands, or by *ordination at large*, if they should think proper. . . ."[9] The request was signed by a church committee consisting of two of Haynes' former officers, Timothy Robinson and Aaron Coe. Accordingly, on November 9, 1785, Lemuel Haynes became the first black to be ordained by any religious organization in America.[10] The ordination took place in Torrington, where Haynes had supplied the pulpit since the previous summer.

The wording of the request for Haynes' ordination suggested some of the larger issues creating discord within the Congregational establishment at this time. The generation to which Haynes was born had experienced drastic upheaval as a result of the evangelizing of George Whitefield and the Great Awakening. Major controversies erupted over the constitution of the church, the way of salvation, and the problem of assurance.[11] Within each of these categories there were specific issues. One of them, which was involved in Haynes' ordination, was the question of itinerant versus a settled ministry. Traditional Congregationalism in Massachusetts adhered to the Cambridge Platform of 1648, which refused to sanction ordination of men to the church at large.[12] Although he had served a Massachusetts church, Haynes was both licensed and ordained by Connecticut clergy, many of whom were guided by the Saybrook Platform of 1708 and supported itinerant revivalism.

Haynes' ministry was thus bound from the outset with the revivalistic heritage of the Great Awakening that continued to be a divisive factor in New England's religious life. The ecclesiastical fragmentation of the church at midcentury gave rise to three factions: the "New Lights," who favored revival, insisting on the necessity of conscious conversion and accepting concomitant emotional extravagance; the "Old Lights," who opposed revival, emphasizing morality and rationalism in theology; and the moderates, who "recognized the hand of God in the revival and had participated wholeheartedly in it, seeking at the same time to restrain the excesses. . . ."[13] Haynes was ideologically allied to the latter group, the New Light moderates. Reared by a Separate master and taught by "a faithful, evangelical minister," he "adopted the same principles as Edwards and Whitefield . . . entering with all his heart upon the work of promoting revivals of religion."[14] Haynes' sermons themselves best illustrate his evangelical Calvinistic theological stance, consistently indicating an unwavering belief in predestination and personal election. A letter to a fellow pastor revealed his attitude toward a community where this tradition was wavering: "Infidelity and stupidity are very prevalent. Corrupt doctrines are circulated; and Arminianism is not without its votaries."[15]

When Haynes came to Torrington he was confronted with a manifestation of New England's religious controversy. The church had become divided, as had others, on the question of what constituted true Congregational practice. Many churches had adopted the "half-way covenant," i.e., the custom of administering the rite of baptism to children of people who, although pious and moral, did not otherwise qualify as communicants. Further, most churches had joined in "consociations," i.e., organizations that provided fellowship but also acted as standing councils with authority over member churches in contradiction to a tradition that recognized each congregation as autonomous in its government. These differences had created a schism in the Torrington church. In the fall of 1785, the strict Congregationalists (or Separates, as they were also known) covenanted together to support a gospel minister. In March 1786, they invited Haynes to "preach with us some time longer."[16] Those members of the church who favored existing practices refused to sustain Haynes' ministry and worshipped in nearby Goshen. It was clearly the Separates who had hired and supported him.[17]

The question of color was also a significant factor that kept the Torrington church from settling Haynes as its pastor. His preaching had impressed not only his own congregation but also listeners from other churches. It was, however, a source of resentment among the faithful of one neighboring congregation "that their people would go away from home, and especially to hear that colored man preach."[18] The following anecdote concerning a church member opposed to Haynes' employment attested to existing prejudices: the man had stayed away from meeting but "at length, curiosity conquered prejudice so far that he went to the house of God, and from designed disrespect, sat with his hat on his head. . . . 'The preacher had not proceeded far in his sermon,' said the man, 'before I thought him the *whitest* man I ever saw, my hat was instantly thrown under the seat, and I found myself listening with the most profound attention.' "[19]

Early in his stay at Torrington, Haynes set out on a brief missionary tour of Vermont, renewing acquaintances and preaching in the Rutland area before returning to Connecticut. Three years later, in 1788, he received a call from Rutland and became the second pastor of the west parish on March 28 of that year.

The Rutland church had its genesis in 1773, in Simsbury, Connecticut. Rev. Benajah Roots, who had been dismissed by his Simsbury congregation the year before, immigrated with some of his followers to Rutland, joining other Simsbury dissidents who had preceded him.[20] Eventually, doctrinal differences split the new church; formal division was consummated in October 1797. The west parish remained a conservative stronghold, while the east parish adhered to less stringent practices, including adoption of the half-way covenant.[21]

The northern frontier had been populated primarily by Connecticut folk seeking escape from constraint by the political and religious establishment of the older eastern settlements. These pioneers represented a variety of conflicting philosophical persuasions. They had in common only the desire to find a setting where they could live according to their convictions without harassment. The Republic of Vermont's first constitution patently manifested these sentiments. Written in 1777, this was probably the most radical document of its kind, allowing for almost complete freedom of religious expression as well as outlawing slavery of any kind within its jurisdiction.

Although there may have been instances of de facto slave holding, the legal process, buttressed by the general sentiment, acted to support the natural rights of man. Free persons of color were to be found in various towns throughout Vermont. In the late eighteenth century, there were some 250 blacks living in communities in the Connecticut River Valley. They were not, however, usually recognized as equals by other Vermonters, and most occupied menial jobs.[22]

The Green Mountains separated Vermont sociologically as well as geographically. Shaped by the early influx of devout Calvinists from southern New England, the eastern portion along the Connecticut River Valley was both more populous and more traditional. One of Connecticut's best-known evangelists, Eleazar Wheelock, settled here, founding Dartmouth College in 1769, and establishing a presbyterian system of governance for Congregational churches on both sides of the river. The region was also known for its political conservatism, keeping "Vermont in the Federalist column until the triumph of Jefferson in 1800."[23]

West of the mountains, too, many communities were founded by Connecticut emigrants but these were of a different stamp. They were political radicals, religious dissenters, and others who came to make a new start on the frontier. It was here that the strict Congregational and Baptist churches were gathered, but it was also the home of the "infamous" revolutionary and Deist, Ethan Allen, and a center of support for Jeffersonian democracy. The area was described as a "Nazareth of anti-federalism" in which "every popular heresy distasteful to the older settlements flourished. . . ."[24] There were only a handful of Congregational ministers and a few small churches in this part of the state. The town of Rutland, where Lemuel Haynes was to spend thirty of his thirty-four years in Vermont, stands in the middle of this part of the state, roughly twenty miles from the New York border.

In Rutland, as in Torrington, there was awareness of Haynes as a black. Young people of his congregation were often taunted about their colored minister. Although Haynes himself was not outspoken on contemporary race relations, his opposition to slavery is incontrovertibly documented in an early manuscript. In "Liberty Further Extended: Or Free thoughts on the illegality of Slave-keeping; Wherein those arguments that Are useed [sic] in its vindication Are plainly confuted. Together with an humble Address to such as are Concearned in the practise," a young Haynes passionately condemned with political, theological, and moral arguments the institution of slavery. The manuscript is undated, but internal evidence shows it was probably written in 1776.[25] Haynes was also known as an intimate of Richard Skinner, one of Vermont's strongest antislavery governors, and a friend of Stephen Bradley, who introduced in the Senate the bill that abolished the slave trade in the United States.[26]

One of Haynes' few known references to slavery appears in a Fourth of July sermon in which he contrasted European despotism with American republicanism:

> . . . under a monarchical government, people are commonly ignorant; they know but little more than to bow to despots, and crouch to them for a piece of bread.
>
> The propriety of this idea will appear strikingly evident by pointing you to the poor Africans, among us. What has reduced them to their present pitiful, abject state? Is it any distinction that the God of nature hath made in their formation? Nay—but being subjected to slavery, by the cruel hands of oppressors, they have been taught to view themselves as a rank of being far below others, which has suppressed, in a degree, every principle of manhood, and so they become despised, ignorant, and licentious. This shows the effects of despotism, and should fill us with the utmost detestation against every attack on the rights of men: while we cherish and diffuse, with a laudable ambition, that heaven-born liberty wherewith Christ hath made us free.[27]

An entry in the West Rutland church records testifies to the presence of "poor Africans, among us." On page 141, Haynes registered the death in December 1804 of "Moses Ames' Black Boy."[28]

The post-revolutionary zeitgeist in Vermont was one of free-thinking liberalism that increasingly rejected Calvinist doctrine in favor of rational theology and the natural rights of man. Ethan Allen's *Reason, the Only Oracle of Man* and the writings of Thomas Paine were widely circulated and read by the growing number of Republicans. These attitudes were anathema to Haynes, who wrote to an associate in Granville: "As you observe, Paine has his advocates. I have attended to all his writings on theology, and can find little else but invective and the lowest kind of burlesque."[29]

The standing order Congregational clergy viewed politics and religion as inextricably joined. Their equation of infidelity with Republicanism solidified their traditional support of the Federalists. In a sermon delivered at the Rutland town meeting, September 4, 1798, Haynes cited civil authority as a preordained instrument of God, damned the insidious influence of the French Revolution, and praised the virtues of Washington and Adams. The text is prefaced by this notice:

> The author is not insensible of the reproach to which the following publication may subject him, at a time of so great civil dissension; and has consented to have it appear abroad with a degree of reluctance. However as all view it a detraction of their liberty, when they are not allowed with honesty and candor to speak their own sentiments: he presumes it will be a sufficient defence against any imputations from those who may differ with him in opinion.[30]

Although Haynes' political position remained unalterably conservative, he sometimes voiced his views with reluctance. In a letter written in 1797 to a correspondent in Granville, Haynes said: "Dissensions about politics have had an unfortunate influence on religion, as they have greatly tended to alienate the affections of the people from each other. . . ." Again, in September 1801: "I am preparing another political discourse for the press, delivered on the 4th of July [quoted above]. I feel an aversion to preach, and especially to print, on the subject, but find it unavoidable without giving offence."[31]

Federalism reached its zenith in 1798, gradually yielding to the swelling opposition thereafter. The beginning of its decline in Vermont was manifest in the election of 1800. Every county west of the mountains was carried by Thomas Jefferson although the eastern part of the state continued to support the Federalist party and its candidate, John Adams. The War of 1812 marked the Federalists' last stand as a political force. The conflict per se was not a popular cause in Vermont and it brought to a boil hostilities that had been simmering for some time.

Haynes did not hesitate to make public his opposition to the war. In a sermon delivered to the Washington Benevolent Society in Brandon, Vermont, on February 22, 1813, he spoke again of the rule of government as ordained by God and therefore to be upheld. But this sanction applied only to the institution; it did not necessarily include administrators:

> . . . for, if the person who possesses the supreme power in any state, exercises it in destroying the fundamental laws, and to the ruin of the people, such a ruler is not from God; is not authorized by him, and *ought to be resisted*. . . .

When we are called upon by civil authority to engage in war, 'tis the duty of men, if they would not be guilty of blood, to examine the matter for themselves, whether there be just cause of war.

Haynes apparently bore in mind the biases of his intended audience. The address is unmistakably an antiwar tract. Yet the tenor of his rhetoric was, in places, almost conciliatory. His text continued:

Are not men often too lavish of their invectives on the present administration, and too hasty in judging and condemning without evidence? . . . Would not a more mild and dispassionate mode of conduct be more becoming, and have more influence?

A note of caution was also evident in his attempt to meet in advance one probable criticism. He answered the perennial complaint that "ministers of the gospel ought not to meddle with politics" by quoting Ezekiel 33:6,

If the watchman see the sword come, and blow not the trumpet, and the people not be warned; if the sword come and take away any person from among them, he is taken away in iniquity; *but his blood will I require at the watchman's hands.*[32]

More striking was Haynes' effort not to identify himself too closely with the controversial organization before which he was speaking. The Washington Benevolent Society was largely a clandestine ploy of the Federalists to further their political ends. In the guise of a secret association whose purposes were purely social, branches of the Society spread rapidly throughout New England, especially in Vermont. The growth of the organization led to disagreements within churches, neighborhoods, and families. Furthermore, "churches [were] separating, dissolving, and dismissing their pastors in various places amidst the ravages of disunion in consequence of the Washington Benevolent Societies."[33] Haynes concluded the sermon quoted above with this disclaimer:

My friends, secret combinations are viewed with a jealous eye; they can do mischief in the dark. Whether your Society deserves this epithet, is not for me to determine, as I am not a member of your body.[34]

The West Rutland congregation did not escape the internal conflict spawned by the Society. In March 1812, Deacon Wait Chatterton accused a fellow deacon, Timothy Boardman, of membership in this group and requested the church to inquire into the matter "that he may be able to pluck the mote out of his brother's eye." Haynes wrote this account of the meeting:

> Deacon Boardman, being asked whether he was a member of the Washingtonian Society, answered in the affirmative . . . and [said that] he believed all good men ought to [be]. As evidence, Mr. Howe was then called upon under oath to declare . . . what he knew about this Society, it was as followeth, viz:
> ". . . I saw a letter [but] I knew nothing from whence it came [as] I saw no subscription. It called on us to persuade young men not to enlist into the service of the United States."[35]

Further consideration of the complaint was scheduled but the disposition of the charge against Deacon Boardman was not recorded.

The decade following the election of Jefferson was, paradoxically, a time of renewed religious fervor in Vermont. "The Holy Spirit came down like a mighty rushing wind, bearing away all opposition."[36] In 1803, Haynes wrote, "Professors are alive. Never did I behold such a winter as the past."[37]

The next year was a particularly active one for Haynes. The *Connecticut Evangelical Magazine* reported his participation in an ordination and other activities as a member of a committee, chosen by the Consociations of the Western Districts of Vermont, whose purpose was to raise money to support missions. Haynes himself was appointed by the Connecticut Missionary Society to bring the gospel to the more remote sections of Vermont. Of his tour, undertaken late that summer, Haynes recorded:

> August, 31, 1804, I sat [sic] out on a mission of five weeks. In that time, I delivered 36 sermons, administered the Lord's supper three times, assisted in the formation of one church; baptized one adult and six children. . . .
> In general, I had the most cordial reception, and in many places the word seemed to take effect. On the whole, I obtained satisfactory evidence of the great utility of missionary exertions.[38]

In a letter written a few months later, Haynes remarked, "The alteration in this state within the last two or three years is surprising. Thousands have been converted. The call almost everywhere now is—*preach! preach!*"[39]

The year 1804 was significant in another respect. Haynes was awarded the master's degree, *honoris causa*, by Middlebury College, perhaps the first black ever to be so recognized.

Among those who knew him there was consensus about Haynes' personal qualities. His speech, as were his sermons, was plain and direct. He also possessed an unusual memory, causing more than one correspondent to comment on his ability to cite Scripture verbatim. He was a sober, righteous man dominated by a sense of mission and not given to levity, although he had a reputation for acerbic wit. An often-told anecdote testifies to the readiness of Haynes' wit: following the election of Andrew Jackson, a group of supporters was celebrating his victory. Haynes mistakenly entered the room, whereupon he was pressed to join the group and to propose a toast. Raising his glass, Haynes pronounced, "Andrew Jackson, Psalm 109, verse 8," and left. Someone later looked up the passage to discover it read, "Let his days be few, and let another take his office."[40]

In June 1805 an event occurred that demonstrated Haynes' ready mind and command of Scripture. This was his well-publicized exchange with Hosea Ballou. Ballou, who was to become one of the leading Universalist theologians, had been settled recently over a congregation in eastern Vermont. Rising interest in Universalist thought, which held that all believers might achieve salvation through the blessing of the gospel in contradiction to the doctrine of the elect, made Ballou a popular and much sought-after speaker. Accordingly, Ballou was asked by several people to preach in West Rutland. Haynes had been urged repeatedly to come and debate with Ballou and had refused, but eventually relented to the extent that he agreed to attend the meeting.

Ballou took as his text I John 4:10, 11:

> Herein is love, not that we loved God, but that he loved us, and sent his Son to be the propitiation for our sins. Beloved, if God so loved, we ought also to love one another.

When Ballou finished preaching he invited Haynes to comment. Without direct reference to Ballou's sermon Haynes spoke extemporaneously on the text Genesis 3:4: "And the serpent said unto the woman, 'Ye shall not surely die.' " His sermon was a witty satire in which he implicitly equated the devil, as a serpent in Eden, with the first Universalist itinerant preacher. He closed with the comment that

> As the author of the foregoing has confined himself wholly to the character of Satan, he trusts no one will feel himself personally injured by this short sermon: But should any imbibe a degree of friendship for this aged divine, and

think I have not treated this Universalist Preacher with the respect and veneration that he justly deserves, let them be so kind as to point it out, and I will most cheerfully retract; for it has ever been a maxim with me, *Give the devil his due*.[41]

The matter did not end here; in December Haynes published this sermon, probably the best known of his written works. Subsequently as many as seventy editions were printed and, well into the nineteenth century, distributed as far away as Europe. Ballou responded the following April by publishing "An Epistle" to Haynes, denouncing his behavior as "the most unchristianlike [that] I ever saw in one who professed to preach Christ and his salvation" and disputing Haynes' assertions point by point.[42] Haynes' vituperative reply appeared a year later. Although Ballou made no answer, both men felt repercussions of the controversy for some time.

In 1807, the General Convention of Congregational and Presbyterian Ministers in Vermont voted to form themselves into the Vermont Missionary Society, and chose Haynes as one of its twelve trustees. Two years later the Society appointed him as a missionary to the northern part of the state.

There was again a "season of refreshment" in 1808; 109 souls were added to the church. Nevertheless, a decline in evangelical spirit had begun, and revival activities dwindled to almost nothing until after the War of 1812. Assessing the state of religion in Rutland, Haynes concluded, "Political distraction, I believe, has extinguished the flame."[43] Despite this, gospel ministry was still welcome in some places. In September 1810, Haynes sent the following letter to Rev. Nathan Perkins of the Connecticut Missionary Society:

Rev. Sir
  I was lately called to administer the Holy Supper at Windham, the southern part of this state; there are a great no. of towns there that seem to hunger after the bread of life, as I hope. They desired me to mention their case to missionaries. Some months ago I was called to attend an ordination in the northern part of the state of New York, toward the river St. Lawrence. The door is abundantly open for gospel labor; I was surprised to see how they need ministerial exertions.
  I am much solicited to take a preaching tour. The Reverend Mr. Washburn discoursed with me on the subject of taking a mission from your Society. I told him that should providence open the door perhaps I might at some future time. I have consulted some of the people of my charge on the subject and think that they will consent to have me go a few weeks should I request it.

Could you deem it expedient to send me a mission, I feel an inclination to comply. I shall (God willing) make returns myself and give an account of my services, as I long to visit my old friends in your parts. My sun is setting. What I do, I must do quickly—However, I am not anxious. Your decision on the subject will be perfectly satisfactory, be it which way it may. I trust it is the language of my heart "send, Lord, by whom thou wilt find."

> Respectfully yours,
> Lemuel Haynes.

The request was received positively. Perkins noted on the verso of the letter, "I am willing and wish Mr. Haynes might be appointed a missionary, for one tour."[44]

There were, in fact, several tours. In 1817 Haynes wrote to the Society's auditor, Rev. Abel Flint, that "A tedious fit of sickness has impeded my exertion," and suggested, "Could you send me to the amount of 30 or 40 dollars more, it would be very acceptable. I am not growing rich by being on mission. Sickness is costly."[45]

Again to the Reverend Dr. Flint he wrote two years later:

. . . the low state of my health has been such and other providential events intervening, I was prevented pursuing the object I proposed when I asked for a mission. . . . My [age] and bodily weakness forbids my undertaking in a work [so] arduous. It is with reluctance I relinquish so pleasing and delightful employment. . . . I have performed 18 weeks services but my mission was for 16 for which I only expect remuneration. . . . What remains due please to send in the mail to me. . . .[46]

Haynes seems to have been well regarded by his fellow Congregational clergy, who elected him moderator of the Vermont General Convention in 1813, and chose him the next year as their delegate to the general meeting in Connecticut. His association with his colleague in the Rutland east parish, Rev. Heman Ball, was particularly cordial. The ordination of Ball as that church's second pastor marked the demise of the half-way covenant and established greater doctrinal closeness between the two congregations.

Initially, Haynes' relationship with his congregation appeared to be harmonious. In 1795 he wrote to a correspondent in Granville that he was "happy among the people of my charge as to union."[47] There was agreement on the rules of Christian conduct. Members were not to

. . . admit of frolicing [sic] or allow of what is called Balls to be holden in their houses—Nor shall any attend such midnight revelings. . . .

> Every member of this Church shall avoid gaming, betting, or laying wagers—Shall not be what is commonly called Tavern-haunters. . . . They shall not frequent horse-races and other occasions of carnal amusements; but endeavor so much as is in them lies to have no fellowship with these unfruitful works of darkness.

Members were also enjoined from traveling on the sabbath, from suing one another except as a last resort, and were required to support the church according to their temporal worth.[48]

The effort to preserve the purity of Christian fellowship sometimes led to preoccupation among members with each other's private lives.[49] The charge against Levi Moses, previously taken to task for his absence from public worship, typified such concerns:

> Is the reason assigned by Br. Moses for killing a deer on the Sabbath which was his extreem [sic] want of provision satisfactory to the Chh. Voted in the negative.[50]

One of the deacons, Wait Chatterton, seemed possessed of exceptional righteousness in this regard. Church records show several occasions (in addition to the previously mentioned complaint against Timothy Boardman) on which Chatterton charged his brethren with wrongdoing. Nor was the pastor exempt from his scrutiny. In November 1813 Haynes entered this statement into the record:

> To the Church of Christ in West Rutland–Brethren, Whereas a serious difficulty has for sometime subsisted between myself and Deacon Chatterton which has an unfavorable influence on religion, and whereas the late council have many of them declared that they did not result on the complaint against me, which was 'dishonesty in talk'; as also I find there is a difference of opinion as to the meaning of the result, and as it was deemed by a part of the council and part of the Church, and on further reflexion [sic] by myself, improper for me to make that vindication necessary for the exonerating of my own character while the complainent was absent: These are ernestly [sic] to request the party complaining and the Church to unite with me in a large council as soon as may be, that the matter may have an hearing which I think I have a right to request [by] reason [of] our Church articles, for the sake of my own character. Above all, for the interest of religion.
>
> Lem. Haynes[51]

The church granted the request and a council consisting of delegates from nearby churches was scheduled to meet in December. Its decision is not known, but subsequent entries in the Rutland church records imply support for Haynes.

The following June at "a regular Church meeting warned for the purpose of settling all burdens and difficulties existing in said Church on account of a publication in the Rutland Herald and other matters of a political nature," Deacon Chatterton proposed, and the church voted, that

> we agree by our resolve to drop all such matters . . . and cordially take each other by the hand and covenant through grace assisting to help each other in the peaceable way to the heavenly Zion.[52]

Nevertheless, the following March Haynes made this entry: "Voted to comply with Deacon Chatterton's request and dismiss him from this Church on his joining with any other Church of Christ."[53] But it was not Chatterton who left.

There were indications of a growing alienation between the pastor and his flock. An increasing number of persons were charged with absenting themselves from public worship. In February 1817 Haynes wrote to a friend in Granville, "I think much of being dismissed from my people, should they be willing," and again, a year later, "My contemporaries are mainly gone. . . . There appears to be a great deal of stupidity among us. . . . I feel sometimes discouraged and worn out with fatigue. I tell my people I wish they would release me, at least for a time. . . ."[54]

When the church met in March 1818 and were asked to "agree to continue the Reverend Lemuel Haynes as our pastor and teacher," they voted no. An ecclesiastical council gathered from neighboring churches was called for the purpose of dismissing Haynes. Meeting in April, the council stated, "We are not disposed to say that the relation is that of a regular Pastor to his Church and people.[55] Yet . . . the relation is such that both Minister and Church greatly needed a Council (as the cause of religion is much concerned)." They concluded:

> altho there appeared no impeachment of the moral or ministerial character of Reverend L. Haynes, yet it was judged by the Council that his usefullness [sic] in this place for the future seemed so improbable that it was unanimously agreed to proceed to dissolve the relation between Pastor and Church.[56]

Changing times, politics, creed, and race—all may have been factors in this decision. "Throughout Vermont, many white Christians failed to live up to the image with which popular history has endowed the freedom-loving

Vermonter. Racist stereotypes of profane 'black fiddlers' and amorous 'negro wenches' were invoked all too frequently as countersymbols of the true Christian."[57] An unidentified contemporary of Haynes remarked:

> The people in Rutland, where he preached thirty years, at length began to think they would appear more respectable with a white pastor than a black one, and therefore, or at least measurably on that account, dismissed him.
> Attending to this, he subsequently used to say, he lived with the people in Rutland thirty years, and they were so sagacious that at the end of that time they found out he was *a nigger*, and so turned him away.[58]

It is a telling irony that nearly 100 years later the same church in West Rutland that Haynes had served considered and decided against hiring a black minister.[59]

Haynes' farewell sermon and valedictory address revealed his ambivalence about the separation. In the sermon, entitled *The Sufferings, Support, and Reward of Faithful Ministers Illustrated*, he said bitterly:

> It may be the case that people may make violent attacks on a minister's character, and do all they can to destroy his influence, and come forward with this hypocritical plea, 'The man's usefulness is at an end'; and so cloak their wickedness and deceit under the garb of religion.

The valedictory was both poignant and reproachful:

> I have sometimes thought that perhaps God designed that I should spend the few of my remaining days among you . . . but the ways of God are mysterious, who often destroys the hope of man.
> On the separation of a minister from his people, there are often very criminal causes existing. . . . There may be *pretended* reasons, while the truth may be kept out of sight, to escape censure. Ecclesiastical councils may think it inexpedient to make any inquiry into the matter. . . .
> Much has been said on the subject of my dismission—that it has been in consequence of my request. . . . I should have chosen to continue with you at the expense of temporal emolument; but, considering the divisions existing, and the uncommon stupidity prevalent, I have been fully satisfied that it is my duty to be dismissed. . . .
> My dear brethren and friends, I did not realize my attachment to you before the parting time came. Many disagreeable things have taken place; but still I feel my heart going out towards this people. . . . You will accept my warmest gratitude for the many instances of kindness shown me.[60]

When Haynes left Rutland in May 1818 he was sixty-five years old; his health and vigor were declining. Within a short time, he was asked to preach in Manchester, Vermont, in the southwestern part of the state. His brief stay there was pleasant and uneventful except for one major occurrence—the Boorn murder case.

Russell Colvin, a Manchester resident known to be mentally unstable, had been missing for several years. He had disappeared on various occasions before without arousing much local concern. What made things different this time was his wife Sally's pregnancy. In order for her to make any claim against the child's putative father, her husband's death first had to be established. Sally's situation stirred community interest in Colvin's whereabouts. Through a combination of specious evidence, garbled testimony, and confession under pressure, Sally's brothers, Stephen and Jesse Boorn, were convicted of murdering Colvin despite the absence of a body. A newspaper account of the affair resulted in the reappearance of the deranged Colvin, accompanied by his employer. The prisoners were set free and Colvin returned to the farm in New Jersey where he had been working.

Haynes was pastor to the Boorn brothers. He visited them daily in prison and became convinced of their innocence. The Sunday after they were freed, Haynes preached a sermon entitled *The Prisoner Released. A Sermon, delivered at Manchester, Vermont, Lord's Day, Jan. 9th, 1820. On the remarkable interposition of Divine Providence in the deliverance of Stephen and Jesse Boorn, who had been under sentence of death for the supposed murder of Russel Colvin. . . .* He published this with *Mystery Developed*, a pamphlet giving his account of the case.

Although Haynes and his Manchester congregation were on good terms, it was clear that the parish needed the energies of a younger man. In 1822 Haynes accepted the invitation of the church in Granville, New York, just across the Vermont border. For eleven years he continued to minister as his diminishing strength permitted. His final illness, a gangrenous infection of one of his feet, began in March 1833. He met with his congregation until May, when his condition made the effort impossible. On September 28, 1833, at the age of eighty, he died.

Lemuel Haynes was a man of rare integrity. His energies were committed wholly and without distraction to helping sinners achieve "hope unto salvation." The fate of blacks per se was not his primary concern; he believed all men were by nature equally depraved and equally in danger of eternal damnation.

He seemed to maintain habitual communion with the Father of Spirits. He forgot himself while the glory of the Lord and the interest of Zion lay near his heart. He was like one standing on the verge of two worlds, viewing alternately the one and the other, and taking his measure in due regard to both.[61]

NOTES

1. Timothy M. Cooley, *Sketches of the Life and Character of the Rev. Lemuel Haynes* (New York: Harper & Bros., 1837), p. 28.
2. For a fuller discussion of Haynes' parentage, see Richard D. Brown, " 'Not Only Extreme Poverty, but the Worst Kind of Orphanage'; Lemuel Haynes and the Boundaries of Racial Tolerance on the Yankee Frontier, 1770-1820," *New England Quarterly*, LXI:4 (December 1988): footnote p. 505.
3. Cooley, p. 30.
4. *Ibid.*, p. 31.
5. Ruth Bogin, " 'Liberty Further Extended': A 1776 Antislavery Manuscript by Lemuel Haynes," *The William and Mary Quarterly*, 3d ser., XL (January 1983): 86. See also Albion B. Wilson, *History of Granville, Massachusetts* (Hartford: n.p., 1954), pp. 64, 190-91.
6. Cooley, pp. 46-47. Robinson was also one of those people, many of them Connecticut clergy, who provided links between Haynes' early days in Connecticut and his later ministry in Vermont.
7. For a full treatment of the poem, see Ruth Bogin, " 'The Battle of Lexington': A Patriotic Ballad by Lemuel Haynes," *The William and Mary Quarterly*, 3d ser., XLII:4 (October 1985): 499-506.
8. Cooley, p. 59.
9. *Ibid.*, p. 71. Emphasis mine.
10. Gregor Hileman, "The Remarkable Life of a 'Poor, Hell-Deserving Sinner,' " *Middlebury College News Letter* 47 (Spring 1973): 7.
11. C.C. Goen, *Revivalism and Separatism in New England, 1740-1800: Strict Congregationalists and Separate Baptists in the Great Awakening* (New Haven: Yale University Press, 1962), p. 8.
12. *Ibid.*, p. 9.
13. *Ibid.*, pp. 33-34. Goen also says the Old Lights "constituted the core of the Arminian movement out of which Unitarianism later developed."
14. Cooley, pp. 42, 89.
15. *Ibid.*, p. 84.
16. Samuel Orcutt, *History of Torrington, Connecticut* (Albany: printed by J. Munsell, 1878), p. 32.
17. Goen, p. 309. He asserts Haynes split the church by preaching New Light doctrines and that it reunited when he left.

18. Orcutt, p. 475.
19. Cooley, p. 73.
20. Stephen A. Freeman, "Puritans in Rutland, Vermont, 1770-1818," *Vermont History* 33 (April 1965): 343.
21. John E. Goodrich, "Immigration to Vermont," *Proceedings of the Vermont Historical Society* 1907-1908, p. 72.
22. Randolph A. Roth, *The Democratic Dilemma: Religion, Reform, and the Social Order in the Connecticut River Valley of Vermont, 1791-1850* (New York: Cambridge University Press, 1987), pp. 23-24.
23. David M. Ludlum, *Social Ferment in Vermont, 1791-1850* (New York: Columbia University Press, 1939), p. 11.
24. *Ibid.*, pp. 12, 14.
25. Bogin, *op. cit.*, p. 90.
26. Charles E. Tuttle, "Vermont and the Antislavery Movement" (B.A. thesis, Harvard University, 1937), pp. 27-28, and Hosea Beckley, *The History of Vermont* (Brattleboro, Vt.: George H. Salisbury, 1846), p. 201.
27. Lemuel Haynes, *The Nature and Importance of True Republicanism* (Rutland, Vt.: printed by William Fay, 1801), pp. 11-12.
28. *Book Record*, First Congregational Church (West Parish), Rutland, Vt., 2 v. Typewritten transcript of the original, p. 141. I am grateful to Mr. and Mrs. George Covalt of the West Rutland United Church and Mr. Frederic Elwert of the Rutland Historical Society for making these records available to me.
29. Cooley, p. 83.
30. Lemuel Haynes, *The Influence of Civil Government on Religion* (Rutland, Vt.: printed by John Walker, 1798), p. 2.
31. Cooley, pp. 85-86.
32. Lemuel Haynes, *Dissimulation Illustrated* (Rutland, Vt.: printed by Fay and Davison, 1814), p. 7. In this sermon Haynes also makes reference to the issue of slavery, criticizing Jefferson as lacking the same concern for the slaves in Virginia that he had shown for impressed American seamen, and praising Washington for emancipating his slaves.
33. William A. Robinson, "The Washington Benevolent Society in New England," *Massachusetts Historical Society. Proceedings* 49 (October 1915-June 1916): 280-81.
34. Haynes, *Dissimulation Illustrated*, p. 24. In his unpublished Harvard College B.A. honors thesis, Charles E. Tuttle asserts that Haynes was, in fact, a member of this organization, that his name appears on page 2 of the Washington Benevolent Society of Massachusetts Directory (see Tuttle, *op. cit.*, pp. 19-20). One can only speculate that Haynes may have joined after delivering his sermon in Brandon.
35. *Book Record*, 1:15.
36. Cooley, p. 83.
37. *Ibid.*, p. 91.
38. "A Circular Letter to the Churches and Congregations in the Western Districts of the State of Vermont," *Connecticut Evangelical Magazine*, May 1806, p. 434.
39. Cooley, p. 151.

40. Asa Fitch, "Anecdotes of Rev. Mr. Haynes," *Historical Notes of Washington County, New York* (Microfilm), Film 197.

41. Lemuel Haynes, *A Sermon Delivered at Rutland, West-Parish (Vermont) in the Year 1805* (n.p., n.d.; reprint ed. Providence: n.p., 1822), p. 11.

42. Hosea Ballou, *An Epistle to the Reverend Lemuel Haynes* (Schenectady: Ryer Schermerhorn, 1807), p. 7.

43. Cooley, pp. 91-92.

44. Lemuel Haynes to Nathan Perkins, 29 September 1810, Archives of the Connecticut Conference of Congregational Christian Churches, Hartford.

45. Lemuel Haynes to Abel Flint, 7 April 1817, Archives of the Connecticut Conference of Congregational Christian Churches, Hartford.

46. *Ibid.*, 29 December 1819.

47. Cooley, p. 82.

48. *Book Record*, 1:13-14.

49. Goen, p. 166.

50. *Book Record*, 1:22. Fortunately for Br. Moses, the Church rescinded this vote at its next meeting.

51. *Ibid.*, 1:16.

52. *Ibid.*, 1:18.

53. *Ibid.*, 1:21.

54. Cooley, pp. 157, 159.

55. This curious entry appears on page 5, vol. 2 of the West Rutland Church *Book Record*: "Rev. Lemuel Haynes, by vote of the Church 28th March AD 1788, took pastoral watch and care of the Church, and was dismissed by an ecclesiastical Council 29th April AD 1818, although he was never installed Pastor of this Church."

56. *Book Record*, 1:23-25.

57. Roth, *op. cit.*, p. 208.

58. Asa Fitch, *op. cit.*

59. Robert W. Mitchell, address in observance of the designation of Haynes' home as an historic site by the U.S. Department of Interior, South Granville, N.Y., July 20, 1980.

60. Cooley, pp. 185-204.

61. *Ibid.*, p. 291. Research for this essay was supported through the Fisk University Library Research Program in Ethnic Studies Librarianship.

Black Preacher
to White America

A Poem, Occasioned by the Sudden and Surprising Death of Mr. Asa Burt

Lemuel Haynes' authorship of this poem has only recently come to light. The American Antiquarian Society discovered the attribution in Roderick H. Burnham's 1892 genealogy of the Burt family. Two broadside copies of the poem are known to exist, one at the Connecticut Historical Society printed in Hartford, and one at Boston Public Library printed by Tracy and Bliss, Lansington. Neither indicates a publication date.

———

A POEM, Occasioned by the sudden and surprising Death of Mr. ASA BURT, of *Granville*; who was mortally wounded by Falling a Tree, on the 28th of January, 1774, in the 37th Year of his age, and expired in a few Hours after he received the wound.

I.
Awake my drousy Muse within,
Attend with awe profound;
Wilt thou be loth for to begin
The awful Theme to found?
II.
Can we forget the signal Rod
That hath amongst us been,
Nor mind the Providence of God,
Which we have lately seen?

3

III.

What awful News was that we heard?
    O! 'twas a dreadful Day!
When Death so suddenly appear'd,
    And took a Friend away.

IV.

He went into the verdant Wood,
    As Business did him call;
A tow'ring Tree that by him stood,
    He did attempt to fall.

V.

The Tree he cut, and to prevent
    All harm, he backward flee'd,
And lo! a cruel Limb was sent,
    Which light upon his Head!

VI.

No help from Man could he obtain,
    All earthly helps were fled,
Elixir Blood like trickling Rain
    Ran from his wounded Head.

VII.

At length the awful News was heard,
    And help did quickly come:
His weeping friends straitway appear'd
    And brought him to his Home.

VIII.

All Means was us'd for to revive
    To former Health again,
And keep the dying Man alive,
    But Means were all in vain.

IX.

Before the Evening Shades were drew,
    Death stop'd his vital Breath,
His Body fell a Victim to
    The Hands of potent Death.

X.

Look how the ghastly structure lies!
    O! who could bear the Sight?

Grim Death has closed up his Eyes,
  His Soul hath took its flight.
XI.

The Grave lies waiting with Desire,
  For to receive her prey,
And Friends with one accord conspire
  To carry him away.
XII.

But Oh! must he forever leave
  His Friends, that loving were,
And go down to the silent Grave,
  To sleep in Darkness there?
XIII.

Methinks I hear him loving say,
  "Farewell my Parents kind,
"My loving Wife, I must away
  "And leave you all behind.
XIV.

"Farewell my Children that appear
  "Clad with juvenile Charms;
"Not long ago your Father dear,
  "Could clasp you in his arms.
XV.

"My Neighbours which I often saw,
  "Who lay so near my heart,
"Death's antient unrelented law,
  "Constrains me to depart."
XVI.

The silent Eloquence I felt,
  'Twas of propitious kind,
O! the Benevolence that dwelt
  In that aetherial Mind!
XVII.

Stop fancy come lift up thine Eyes,
  If haply thou canst tell,
Who were his Pilots through the Skies,
  Mark the transition well.

XVIII.
Kind Charity, I will invoke
  Thine aid, to guide me on;
Trace every Foot-step which he took,
  Tell whether he is gone.

XIX.
Do not I see an Angel bright,
  Clad with seraphick Charms,
Conduct him to the realms of Light,
  From all opposing Harms?

XX.
Does Fancy aid my vulgar Song?
  Or do I see him there,
Cloathed in Garments white and long,
  All beautiful and fair.

XXI.
Hark! hear him sing that lovely Song.
  And with his kindred join,
Assisting the triumphant throng
  In Concerts all divine.

XXII.
But Oh! what bitter groans I hear,
  (Like Rachel much distress'd)
Lamenting for a Husband dear,
  With heavy Grief oppress'd.

XXIII.
Madam, O let thy Tears suffice,
  Not murmer at the Rod,
With humble Chearfulness arise,
  And bless the Name of GOD.

XXIV.
At first Afflictions may seem hard,
  And penetrate severe,
Yet they will profit afterward,
  To them that faithful are.

XXV.
Justice is God's own Attribute,
  With Wisdom 'tis subjoin'd;

Why should a mortal Worm dispute
   And call a God unkind?
          XXVI.
Give up thy Children to the Lord,
   Which young and tender are;
Venture thyself upon his word,
   And then thou need'st not fear.
          XXVII.
How doth the Covenant extend
   To Children, (proving true)
He'll be their Father and their Friend
   And he thine Husband too.
          XXVIII.
O meditate on sudden Death,
   And ever keep it near,
Be ready to resign your Breath,
   When you the Summons hear.
          XXIX.
Walk chearful on in Wisdom's ways
   That when thou com'st to die,
Thou may'st behold thy Husband's Face,
   To all Eternity.
          XXX.
Heaven won't admit a single Sigh,
   Nor feel a twinging pain:
Death's Empire shall in ruin lye,
   And never rise again.
          XXXI.
And now, come let us one and all,
   Be actually prepar'd,
And hearken to the awful call
   That we have lately heard.
          XXXII.
O! why should we gon on so hard,
   And boast of Days to come,
When Death stands with a naked sword
   To cast us in the Tomb.

XXXIII.

We know we do exist to Day,
But yet we cannot tell
But the next Moment we must say
Unto the World farewell.

XXXIV.

Lord, guide us by thy Counsels here,
That when we come to die,
Angels our precious souls may bear
Up to thy Throne on high.

The Battle of Lexington

The manuscript of this poem was recently discovered by Professor Ruth Bogin in the Houghton Library at Harvard, and she published it with an introduction in *The William and Mary Quarterly* in 1985. She reproduced Haynes' corrected manuscript exactly, including his punctuation, spelling, and discarded words and verses.

Professor Bogin suggests Haynes composed this "patriotic ballad" shortly after the event. While Haynes did not fight at Lexington, he was a member of a company of Granville militiamen who hastened to the scene at the outbreak of war.

———

A *Poem* on the inhuman Tragedy perpetrated on the 19th of April 1775 by a Number of the Brittish Troops under the Command of Thomas Gage, which Parricides and Ravages are shocking Displays of ministerial & tyrannic Vengeance composed by Lemuel a young Mollato who obtained what little knowledge he possesses, by his own Application to Letters.

1

Some Seraph now my Breast inspire
whilst my *Urania* sings
while She would try her solemn Lyre
Upon poetic Strings.

2

Some gloomy Vale or gloomy Seat
where Sable veils the sky
Become that Tongue that w^d repeat
The dreadfull Tragedy

3

The Nineteenth Day of April last
We ever shall retain
As monumental of the past
most bloody shocking Scene

4

Then Tyrants fill'd wth horrid Rage
A fatal Journey went
& Unmolested to engage
And slay the innocent

5

Then did we see old *Bonner* rise
And, borrowing Spite from Hell
They stride along with magic Eyes
where Sons of Freedom dwell

6

At *Lexington* they did appear
Array'd in hostile Form
And tho our Friends were peacefull there
Yet on them fell the Storm

7

Eight most unhappy Victims fell
Into the Arms of Death
unpitied by those Tribes of Hell
who curs'd them wth their Breath

8

The Savage Band still march along
For *Concord* they were bound
while Oaths & Curses from their Tongue
Accent with hellish Sound

9

To prosecute their fell Desire
At *Concord* they unite
Two Sons of Freedom there expire
By their tyrannic Spite

10

Thus did our Friends endure their Rage
without a murm'ring Word
Till die they must or else engage
and join with one Accord

11

Such Pity did their Breath inspire
That long they bore the Rod
And with Reluctance they conspire
to shed the human Blood

12

But Pity could no longer sway
Tho' 't is a pow'rfull Band
For Liberty now bleeding lay
And calld them to withstand

13

The Awfull Conflict now begun
To rage with furious Pride
And Blood in great Effusion run
From many a wounded Side

14

For Liberty, each Freeman Strives
As its a Gift of God
And for it willing yield their Lives
And Seal it with their Blood

15

Thrice happy they who thus resign
Into the peacefull Grave
Much better there, in Death Confin'd
Than a Surviving Slave

16

This Motto may adorn their Tombs,
(Let tyrants come and view)
"We rather seek these silent Rooms
"Than live as Slaves to You

17

Now let us view our Foes awhile
who thus for blood did thirst
See: stately Buildings fall a Spoil
To their unstoick Lust

18

Many whom Sickness did compel
To seek some Safe Retreat
Were dragged from their sheltering Cell
And mangled in the Street

19

Nor were our aged Gransires free
From their vindictive Pow'r
On yonder Ground lo: there you see
Them weltering in their Gore

20

Mothers with helpless Infants strive
T' avoid the tragic Sight
All fearfull wether yet alive
Remain'd their Soul's delight

21

Such awefull Scenes have not had Vent
Since Phillip's War begun
Nay sure a Phillip would relent[?]
And such vile Deeds would shun

22

But Stop and see the Pow'r of God
Who lifts his Banner high
Jehovah now extends his Rod
And makes our Foes to fly

23

Altho our Numbers were but few
And they a Num'rous Throng
Yet we their Armies do pursue
And drive their Hosts along

24

One Son of Freedom could annoy
A Thousand Tyrant Fiends
And their despotick Tribe destroy
And chace them to their Dens

25

Thus did the Sons of Brittain's King
Recieve a sore Disgrace
Whilst *Sons of Freedom* join to sing
The Vict'ry they Imbrace

26

Oh! Brittain how art thou become
Infamous in our Eye
Nearly allied to antient Rome
That Seat of Popery

27

Our Fathers, tho a feeble Band
Did leave their native Place
Exiled to a desert Land
This howling Wilderness

28

A Num'rous Train of savage Brood
Did then attack them round
But still they trusted in their God
Who did their Foes confound

29

Our Fathers Blood did freely flow
To buy our Freedom here
Nor will we let our freedom go
The Price was much too dear

30

Freedom & Life, O precious Sounds
yet Freedome does excell
and we will bleed upon the ground
or keep our Freedom still

31

But oh! how can we draw the Sword
Against our native kin
Nature recoils at such a Word
And fain w^d quit the Scene

32

We feel compassion in our Hearts
That captivating Thing
Nor shall Compassion once depart
While Life retains her String

33

Oh England let thy Fury cease
At this convulsive Hour
Consult those Things that make for Peace
Nor foster haughty Power

34

Let Brittain's king call home his Band
of Soldiers arm'd to fight
To see a Tyrant in our Land
Is not a pleasing Sight

35

Allegiance to our King we own
And will due Homage pay
As does become his royal Throne
Yet in a *legal Way*

36

Oh Earth prepare for solemn Things
Behold an angry god
Beware to meet the King of Kings
Arm'd with an awefull Rod

37

Sin is the Cause of all our Woe
That sweet deluding ill
And till we let this darling go
There's greater Trouble still

Liberty Further Extended

Haynes' remarkable essay "on the illegality of Slave-keeping" was found at Harvard by Professor Ruth Bogin, who edited and introduced it in *The William and Mary Quarterly* in 1983. All the original spellings, structure, and punctuation of the manuscript have been preserved.

Liberty Further Extended: Or Free thoughts on the illegality of Slave-keeping; Wherein those arguments that Are useed in its vindication Are plainly confuted. Together with an humble Address to such as are Concearned in the practise.

By Lemuel Haynes.

We hold these truths to be self-Evident, that all men are created Equal, that they are Endowed By their Creator with Ceartain unalienable rights, that among these are Life, Liberty, and the pursuit of happyness.

Congress

The Preface. As *Tyrony* had its Origin from the infernal regions: so it is the Deuty, and honner of Every son of freedom to repel her first motions. But while we are Engaged in the important struggle, it cannot Be tho't impertinent for us to turn one Eye into our own Breast, for a little moment, and See, whether thro' some inadvertency, or a self-contracted Spirit, we Do not find the monster Lurking in our own Bosom; that now while we are inspir'd with so noble a Spirit and Becoming Zeal, we may Be Disposed to tear her from us. If the following would produce such an Effect the auther should rejoice.

It is Evident, by ocular demonstration, that man by his Depravety, hath procured many Courupt habits which are detrimental to society; And altho' there is a way pre[s]crib'd Whereby man may be re-instated into the favour of god, yet these courupt habits are Not Extirpated, nor can the subject of renovation Bost of perfection, 'till he Leaps into a state of immortal Existance. yet it hath pleas'd the majesty of Heaven to Exhibet his will to men, and Endow them With an intulect Which is susceptible of speculation; yet, as I observ'd before, man, in consequence of the fall is Liable to digressions. But to proceed,

Liberty, & freedom, is an innate principle, which is unmovebly placed in the human Species; and to see a man aspire after it, is not Enigmatical, seeing he acts no ways incompatible with his own Nature; consequently, he that would infring upon a mans Liberty may reasonably Expect to meet with oposision, seeing the Defendant cannot Comply to Non-resistance, unless he Counter-acts the very Laws of nature.

Liberty is a Jewel which was handed Down to man from the cabinet of heaven, and is Coaeval with his Existance. And as it proceed from the Supreme Legislature of the univers, so it is he which hath a sole right to take away; therefore, he that would take away a mans Liberty assumes a prerogative that Belongs to another, and acts out of his own domain.

One man may bost a superorety above another in point of Natural previledg; yet if he can produse no convincive arguments in vindication of this preheminence his hypothesis is to Be Suspected. To affirm, that an Englishman has a right to his Liberty, is a truth which has Been so clearly Evinced, Especially of Late, that to spend time in illustrating this, would be But Superfluous tautology. But I query, whether Liberty is so contracted a principle as to be Confin'd to any nation under Heaven; nay, I think it not hyperbolical to affirm, that Even an affrican, has Equally as good a right to his Liberty in common with Englishmen.

I know that those that are concerned in the Slave-trade, Do pretend to Bring arguments in vindication of their practise; yet if we give them a candid Examination, we shall find them (Even those of the most cogent kind) to be Essencially Deficient. We live in a day wherein *Liberty & freedom* is the subject of many millions Concern; and the important Struggle hath alread caused great Effusion of Blood; men seem to manifest the most sanguine resolution not to Let their natural rights go without their Lives go with them; a resolution, one would think Every one that has the Least Love to his country, or futer posterity, would fully confide in, yet while we are so zelous to maintain, and foster our own invaded rights, it cannot be tho't impertinent for us Candidly to reflect on our own conduct, and I doubt not But that we shall find that subsisting in the midst of us, that may with propriety be stiled *Opression*, nay, much greater opression, than that which Englishmen seem so much to spurn at. I mean an oppression which they, themselves, impose upon others.

It is not my Business to Enquire into Every particular practise, that is practised in this Land, that may come under this Odeus Character; But, what I have in view, is humbly to offer som free thoughts, on the practise of *Slave-keeping*. Opression, is not spoken of, nor ranked in the sacred oracles, among the Least of those sins, that are the procureing Caus of those signal Judgments, which god is pleas'd to bring upon the Children of men. Therefore let us attend. I mean to white [write] with freedom, yet with the greatest Submission.

And the main proposition, which I intend for some Breif illustration is this, Namely, That an *African*, or, in other terms, *that a Negro may Justly Chalenge, and has an undeniable right to his* ["freed(om)" is blotted out] *Liberty: Consequently, the practise of Slave-keeping, which so much abounds in this Land is illicit.*

Every privilege that mankind Enjoy have their Origen from god; and whatever acts are passed in any Earthly Court, which are Derogatory to those Edicts that are passed in the Court of Heaven, the act is *void*. If I have a perticular previledg granted to me by god, and the act is not revoked nor the power that granted the benefit vacated, (as it is imposable but that god should Ever remain immutable) then he that would infringe upon my Benifit, assumes an unreasonable, and tyrannic power.

It hath pleased god to *make of one Blood all nations of men, for to dwell upon the face of the Earth.* Acts 17, 26. And as all are of one Species, so there are the same Laws, and aspiring principles placed in all nations; and the Effect that these Laws will produce, are Similar to Each other. Consequently we may suppose, that what is precious to one man, is precious to another, and what is irksom, or intolarable to one man, is so to another, consider'd in a Law of Nature. Therefore we may reasonably Conclude, that Liberty is Equally as pre[c]ious to a *Black man*, as it is to a *white one*, and Bondage Equally as intollarable to the one as it is to the other: Seeing it Effects the Laws of nature Equally as much in the one as it Does in the other. But, as I observed Before, those privileges that are granted to us By the Divine Being, no one has the Least right to take them from us without our consen[t]; and there is Not the Least precept, or practise, in the Sacred Scriptures, that constitutes a Black man a Slave, any more than a white one.

Shall a mans Couler Be the Decisive Criterion whereby to Judg of his natural right? or Becaus a man is not of the same couler with his Neighbour, shall he Be Deprived of those things that Distuingsheth [Distinguisheth] him from the Beasts of the field?

I would ask, whence is it that an Englishman is so far Distinguished from an Affrican in point of Natural privilege? Did he recieve it in his origenal constitution? or By Some Subsequent grant? Or Does he Bost of some hygher Descent that gives him this pre-heminance? for my part I can find no such revelation. It is a Lamantable consequence of the fall, that mankind, have an insatiable thurst after Superorety one over another: So that however common or prevalent the practise may be, it Does not amount, Even to a Surcomstance, that the practise is warrentable.

God has been pleas'd to distiungs [distinguish] some men from others, as to natural abilitys, But not as to natural *right*, as they came out of his hands.

But sometimes men by their flagitious practise forfeit their Liberty into the hands of men, By Becomeing unfit for society; But have the *affricans* Ever as a Nation, forfited their Liberty in this manner? What Ever individuals have done; yet, I Believe, no such Chaleng can be made upon them, as a Body. As there should be Some rule whereby to govern the conduct of men; so it is the Deuty, and intrest of a community, to form a system of *Law*, that is calculated to promote the commercial intrest of Each other: and so Long as it produses so Blessed an Effect, it should be maintained. But when, instead of contributing to the well Being of the community, it proves banefull to its subjects over whome it Extends, then it is hygh time to call it in question. Should any ask, where shall we find any system of Law whereby to regulate our moral Conduct? I think their is none so Explicit and indeffinite, as that which was given By the Blessed Saviour of the world. *As you would that men should do unto you, do you Even so to them.* One would think, that the mention of the precept, would strike conviction to the heart of these Slavetraders; unless an aviricious Disposision, governs the Laws of humanity.

If we strictly adhear to the rule, we shall not impose anything upon Others, But what we should Be willing should Be imposed upon us were we in their Condision.

I shall now go on to consider the manner in which the Slave-trade is carried on, By which it will plainly appear, that the practise is vile and atrocious, as well as the most inhuman. it is undoubtedly true that those that Emigrate slaves from *Africa* Do Endevour to rais mutanies among them in order to procure slaves. here I would make some Extracts from a pamphlet printed in Philadelphia, a few years ago: the varacity of which need not be scrupled, seeing it agrees with many other accounts.

N. *Brue*, Directory of the *French* factory at *Senegal*, who Lived twenty-seven years in that country says, "that the *Europeans* are far from desiring to act as peace-makers among the *Negros*, which would Be acting contrary to their intrest, since the greater the wars, the more slaves are procured." *William Boseman*, factor for the Duch at *Delmina*, where he resided sixteen years, relates, "that one of the former Comma[n]ders hired an army of the Negros, of *Jefferia*, and *Cabesteria*, for a Large Sum of money, to fight the Negros of *Commanry* [?], which occasioned a Battle, which was more Bloody than the wars of the Negros usually are: And that another Commander gave at one time five *hundred* pounds, and at another time Eight hundred pounds, to two other Negro nations, to induce them to take up arms against their Country people." This is confirmed by *Barbot*, agent general of the french African company, who says, "The *Hollanders*, a people very zelous for their Commerce at the Coasts, were very studious to have the war carried on amongst the Blacks, to distract, as Long as possible, the trade of the other Europeans and to that Effect, were very ready to assist upon all occasions, the Blacks, their allies, that they mite Beat their Enemies, and so the Commerce fall into their hands." And one *William Smith*, who was sent By the *African* company, to visit their settlements in the year 1726, from the information he reciev'd from one, who had resided ten years, viz. "that the Discerning Natives accounted it their greatest unhappyness that they were Ever visited by the *Europeans*:—that we Christians introduced the traffick of Slaves, and that Before our comeing they Lived in peace; But, say they, it is observable, that Wherever Christianity comes, there comes with it a Sword, a gun, powder, and Ball." And thus it Brings ignominy upon our holy religion, and mak[e]s the Name of Christians sound Odious in the Ears of the heathen. O Christianity, how art thou Disgraced, how art thou reproached, By the vicious practises of those upon whome thou dost smile! Let us go on to consider the great hardships, and sufferings, those Slaves are put to, in order to be transported into these plantations. There are generally many hundred slaves put on board a vessel, and they are Shackkled together, two by two, wors than Crimanals going to the place of Execution; and they are Crouded together as close as posable, and almost naked; and their sufferings are so great, as I have Been Credibly informed, that it often Carries off one third of them on their passage; yea, many have put an End to their own Lives for very anguish; And as some have manifested a

21

Disposision to rise in their Defence, they have Been put to the most Cruel torters, and Deaths as human art could inflict. And O! the Sorrows, the Greif the Distress, and anguish which attends them! and not onely them But their frinds also in their Own Country, when they must forever part with Each Other? What must be the plaintive noats that the tend[er] parents must assume for the Loss of their Exiled *Child*? Or the husband for his Departed wife? and how Do the Crys of their Departed friends Eccho from the watry Deep! Do not I really hear the fond mother Expressing her Sorrows, in accents that mite well peirce the most obdurate heart? "O! my Child, why why was thy Destiny hung on so precarious a theread! unhappy fate! O that I were a captive with thee or for thee! [About seventy-five words are crossed out and utterly illegible. The mother's words continue:] Cursed Be the Day wherein I Bare thee, and Let that inauspicious Night be remembered no more. Come, O King of terrors. Dissipate my greif, and send my woes into oblivion."

But I need Not stand painting the Dreery Sene. Let me rather appeal to tender parents, whether this is Exaggarating matters? Let me ask them what would be their Distress. Should one of their Dearest *Children* Be snach'd from them, in a Clendestine manner, and carried to *Africa*, or some othe forreign Land, to be under the most abject Slavery for Life, among a strang people? would it not imbitter all your Domestic Comforts? would he not Be Ever upon your mind? nay, Doth not nature Even recoil at the reflection?

And is not their many ready to say, (unless void of natural Effections) that it would not fail to Bring them Down with sorrow to the grave? And surely, this has Been the awfull fate of some of those *Negros* that have been Brought into these plantations; which is not to be wondered at, unless we suppose them to be without natural Effections: which is to rank them Below the very Beasts of the field.

O! what an Emens Deal of Affrican-Blood hath Been Shed by the inhuman Cruelty of Englishmen! that reside in a Christian Land! Both at home, and in their own Country? they being the fomenters of those wars, that is absolutely necessary, in order to carry on this cursed trade; and in their Emigration into these colonys? and By their merciless masters, in some parts at Least? O ye that have made yourselves Drunk with human Blood! altho' you may go with impunity here in this Life, yet God will hear the Crys of that innocent Blood, which crys from the Sea, and from the ground against you, Like the Blood of Abel, more pealfull [?] than thunder, *vengence! vengence!* What will you Do in that Day when God shall make inquisision for Blood? he will make you Drink the phials of his indignation which Like a potable Stream shall Be poured out without the Least mixture of mercy; Believe it, Sirs, their shall not a Drop of Blood, which you have Spilt unjustly, Be Lost in forgetfullness. But it Shall Bleed affresh, and testify against you, in the Day when God shall Deal with Sinners.

We know that under the Levitical Oeconomy, *man-stealing* was to Be punished with Death; so [?] we Esteem those that Steal any of our Earthy Commadety gilty of a very heinous Crime:

What then must Be an adiquate punishment to Be inflicted on those that Seal [steal] men?

Men were made for more noble Ends than to be Drove to market, like Sheep and oxen. "Our being Christians, (says one) Does not give us the Least Liberty to trample on heathen, nor Does it give us the Least Superority over them." And not only are they gilty of *man-stealing* that are the immediate actors in this trade, But those in these colonys that Buy them at their hands, ar far from Being guiltless: for when they saw the theif they consented with him. if men would forbear to Buy Slaves off the hands of the Slave-merchants, then the trade would of necessaty cease; if I buy a man, whether I am told he was stole, or not, yet I have no right to Enslave him, Because he is a human Being: and the immutable Laws of God, and indefeasible Laws of nature, pronounced him free.

Is it not exceeding strang that mankind should Become such mere vassals to their own carnal avarice as Even to imbrue their hands in inocent Blood? and to Bring such intollerable opressiones upon others, that were they themselves to feel them, perhaps they would Esteem Death preferable—pray consider the miserys of a Slave, Being under the absolute controul of another, subject to continual Embarisments, fatiues, and corections at the will of a master; it is as much impossable for us to bring a man heartely to acquiesce in a passive obedience in this case, as it would be to stop a man's Breath, and yet have it caus no convulsion in nature. those negros amongst us that have Children, they, viz. their *Children* are brought up under a partial Disapilne: their white masters haveing but Little, or no Effection for them. So that we may suppose, that the abuses that they recieve from the hands of their masters are often very considerable; their parents Being placed in such a Situation as not being able to perform relative Deutys. Such are those restrictions they are kept under By their task-masters that they are render'd incapable of performing those morral Deutys Either to God or man that are infinitely binding on all the human race; how often are they

Seperated from Each other, here in this Land at many hundred miles Distance, Children from parents, and parents from Children, Husbands from wives, and wives from Husbands? those whom God hath Joined together, and pronounced one flesh, man assumes a prerogative to put asunder. What can be more abject than their condission? in short, if I may so speak 'tis a hell upon Earth; and all this for filthy Lucres sake: Be astonished, O ye Heavens, at this! I believe it would Be much Better for these Colonys if their was never a Slave Brought into this Land; theirby our poor are put to great Extremitys, by reason of the plentifullness of Labour, which otherwise would fall into their hands.

I shall now go on to take under Consideration some of those *arguments* which those that are Concern'd in the Slave-trade Do use in vindication of their practise; which arguments, I shall Endevour to Shew, are Lame, and Defective.

The first argument that I shall take notice of is this viz. *that in all probability the Negros are of Canaans posterity, which ware Destined by the almighty to Slavery; theirfore the practise is warrantable.* To which I answer, Whethear the Negros are of Canaans posterity or not, perhaps is not known By any mortal under Heaven. But allowing they were actually of Canaans posterity, yet we have no reason to think that this Curs Lasted any Longer than the comeing of Christ: when that Sun of riteousness arose this wall of partition was Broken Down. Under the *Law*, their were many External Cerimonies that were tipecal of Spiritual things; or which Shadowed forth the purity, & perfection of the Gospel: as Corporeal *blemishes*, Spurious *Birth*, flagicious *practises*, debar'd them from the congregation of the Lord: theirby Shewing, the intrinsick purity of heart that a Conceal'd Gospel requir'd as the pre-requisite for heaven, and as *Ham* uncovered his fathers nakedness, that is, Did not Endevour to Conceal it, but gaz'd perhaps with a Lascivious Eye, which was repugnant to the Law which was afterwards given to the Children of Isarel [Israel]: So it was most [?] Necessary that god Should manifest his Signal Disapprobation of this hainous Sin, By makeing him and his posterity a publick Example to the world, that theirby they mite be set apart, and Seperated from the people of God as unclean. And we find it was a previlege Granted to God's people of old, that they mite Enslave the *heathen, and the Stranger that were in the Land*; theirby to Shew the Superior previleges God's people Enjoy'd above the rest of the world: So that we, Gentiles were then Subject to Slavery, Being then heathen; [illegible] So that if they will keep Close to the Letter they must own themselves yet Subject to the yoak; unless we Suppose them *free* By Being Brought into the same place, or haveing the same previleges with the Jews; then it follows, that we may inslave all Nations, be they White or Black, that are heathens, which they themselves will not allow. We find, under that Dispensation, God Declareing that he would *visit the iniquity of the fathers upon the Children, unto the third, and fourth generation, &c*. And we find it so in the case of *Ham*, as well as many others; their posterity Being Extrinsically unclean.

But now our glorious hygh preist hath visably appear'd in the flesh, and hath Establish'd a more glorious Oeconomy. he hath not only visably Broken Down that wall of partision that interposed Between the ofended majesty of Heaven and rebellious Sinners and removed those tedeous forms under the Law, which savoured so much of servitude, and which *could never make the comers thereunto perfect*, By rendering them obselete: But he has removed those many Embarisments, and Distinctions, that they were incident to, under so contracted a Dispensation. So that whatever *Bodily imperfections*, or whatever *Birth* we sustain, it Does not in the Least Debar us from Gospel previlege's. Or whatever hainous practise any may be gilty of, yet if they manifest a gospel [?] repentance, we have no right to Debar them from our Communion. and it is plain Beyond all Doubt, that at the comeing of Christ, this curse that was upon *Canaan*, was taken off; and I think there is not the Least force in this argument than there would Be to argue that an imperfect Contexture of *parts*, or Base *Birth*, Should Deprive any from Gospel previleges; or Bring up any of those antiquated Ceremonies from oblivion, and reduse them into practise.

But you will say that Slave-keeping was practised Even under the Gospel, for we find *paul*, and the other apostles Exhorting *Servants to be obedient to their masters*. to which I reply, that it mite be they were Speaking to Servants in *minority* in General; But Doubtless it was practised in the Days of the Apostles from what *St. paul* Says, *1. Corin. 7 21. art thou called, being a servant? care not for it; but if thou mayest Be made free, use it rather*. So that the Apostle seems to recomend freedom if attainable, q.d. "if it is thy unhappy Lot to be a slave, yet if thou art Spiritually free Let the former appear so minute a thing when compared with the Latter that it is comparitively unworthy of notice; yet Since freedom is so Exelent a Jewel, which none have a right to Extirpate, and if there is any hope of attaining it, use all Lawfull measures for that purpose." So that however Extant or preval[e]nt it mite Be in that or this age; yet it does not in the Least reverse

25

the unchangeable Laws of God, or of nature; or make that Become Lawfull which is in itself unlawfull; neither is it Strange, if we consider the moral Depravity of mans nature, thro'out all ages of the world, that mankind should Deviate from the unering rules of Heaven. But again, another argument which some use to maintain their intollerable opression upon others is this, viz., *that those Negros that are Brought into these plantations are Generally prisoners, taken in their wars, and would otherwise fall a sacrifice to the resentment of their own people.* But this argument, I think, is plainly confuted By the forecited account which Mr. *Boasman* gives, as well as many others. Again, some say they *Came honestly By their Slaves, Becaus they Bought them of their parents,* (that is, those that Brought them from Africa) *and rewarded them well for them.* But without Doubt this is, for the most part fals; But allowing they Did actually Buy them of their parents, yet I query, whether parents have any right to sel their Children for Slaves: if parents have a right to Be free, then it follows that their Children have Equally as good a right to their freedom, Even *Hereditary.* So, (to use the words of a Learned writer) "one has no Body to Blame But himself, in case he shall find himself Deprived of a man whome he tho't By Buying for a price he had made his own; for he Dealt in a trade which was illicit, and was prohibited by the most obvious Dictates of Humanity. for these resons Every one of those unfortunate men who are pretended to be Slaves, has a right to Be Declared free, for he never Lost his Liberty; he could not Lose it; his prince had no power to Dispose of him. of cours the Sale was *ipso Jure* void."

But I shall take notice of one argument more which these Slave-traders use, and it is this, viz. *that those Negros that are Emigrated into these colonies are brought out of a Land of Darkness under the meridian Light of the Gospel; and so it is a great Blessing instead of a Curs.* But I would ask, who is this that Darkneth counsel By words with out knoledg? Let us attend to the great appostle Speaking to us in *Rom. 3.8.* where he reproves some slanderers who told it as a maxim preached By the apostles that they said *Let us Do Evil that Good may come, whose Damnation* the inspired penman pronounces with an Emphasis *to Be Just.* And again *Chap.* 6 vers 1. where By way of interagation he asks, *Shall we continue in Sin that grace may abound?* The answer is obvious, *God forbid.* But that those Slavemerchants that trade upon the coasts of Africa do not aim at the Spiritual good of their Slaves, is Evident By their Behaviour towards them; if they had their Spiritual good at heart, we should Expect that those Slave-merchants that trade upon their coasts, would, insted of Causing quarrelings, and Blood-Shed among them, which is repugnant to Christianity, and below the Character of humanity, Be Sollicitous to Demean Exampleary among them, that By their wholesom conduct, those heathen mite be Enduced to Entertain hygh, and admiring tho'ts of our holy religion. Those Slaves in these Colonies are generally kept under the greatest ignorance, and Blindness, and they are scersly Ever told by their white masters whether there is a Supreme Being that governs the univers; or wheather there is any reward, or punishments Beyond the grave. Nay such are those restrictions that they are kept under that they Scersly know that they have a right to Be free, or if they Do they are not allowed to Speak in their defence; Such is their abject condission, that that *genius* that is peculiar to the human race, cannot have that Cultivation that the polite world is favour'd with, and therefore they are stiled the ignorant part of the world; whereas were they under the Same advantages to git knoledge with them, perhaps their progress in arts would not be inferior.

But should we give ourselves the trouble to Enquire into the grand motive that indulges men to concearn themselves in a trade So vile and abandon, we Shall find it to Be this, Namely, to Stimulate their Carnal avarice, and to maintain men in pride, Luxury, and idleness, and how much it hath Subserv'd to this vile purpose I Leave the Candid publick to Judge: I speak it with reverence yet I think all must give in that it hath such a tendency.

But altho god is of Long patience, yet it does not Last always, nay, he has *whet* his *glittering Sword, and his hand hath already taken hold on Judgement;* for who knows how far that the unjust Oppression which hath abounded in this Land, may be the procuring cause of this very Judgement that now impends, which so much portends *Slavery?*

for this is God's way of working, Often he brings the Same Judgements, or Evils upon men, as they unriteously Bring upon others. As is plain from *Judges* 1 and on.

But Adoni-bezek fled, and they persued after him, and caut him, and cut off his thumbs, and his great toes.

And Adoni-besek said, threescore and ten kings haveing their thumbs and their great toes cut off gathered their meat under my table: as I have Done, So god hath requited me.

And as wicked *Ahab,* and *Jezebel* to gratify their covetousness caused *Naboth* to be put to Death, and as *Dogs* licked the Blood of *Naboth,* the word of the Lord was By the prophet *Elijah, thus Saith the Lord, in the place where Dogs Licked the Blood of Naboth, Shall Dogs Lick thy Blood Even thine. See 1 Kings 21. 19. And of Jezebel also Spake the Lord, Saying, The Dogs Shall Eat Jezebel By the walls of Jezreel. vers 23.*

And we find the Judgement actually accomplished upon *Ahab* in the 22. Chap. & 38. vers.

And upon *Jezebel* in the 9 chap. 2 of *Kings*.

Again *Rev. 16.6. for they have Shed the Blood of Saints and prophets, and thou hast given them Blood to Drink; for they are worthy. And chap. 18.6. Reward her Even as She rewarded you.* I say this is often God's way of Dealing, by retaliating Back upon men the Same Evils that they unjustly Bring upon others. I Don't Say that we have reason to think that *Oppression* is the alone caus of this Judgement that God is pleas'd to Bring upon this Land, Nay, But we have the greatest reason to think that this is not one of the Least. And whatever some may think that I am instigated By a fals zeal; and all that I have Said upon the Subject is mere Novelty: yet I am not afraid to appeal to the consience of any rational and honnest man, as to the truth of what I have just hinted at; and if any will not confide in what I have humbly offer'd, I am persuaded it must be such Short-Sited persons whose Contracted Eyes never penitrate thro' the narrow confines of Self, and are mere Vassals to filthy Lucre.

But I Cannot persuade myself to make a period to this Small *Treatise*, without humbly addressing myself, more perticularly, unto all such as are Concearn'd in the practise of *Slave-keeping*.

Sirs, Should I persue the Dictates of nature, resulting from a sense of my own inability, I should be far from attempting to form this address: Nevertheless, I think that a mere Superficial reflection upon the merits of the Cause, may Serve as an ample apology, for this humble attempt. Therefore hopeing you will take it well at my hands, I persume, (tho' with the greatest Submission) to Crave your attention, while I offer you a few words.

Perhaps you will think the preceeding pages unworthy of Speculation: well, Let that be as it will; I would Sollicit you Seriously to reflect on your conduct, wheather you are not gilty of unjust Oppression. Can you wash your hands, and say, I am Clean from this Sin? Perhaps you will Dare to Say it Before men; But Dare you Say it Before the tremendous tribunal of that God Before Whome we must all, in a few precarious moments appear? then whatever fair glosses we may have put upon our Conduct, that god whose Eyes pervade the utmost Extent of human tho't, and Surveys with one intuitive view, the affairs of men; he will Examin into the matter himself, and will set Every thing upon its own Basis; and impartiallity Shall Be Seen flourishing throughout that Sollemn assembly. Alas! Shall men hazard their precious Souls for a little of the transetory things of time. O *Sirs!* Let that pity, and compassion, which is peculiar to mankind, Especially to Englishmen, no Longer Lie Dormant in your Breast: Let it run free thro' Disinterested Benevolence. then how would these iron yoaks Spontaneously fall from the gauled Necks of the oppress'd! And that Disparity, in point of Natural previlege, which is the Bane of Society, would Be Cast upon the utmost coasts of Oblivion. If this was the impulsive Exercise that animated all your actions, your Conscience's wold Be the onely Standard unto which I need appeal. think it nor uncharitable, nor Censorious to say, that whenever we Erect our Battery, so as it is Like to prove a Detriment to the intrest of any, we Loos their attention. or, if we Don't Entirely Loos that, yet if true Christian candour is wanting we cannot Be in a Sutiable frame for Speculation: So that the good Effect that these Otherwise mite have, will prove abortive. If I could once persuade you to reflect upon the matter with a Single, and an impartial Eye, I am almost assured that no more need to be Said upon the Subject: But whether I shall Be so happy as to persuade you to Cherish such an Exercise I know not: yet I think it is very obvious from what I have humbly offer'd, that so far forth as you have Been Concerned in the *Slave-trade*, so far it is that you have assumed an oppressive, and tyrannic power. Therefore is it not hygh time to undo these heavy Burdens, and Let the Oppressed go free? And while you manifest such a noble and magnanimous Spirit, to maintain inviobly your own Natural rights, and militate so much against Despotism, as it hath respect unto yourselves, you do not assume the Same usurpations, and are no Less tyrannic. Pray let there be a congruity amidst you Conduct, Least you fall amongst that Class the inspir'd pen-man Speaks of. *Rom.* 2.21 and on. *thou therefore which teacheth another, teachest thou not thy Self? thou that preachest a man Should not Steal, Dost thou Steal? thou that sayest, a man Should not Commit adultery, Dost thou Commit adultery? thou that abhoreth idols, Dost thou Commit Sacrilege? thou that makest thy Bost of the Law, through Breaking the Law Dishonnerest thou God?* While you thus Sway your tyrant Scepter over others, you have nothing to Expect But to Share in the Bitter pill. 'Twas an Exelent note that I Lately read in a modern peice, and it was this. "O when shall America be consistantly Engaged in the Cause of Liberty!" If you have any Love to yourselves, or any Love to this Land, if you have any Love to your fellow-men, Break these intollerable yoaks, and Let their names Be remembered no more, Least they Be retorted on your own necks, and you Sink under them; for god will not hold you guiltless.

Sirs, the important Caus in which you are Engag'd in is of a[n] Exelent nature, 'tis ornamental to your Characters, and will, undoubtedly, immortalize your names thro' the Latest posterity. And it is pleasing to Behold that patriottick Zeal which fire's your Breast; But it is Strange that you Should want the Least Stimulation to further Expressions of so noble a Spirit. Some gentlemen have Determined to Contend in a Consistant manner: they have *Let the oppressed go free;* and I cannot think it is for the want of such a generous princaple in you, But thro' some inadvertancy that [end of extant manuscript].

A Sermon on
John 3:3

Studying theology on his own, the young Haynes composed this sermon. It was the Rose family custom to read published sermons at Saturday evening worship. Haynes read this one, Deacon Rose asked who the author was (assuming it to be Whitefield), and Haynes modestly confessed it was his own work.

———

John iii., 3:—"Jesus answered and said unto him, Verily, verily, I say unto thee, except a man be born again, he cannot see the kingdom of God."

This chapter contains a conference between our blessed Lord and Nicodemus, a ruler of the Jews. This great man came to our Saviour by night, and addressed him in this manner: "Rabbi," says he, "we know that thou art a teacher come from God, for no man can do the miracles that thou doest except God be with him." Doubtless he had a rational conviction, from the many miracles that Christ did, that he was come from God. Our blessed Lord did not stand to show who he was, but, like a wise and kind teacher, takes occasion to inculcate the importance of the great doctrine of regeneration; and tells him, with a double asseveration, that, except a man be born again, he cannot see the kingdom of God. But, as great as this man was, we find that he was ignorant in a fundamental point in religion. It appeared a paradox unto him; for he, supposing our Lord must mean a natural birth, asks him, as in ver. 4, "How can a man be born when he is old? Can he enter the second time into his mother's womb, and be born?" Christ, in order further to explain his meaning, and to show that it was not a natural birth that he had reference to, adds, "Verily, verily, I say unto thee, except a man be born of water and of the Spirit, he cannot enter into the kingdom of God." By which, perhaps, we may understand, that, as water is often made use of in the Scriptures as a symbolical representation of the regenerating and sanctifying influences of the Holy Spirit on the hearts of the children of men, so, unless we are born of the *water* of the Spirit (as divines interpret it), we cannot see the kingdom of God.

Our Lord proceeds to tell him, That which is born of the flesh is flesh, and that which is born of the spirit is spirit. *Q.d.,* It would be to no purpose if a man should have another natural birth, seeing it would not alter his nature; for that which is born of the flesh is flesh; let it be born ever so many times of the flesh, it would still remain fleshly; and that which is born of the spirit is spirit. "Marvel not that I said unto thee, Ye must be born again." And now it seemed a greater mystery to Nicodemus than ever; therefore he cries out, as in ver. 9, "How can these things be?"

Thus you see, as I observed before, that, although Nicodemus was a great man, a ruler of the Jews, he was ignorant about the new birth. And doubtless it is so now. There are many of the great ones of the earth—tell them about experimental religion—tell them that they must feel the Holy Spirit working powerfully on their hearts—that they must be born again—they are ready to cry out, with this master in Israel, *How can these things be?*

But, to return to the words first read. . . . . . In speaking something from these words I shall pursue the following method:—

I.   Show the necessity of regeneration, or of our being born again.

II. Explain the nature of the new birth, or what it is to be born again.

III. Show what we are to understand by *seeing the kingdom of God.*

IV. Make some remarks.

1. This will appear, if we consider that state that mankind are in antecedent to the new birth. And if we view mankind as they come into the world, we shall then find them *haters of God—enemies to God—estranged from God*—nay, the very heart is enmity itself against all the Divine perfections; and we shall find them acting most freely and most voluntarily in these exercises. There is no state or circumstance that they prefer to the present, unless it be one whereby they may dishonour God more, or carry on their war with heaven with a higher hand. They have no relish for divine things, but hate, and choose to remain enemies to, all that is morally good. Now, that this is actually the case with sinners, is very evident from the Scriptures. We are told in the chapter of which the text is a part, that that which is born of the flesh is flesh, and that which is born of the spirit is

spirit; which teaches us that there is nothing truly spiritual or holy in the first birth, but that this comes by the second, or by the renewings of the Holy Ghost. Christ tells the Jews that they hated him without a cause. And the inspired apostle says, "That the carnal mind is enmity against God, for it is not subject to the law of God, neither indeed can be. So, then, they that are in the flesh cannot please God."—Rom. viii., 7, 8. Therefore,

2. Seeing this is the state that mankind are in antecedent to the new birth, it is not fit or reasonable that God should bring them into favour with himself, or be at peace with them, without regeneration. Nay, he cannot, consistent with his perfection, for this would be for him to connive at wickedness when he tells us that he can by no means clear the guilty. And,

3. To suppose that sinners can see the kingdom of God or be happy in the Divine favour without regeneration or the new birth, is a perfect inconsistency, or contrary to the nature of the thing. The very essence of religion consists in love to God; and a man is no further happy in the favour of God than he loves God. Therefore, to say we enjoy happiness in God, and at the same time hate God, is a plain contradiction.

4. It is evident from Scripture that those to whom God gives a title to his spiritual kingdom are regenerated or born again, and those that are not, and remain so, shall be miserable. This is not only asserted in the text by the Son of God, who was co-equal, co-eternal, and co-essential with the Father—whose words stand more permanent than the whole fabric of heaven and earth—and who stands at the gate of the universe, and will not alter the things that have gone out of his mouth; I say, it was not only spoken by this glorious being who cannot lie, by his own lips, with a repeated *verily*, but has been confirmed by those whom he inspired, and who, we are assured, had the mind of Christ. St. Paul gives us the character of a good man, or one entitled to the heavenly world, 2 Cor. v., 17: "If any man be in Christ Jesus, he is a new creature; old things are passed away, behold, all things are become new." And they are said to be renewed in the spirit of their mind, Eph. iv., 23. Compare Rom. xii., 2. And to be born of God, John i., 13. And they are spoken of as being lovers of God, Prov. viii., 17. And [respecting] those that are not of this character, or that remain enemies to God, he tells us that he will pour out his fury upon them. Hence we read that the wicked shall be turned into hell, even all the nations that forget God; and that without holiness no man shall see the Lord. And St. John the Divine, having a view of the glory of the heavenly world, says that there shall in no wise enter into it any thing that defileth, neither whatsoever

worketh abomination, or maketh a lie, but they which are written in the Lamb's book of life. Thus we see the propriety of our Lord's assertion, that, except a man be born again, he cannot see the kingdom of God.

But, as I mean to handle the subject with the utmost brevity, I pass on,

II. To show the nature of regeneration, or what it is to be born again. And here,

1. I would consider the agent, or who it is that effects this great work. And if we consider that state that mankind are in by nature, as has been described above, we need not stand long to know who to attribute this work to. It is a work too great to attribute to men or angels to accomplish. None but He who, by one word's speaking, spake all nature into existence, can triumph over the opposition of the heart. This is the work of the Holy Spirit, who is represented in Scripture as emanating from the Father and the Son, yet co-equal with them both. It is God alone that slays the native enmity of the heart—that takes away those evil dispositions that govern the man—takes away the heart of stone and gives a soft heart—and makes him that was a hater of God, an enemy to God, to become friendly to his divine character. This is not wrought by any efficiency of man, or by any external motives, or by any light let into the understanding, but of God. Hence we read that those that receive Christ are born, not of blood, nor of the will of the flesh, nor of the will of man, but of God.—John i., 13. And that it is the gift of God.—Eph. ii., 8. Also that it is God which worketh in us.—Phil. ii., 13.

Thus, I say, the man is entirely passive in this work, but it is all wrought immediately by a Divine agency.

> In regeneration man is wholly passive; in conversion he is active. Regeneration is the motion of God in the creature; conversion is the motion of the creature to God, by virtue of that first principle whence spring all the acts of believing, repenting, and quickening. In all these man is active; in the other he is merely passive.
>
> —Charnock

The man now becomes a new creature. Although he cannot discern what is the way of the spirit (as the wise man observes), or how God thus changes the heart, yet he knows that he has different feelings from what he had before. Therefore,

2. It is necessary that we consider those things that are the attendants or consequences of regeneration or the new birth; for there are no gracious or

holy exercises that are prior thereto, to be sure, in the order of nature. Some seem to suppose faith to be before regeneration, but a little reflection upon the matter will show this to be wrong. By *faith* we are to understand a believing of those truths that God has exhibited in his word with a *friendly heart*. Now, to suppose that a man believes with this friendly heart antecedent to regeneration, is to suppose that a man is a friend to God while in a state of unregeneracy, which is contradictory to Scripture. Now, if to believe with a friendly and right-disposed heart is absolutely necessary in order to constitute a true faith, and such a heart is peculiar to the regenerate only, then we must be possessed with this heart (which is given in regeneration) before there can flow from it any such exercises. So that the man must become a good man, or be regenerated, before he can exercise faith, or love, or any grace whatever. Hence we read of men's receiving Christ, and then becoming the sons of God.—John i., 12. Therefore, what lies before us is to show what those fruits and effects are, and what are those inward feelings that come in consequence of the new birth. And,

1. He loves God supremely. He loves holiness for what it is in itself, because it agrees with his new temper. He chooses and prefers *that* to any thing else. He loves the law of God. He loves the gospel, and every thing that is Godlike. He loves the holy angels and the spirits of just men made perfect. His affections are set on things that are above. His treasure is there, and his heart will be there also. He loves the people of God in this world; nay, wherever moral rectitude is to be seen, he falls in love with it. He loves all mankind with a holy and virtuous love. Although he cannot love those that are the enemies of God with a love of complacency, yet he loves them with the love of benevolence. He is of a noble and generous spirit. He is a well-wisher to all mankind. And this supreme love to God and benevolence to man is spoken of in Scripture as the very essence of true religion.

2. He repents of all his sins. He feels guilty before God. He sees and owns that God is right and he is wrong. He sees and gives in that it would be just with God to consign him over to the regions of despair. Now the man which could take no delight in any thing else but sin, hates it beyond any thing whatever. Now he can acknowledge his sin with holy David—"Against thee, and thee only, have I sinned."—"Hide thy face from my sins, and blot out all mine iniquities." He sees that the sacrifice of God is a broken and a contrite spirit. Like the publican, afraid to look up, he smites upon his breast, saying, *"God be merciful to me, a sinner."*

3. He believes on the Lord Jesus Christ. I just observed what it was to believe. It is believing the record that God has given of his Son with a *friendly heart*. He gives in to the truths of the gospel with his heart, and he knows the truth by his own happy experience.

4. He is disposed to walk in all the ordinances of God blameless.

He evidences by his holy walk that he has a regard for the honour of God. He endeavours to imitate his Divine master in all his imitable perfections. Knowing that he saith "he that abideth in him, ought himself so to walk, even as he has walked." Oh, happy change indeed! The man is made like God in some good measure. He has the same kind of affections and dispositions as there are in God. He has a living principle within him, which is active and vigorous, springing up into everlasting life.

But we pass on to take notice of the third thing in the method, which was,

III. To show what we are to understand by seeing the kingdom of God.

Now we are not to suppose that it is an intuitive view that we have of the kingdom of God, as we behold objects with our eyes; but we are to understand enjoying, or being admitted to possession of, the blessings and entertainments of the heavenly world, or being brought into the Divine favour. He cannot be a partaker of that unspeakable happiness that is in God; he cannot enjoy that blessed intercourse and holy communion that comes to the believer in consequence of his being united to Christ in this world, or be admitted to those more sublime entertainments that are above. Something like this we are to understand by seeing the kingdom of God. But it will not be amiss to inquire a little what is meant by the kingdom of God. And we may understand,

1. The spiritual kingdom of Christ here in this world. I mean that gracious temper of mind, or those holy dispositions that are implanted in the heart by regeneration, and also when a number of such do unite together in an ecclesiastical body. This is called Christ's kingdom, because they not only have Christ's kingdom in their hearts, but also, being visibly united together to promote the cause of Christ, they may, by way of eminence, be so styled. And,

2. We may understand the kingdom of glory, or this principle of divine life consummated in the heavenly world, so that this kingdom that believers have set up in them in this world, is the same in kind as it is in heaven. But when we shall come to put off this tabernacle, and be imbodied spirits in the

upper world, our love will be increased, and we shall drink full draughts out of that crystal stream that glides gently through the paradise of God.

Oh! did believers once know adequately what is prepared for them in the heavenly world, how would they despise all things here below, and long to be on the wing for heaven! Well may it be called a kingdom, where are crowns not of gold, but of glory;—where the King of kings sits amid the heavenly throng, and feeds them with his celestial dainties. And when the body is reunited to the soul at the resurrection, there will no doubt be much higher degrees of glory. Oh! then, let us live as becometh those that are so highly favoured of the Lord.

Application

1. Hence see the propriety of our blessed Lord's assertion in the text, that, except a man be born again, he cannot see the kingdom of God, or enjoy the favour and love of God, either in this world or that to come. If men are totally depraved, as has been considered, from thence arises the absolute necessity of the new birth, and it is no strange or unaccountable thing that men must be born again. There is no obtaining the blessings of heaven without it. Therefore, says our Lord, "Marvel not that I said unto thee, Ye must be born again."

2. Hence learn the folly of all those that rest in any thing short of regeneration or the new birth. For, however far we may go in the things of religion, yet, if we are destitute of this divine and holy principle, we may be assured of it, from scripture as well as from the nature of things, that we cannot see the kingdom of God.

3. Let us examine ourselves whether we are possessed of this holy temper of heart or not. Have we new dispositions?—new affections?—and new desires? Are God and divine things the centre and object of our supreme love? Have we repentance towards God and faith in the Lord Jesus Christ? Have we got that universal benevolence which is the peculiar characteristic of a good man? Do we love the law of God? Have we viewed it in its purity and spirituality? Are we heartily disposed to walk in the ways of holiness? Do we freely and voluntarily choose that way? Are we well pleased with the gospel way of salvation?

Lastly. Let all those that are strangers to the new birth be exhorted no longer to live estranged from God, but labour after this holy temper of mind. Flee to Christ before it is too late. Consider that there is an aggravated condemnation that awaits all impenitent sinners. There is a day of death coming. There is a day of judgment coming. A few turns more upon the stage and we are gone. Oh how will you answer it at the bar of God, for your thus remaining enemies to him? It is sin that separates from God. But it is the *being* or *remaining* such that will eternally separate you from him. Never rest easy till you feel in you a change wrought by the Holy Spirit. And believe it,—until then you are exposed to the wrath of God; and without repentance you will in a few days be lifting up your eyes in torment.

The Lord grant that we may lay these things suitably to heart;—that we, having the kingdom of Christ set up in our hearts here, may grow up to the stature of perfect men in Christ Jesus. This will lay a foundation for union with all holy beings, and with this everlasting happiness in the kingdom of glory is inseparably connected, through Jesus Christ our Lord. Amen.

Outline of a Sermon
on Ps. 96:1

After his examination for ordination to the ministry, Haynes preached this sermon at Wintonbury, Connecticut.

———

"The Lord reigneth, let the earth rejoice."

Ps. 96:1

Doctrine

The absolute government of God affords just matter of rejoicing. Because

1. He has a perfect knowledge of all those events which ever took place in the whole universe. Prov. 15:3.

2. All things are entirely dependent on God for their existence.

3. He is infinitely wise.

This is another essential thing in an absolute governor, that he should know the exact number of events necessary to take place;—when and how they shall take place;—how powerful and how long they must continue to operate; for, if this is not perfectly understood, it will cause the greatest disorder in the system. This wisdom belongs to God, and to him only. Ps. 104:24.

4. He is all-powerful, hence he is called "the Lord Omnipotent." Rev. 19:6.

5. He is perfectly holy. Ps. 145:17.

Objections

1. Does it not look like tyranny for Jehovah to set up as absolute governor of the universe?

2. This doctrine destroys that freedom of the creature, which is necessary in order to render his actions virtuous or vicious.

3. If God is the disposer of all events, and it is [a] matter of joy that he reigns, then we ought to rejoice in all that wickedness and disorder which have taken place in the intellectual system.

4. The absolute supremacy of Jehovah is a licentious doctrine. If all things are dependent on God, then the salvation of the sinner is; therefore I will sit down in indolence; if he should please to save me in my stupid state, well,—if not, I must be lost.

Answer

Two things seem to be taken for granted in such an objection that are not true.

1. That the sinner has some true desire to be reconciled, and that his wickedness does not consist in the voluntary exercises of his heart. But the truth of the case is, his heart is wholly at enmity to God, without the least true desire to be reconciled to him, and in this all his inability and all his sin does radically consist.

2. It seems to suppose that the sinner may possibly obtain salvation while in a state of indolence, which is contrary to the very nature of those things that are required in the gospel, and which are connected with salvation, viz., repentance towards God, and faith in the Lord Jesus Christ. These are opposed to sloth and carelessness. They imply activity. Exertion is the very essence of that salvation which delivers from everlasting destruction. So that, to say that we may possibly obtain salvation while in a state of indolence, is to say we may have a thing, and at the same time not have it. Continuing in a state of stupidity is inseparably connected with everlasting burnings.

Farther, the consequence which the objector draws from the doctrine is not a natural one. Is it not a fearful thing to be in the hands of God? Yes, verily. But to whom? Not to the friends, but to the enemies of God; for to them he is a consuming fire. Their case is truly dangerous; and has the consideration of danger a tendency to make men careless and secure? Nay, it is always in view of danger that persons are exercised with concern and anguish. Did sinners realize these things, they could not live so careless as they do. Therefore, one reason why sinners are so stupified is, that they do not believe divine sovereignty. Hence we see that no such consequence follows from this doctrine. It is true men make this improvement of it. And what is the reason that they draw such frightful consequences? Alas! the reason is too obvious. It is because the carnal mind is enmity towards God.

The Character and Work of a Spiritual Watchman Described

Haynes' first published sermon was preached at the ordination of Reuben Parmelee, the first minister of the seven families who gathered together to form the First Congregational Church, Hinesburgh, Vermont. While most sources assume the sermon was published in 1791, it was probably the first publication of the printing partnership of Collier and Buel of Litchfield, Connecticut, in 1792.

———

The Character and Work of a Spiritual Watchman Described, a Sermon, Delivered at Hinesburgh, February 23, 1791, at the Ordination of the Rev. Reuben Parmelee

"For they watch for your souls as they that must give account."

Hebrews 13:17

Nothing is more evident, than that men are prejudiced against the gospel. It is from this source, that those who are for the defence of it, meet with so much contempt. It is true, they are frail, sinful dust and ashes, in common with other men; yet on account of the important embassy with which they are entrusted, it is agreeable to the unerring dictates of inspiration, to esteem them very highly in love for their work's sake. I Thess. 5:13.

43

To illustrate this sentiment, was the delight of the Apostle in this verse: "Obey them that have the rule over you, and submit yourselves." He was far from inculcating anything that might seem to confront what the Apostle Peter has enjoined, I Peter 5:3, Neither as being lords over God's heritage. The word signifies to *lead*, *guide*, or *direct* (Guyse's paraphrase).

Our text contains an important motive, to excite to attention and respect, that is due to the ministers of Christ, on account of their relation to him; and that is the aspect their work has to a judgement-day: For they watch for your souls, as they that must quickly give account. They are amenable to their great Lord and Master for every sermon they preach, and must give an account of the reception they and their work meet with, among their hearers.—Under the influence of such a thought, let us take notice of a few things, supposed by the work, assigned to ministers in the text.—Say something with respect to their character.—Whence it appears, that they must give account.—When they may be said to be properly influenced by such considerations.

I. There are several ideas suggested by the work assigned to gospel ministers in the text; which is, to *watch for souls*. This supposes,

1. That the soul is of vast importance; else why so much attention paid to it, as to have a guard to inspect it? All those injunctions we find interpreted through the sacred pages, to watchmen to be faithful, are so many evidences of the worth of men's souls. What renders them so valuable, is the important relation they stand in to their Maker. The perfections of the Deity are more illustrated in the redemption of fallen men, than they would have been in the salvation of apostate angels; else why were the latter passed by, while God chose the former as the objects of his attention? God hath from eternity appointed a proper number, for the display of his mercy and justice; means are necessary to fit them for the Master's use; so that the soul in this view, is of infinite importance.

2. Watchmen over the souls of men, implies that they are prone to neglect them, or to be inattentive to their souls. When one is set to inspect, or watch over another, it supposes some kind of incapacity that he is under to take care of himself. The scripture represents mankind by nature as *fools*, *madmen*; and being in a state of *darkness*, etc.

Men in general are very sagacious with respect to temporal affairs, and display much natural wit and ingenuity, in contriving and accomplishing evil designs; but to do good, they have no knowledge. Jer. 4:22. This is an evidence that their inability to foresee danger, and provide against it, is of the moral kind. Was there a disposition in mankind, correspondent to their natural powers, to secure the eternal interest of their souls in the way God has proscribed, watchmen would in a great measure be useless.

3. The work and office of gospel ministers, suggests the idea of enemies invading; that there is a controversy subsisting, and danger approaching. When soldiers are called forth, and sentinels stand upon the wall, it denotes war. The souls of men are environed with ten thousand enemies, that are seeking their ruin. Earth and hell are combined together to destroy. How many already have fell victims to their ferocity! The infernal powers are daily dragging their prey to the prison of hell. Men have rebelled against God, and made him their enemy; yea, all creatures, and all events, are working the eternal misery of the finally impenitent sinner.

4. We are taught in the text and elsewhere, that the work of a gospel minister is not with the temporal, but the spiritual concerns of men: They watch for *souls*. Their conversation is not to be about worldly affairs, but things that relate to Christ's kingdom, which involves the everlasting concerns of men's souls. When a minister's affections are upon this world, his visits among his people will be barren; he will inquire about the outward circumstances of his flock; and perhaps, from pecuniary motives, rejoice at such prosperity. But as though that was of greatest concern, he will have nothing to say with respect to the health, and prosperity of their souls: Have no joys or sorrows, to express, on account of the fruitful or more lifeless state of the inward man.

II. Let us say something with respect to the character of a spiritual watchman.

Natural endowments, embellished with a good education, are qualifications so obviously requisite in an evangelical minister, that it is needless we insist upon them at this time; and that the interest of religion has, and still continues, greatly to suffer for the want of them, is equally notorious.

In the early ages of Christianity, men were miraculously qualified and called into the work of the gospel ministry; but we are far from believing, that this is the present mode by which ordinary ministers are introduced.

1. It is necessary that those who engage in this work, love the cause in which they profess to be embarked; that the love of Christ be shed abroad in the heart: Hence our blessed Lord, by whose repeated interrogations to Simon whether he loved him, has set before us the importance of this

qualification in a spiritual Shepherd. The sad consequences of admitting those into the army, who are in heart enemies to the commonwealth, have often taught men to be careful in this particular. The trust reposed in a watchman is such, as renders him capable of great detriment to the community. He that undertakes in this work from secular motives, will meet with disappointment. What a gross absurdity is this, for a man to commend religion to others, while he is a stranger to it himself! "The pious preacher will commend the Saviour, from the personal fund of his own experience." Being smitten with the love of Christ himself, with what zeal and fervor will he speak of the divine glory! Love to Christ will tend to make a minister faithful, and successful. The importance of this point, urges me to be copious on the subject, were it not too obvious to require a long discussion.

2. Wisdom and prudence are important qualifications in ministers: hence that injunction of the great preacher, Matt. 10:16. Be ye therefore wise as serpents, and harmless as doves. He is a man of spiritual understanding, whose soul is irradiated with the beams of the Son of Righteousness,—has received an unction from the holy one,—is taught by the word and spirit, and walks in the light of God's countenance. He has seen the deceit of his own heart,—knows the intrigues of the enemy,—sees the many snares to which the souls of men are exposed,—and not being ignorant of the devices of Satan, he will endeavour to carry on the spiritual campaign, with that care and prudence, that he shall not get advantage. He knows that he has a subtle enemy to oppose, and human nature, replete with enmity against the gospel; and will endeavour, in every effort, to conduct with that wisdom and circumspection, as shall appear most likely to prove successful.

3. Patience is another qualification very necessary in a spiritual watchman. His breast being inspired with love to the cause, he will stand the storms of temptation; will not be disheartened by all the fatigues, and sufferings, to which his work exposes him; but will endure hardness as a good soldier of Jesus Christ.

4. Courage and fortitude, must constitute a part of the character of a gospel minister. A sentinel, who is worthy of that station, will not fear the formidable appearance of the enemy, nor tremble at their menaces. None of these things will move him, neither will he count his life dear unto him, to defend a cause so very important. He has the spirit of the intrepid Nehemiah, "Should such a man as I flee?" He stands fast in the faith; quits himself like a man, and is strong.

5. Nor must we forget to mention vigilance, or close attention to the business assigned him, as an essential qualification in a minister of Christ. A man does not answer the idea of a watchman, unless his mind is engaged in the business. The word, which we have rendered *watch*, in the text, signifies, in the original, to awake, and abstain from sleeping (Legh's *Critica Sacra*). Indeed all the purposes of a watch set upon the wall, are frustrated, if he sleeps on guard; thereby himself, and the whole army, are liable to fall an easy prey to the cruel depredations of the enemy. The spiritual watchman is not to sleep, but to watch the first motion of the enemy, and give the alarm; lest souls perish through his drowsiness and inattention.

Some further observations with respect to the work of a gospel minister, will be made in their place. We pass,—

III. To shew, That ministers must give account to God of their conduct, more especially as it respects the people of their charge.

This solemn consideration is suggested in the text:—'Tis the design of preaching, to make things ready for the day of judgment. 2 Cor. 2:16. To the one we are the favour of death unto death; and to the other, the favour of life unto life: We are fitting men for the Master's use,—preparing affairs for that decisive court. This supposes, that things must be laid open before the great assembly at the day of judgment; or why is it that there are so many things that relate thereto, and are preparatives therefor.

The work of a gospel minister has a peculiar relation to futurity: An approaching judgment is that, to which every subject is pointing, and which renders every sentiment to be inculcated, vastly solemn, and interesting. Ministers are accountable creatures in common with other men; and we have the unerring testimony of scripture, that God shall bring every work into judgment, with every secret thing, whether it be good, or whether it be evil. Eccle. 12:14. If there is none of our conduct too minute to be cognizable, we may well conclude, that such important affairs, that relate to the work and office of gospel ministers, will not pass unnoticed.

Arguments may be taken from the names given to the ministers of Christ, that they must give account. They are called *soldiers, ambassadors, servants, stewards, angels*, etc. Which points out the relation they and their work stands in to God: That they are sent of God, and are amenable to him that sent them; as a servant or steward, is to give account to his Lord and Master, with respect to his faithfulness, in the trust reposed in him. God tells Ezekiel, If watchmen are not faithful, and souls perish through their neglect, that he would require their blood at the hands of such careless watchmen. It is evident, that primitive ministers were influenced to faithfulness from a view of the solemn account they expected to give at the day of judgment. This gave rise to those words, Acts 4:19. "But Peter and John answered and said unto them, Whether it be right in the sight of God to hearken unto you more than unto God, judge ye." If God's omniscience is a motive to faithfulness, it must be in this view, that he will not let our conduct pass unnoticed, but call us to an account.

It was approaching judgment that engrossed the attention of St. Paul, and made him exhort Timothy to study to approve himself unto God. This made the beloved disciple speak of having boldness in the day of judgment, I John 4:17.

The divine glory is an object only worthy of attention; and to display his holy character, was the design of God in creation; as there was no other beings existing antecedent thereto, to attract the mind of Jehovah; and we are sure that God is pursuing the same thing still, and always will. He is in one mind, and who can turn him? Job 23:13. There is no conceivable object that bears any proportion with the glory of God; and for him ever to aim at any thing else, would be incompatible with his perfections. The day of judgment is designed to be a comment on all other days; at which time God's government of the world, and their conduct towards him, will be publicly investigated, that the equity of divine administration may appear conspicuous before the assembled universe. It is called a day when the son of man is *revealed*. Luke 17:30. The honour of God requires that matters be publicly and particularly attended to; that evidences are summoned at this open court: Hence the saints are to judge the world. I Cor. 6:2.

It will conduce to the mutual happiness of faithful ministers and people, to have matter laid open before the bar of God, as in the words following our text, that they may do it with joy, and not with grief. The apostle speaks of some ministers and people who should have reciprocal joy in the day of the Lord Jesus;—which supposes, that ministers, and the people of their charge, are to meet another day as having something special with each other. The connexion between ministers and people is such, as renders them capable of saying much for, or against, the people of their charge; and of hearers making the same observations with respect to their teachers; and in this way the mercy and justice of God will appear illustrious.

Since, therefore, the work of gospel ministers has such a near relation to a judgment day;—since they are accountable creatures, and their work so momentous;—since it is a sentiment that has had so powerful influence on all true ministers in all ages of the world: Also their connexion is such as to render them capable of saying many things relating to the people of their charge. Above all, since the displays of divine glory are so highly concerned in this matter; we may without hesitation adopt the idea in the text, That ministers have a solemn account to give to their great Lord and Master, how they discharge the trust reposed in them.

IV. We are to inquire, what influence such considerations will have on the true ministers of Christ; or when they may be said to preach and act as those who must give account.

1. Those who properly expect to give account, will be very careful to examine themselves with respect to the motives by which they are influenced, to undertake in this work. He will view himself acting in the presence of an heart-searching God, who requires truth in the inward part, and will shortly call him to an account for all the exercises of his heart. He will search every corner of his soul, whether the divine honour, or something else, is the object of his pursuit. He has been taught, by the rectitude of the divine law, that God will not pass by transgressors, but will judge the secrets of men. The work will appear so great, that nature will recoil at the thought, like Jeremiah, "Ah, Lord God! behold, I cannot speak; for I am a child." Or with the great apostle, "Who is sufficient for these things?" The true disciple of Jesus will not thrust himself forward into the ministry, like a heedless usurper; but with the greatest caution, and self-diffidence.

2. A faithful Watchman will manifest that he expects to give account, by being very careful to know his duty, and will take all proper ways which are in his power, to become acquainted with it. He will study, as the apostle directs Timothy, to shew himself approved unto God. He will give attendance to Reading, Meditation and Prayer; will often call in divine aid, on account of his own insufficiency. As a faithful soldier will be careful to understand his duty; so the spiritual Watchman, will adhere closely to the word of God for his guide and directory.

3. A minister that watches for souls as one who expects to give account, will have none to please but God. When he studies his sermons, this will not be the enquiry, "How shall I form my discourse so as to please and gratify the humours of men, and get their applause?" but "How shall I preach so as to do honor to God, and meet with the approbation of my Judge?" this will be his daily request at the throne of grace. This will be ten thousand

times better to him than the vain flattery of men. His discourses will not be calculated to gratify the carnal heart, but he will not shun to declare the whole counsel of God.

The solemn account that the faithful minister expects to give another day, will direct him in the choice of his subjects; he will dwell upon those things which have a more direct relation to the eternal world. He will not entertain his audience with empty speculations, or vain philosophy; but with things that concern their everlasting welfare. Jesus Christ, and him crucified, will be the great topic and darling theme of his preaching. If he means to save souls, like a skilful physician, he will endeavor to lead his patients into a view of their maladies, and then point them to a bleeding Saviour as the only way of recovery. The faithful Watchman will give the alarm at the approach of the enemy, will blow the trumpet in the ears of the sleeping sinner, and endeavour to awake him.

4. The pious preacher will endeavour to adapt his discourses to the understanding of his hearers. "He will not be ambitious of saying fine things to win applause, but of saying useful things, to win souls." He will consider that he has the weak as well as strong, children as well as adults to speak to, and that he must be accountable for the blood of their souls, if they perish through his neglect. This will influence him to study *plainness* more than politeness; also he will labour to accommodate his sermons to the different states, or circumstances of his hearers; he will have comforting and encouraging lessons to set before the children of God; while the terrors of the law are to be proclaimed in the ears of the impenitent. He will strive to preach distinguishing, that every hearer may have his portion.—The awful scenes of approaching judgment, will have an influence on the Christian preacher with respect to the *manner* in which he will deliver himself. He will guard against that low and vulgar style, that tends to degrade religion; but his language will in some measure correspond with those very solemn and affecting things, that do engage his heart and tongue. He will not substitute a whining tone in the room of a Sermon; which, to speak no worse of it, is a sort of satire upon the Gospel, tending greatly to depreciate its solemnity and importance, and to bring it into contempt; but the judgment will appear so awful, and his attention so captivated with it, that his accents will be the result of a mind honestly, and engagedly taken up with a subject vastly important. "Such a preacher will not come into the pulpit as an actor comes upon the stage, to personate a feigned character, and forget his real one; to utter sentiments, or represent passions not his

own" (Fordyce). It is not to display his talents; but like one who feels the weight of eternal things, he will not address his hearers as though judgment was a mere empty sound; but viewing eternity just before him, and a congregation on the frontiers of it, whose eternal state depends upon a few uncertain moments; Oh! with what zeal and fervor will he speak! How will death, judgment, and eternity appear as it were in every feature, and every word! Out of the abundance of his heart, his mouth will speak. His hearers will easily perceive, that the preacher is one who expects to give account. He will study and preach with reference to a judgment to come, and deliver every sermon in some respects, as if it were his last, not knowing when his Lord will call him, or his hearers to account.—We are not to suppose that his zeal will vent itself in the frightful bellowings of enthusiasm; but he will speak forth the words of truth in soberness, with modesty, and christian decency.

5. They who watch for souls as those who expect to give account, will endeavour to know as much as may be the state of the souls committed to their charge, that they may be in a better capacity to do them good. They will point out those errors and dangers which they may see approaching; and when they see souls taken by the enemy, they will exert themselves to deliver them from the snare of the devil. The outward deportment of a faithful minister will correspond with his preaching: he will reprove, rebuke, warning his people from house to house. The weighty affairs of another world will direct his daily walk and conversation, in all places, and on every occasion.

A few particular Addresses

First, To him who is about to be set apart to the work of the Gospel Ministry in this place.

Dear Sir, From the preceding observations, you will easily see, that the work before you is great and solemn; and I hope this is a lesson you have been taught otherwise; the former acquaintance I have had with you, gives me reason to hope that this is the case. You are about to have these souls committed to your care; you are to be placed as a Watchman upon the walls of this part of Zion; I doubt not but that it is with trembling you enter upon this work. The relation that this day's business has with a judgment to come, renders the scene affecting. Your mind I trust has already anticipated the important moment, when you must meet this people before the bar of God. The good profession you are this day to make is before many witnesses; saints and wicked men are beholding; the angels are looking down upon us; above all, the great God with complacency or disapprobation, beholds the transactions of this day; he sees what motives govern you, and will proclaim it before the assembled Universe. Oh! solemn and affecting thought! The work before you is great, and requires great searching of heart, great self-diffidence, and self abasement. How necessary that you feel your dependance upon God; you cannot perform any part of your work without his help; under a sense of your weakness, repair to him for help. Would you be a successful Minister, you must be a praying, dependant one: do all in the name, and strength of the Lord Jesus. Would you be faithful in watching for the souls of men, you must be much in watching your own heart. If you are careless with respect to your own soul, you will be also with respect to others. Although the work is too great for you, yet let such considerations as these revive your desponding heart. That the cause is good, better than life, you may well give up all for it. 'Tis the cause of God, and that which will prove victorious, in spite of all opposition from men or devils—that God has promised to be with his Ministers to the end of the world—that the work is delightful; Paul somewhere blesses God for putting him into the work of the Ministry—that the campaign is short, your warfare will soon be accomplished—that the reward is great, being found faithful, you will receive a crown of glory, that fadeth not away.

Secondly, We have a word to the church and congregation in this place.

My Brethren and Friends, The importance of the work of a gospel Minister, suggests the weighty concerns of your souls. As Ministers must give account how they preach and behave; so hearers also are to be examined how they hear and improve. You are to hear with a view to the day of judgment, always remembering, that there is no sermon or opportunity that you have in this life, to prepare for another world, that shall go unnoticed at that decisive court. Your present exercises, with respect to the solemn affairs of this day, will then come up to public view.

God, we trust, is this day sending you one to watch for your souls; should not this excite sentiments of gratitude in your breasts? Shall God take so much care of your souls, and you neglect them? How unreasonable will it be for you to despise the pious instruction of your watchmen? You will herein wrong your own souls, and it will be an evidence that you love death. You will bear with him in not accommodating his sermons to your vitiated tastes, because he *must give account*. His work is great, and you must pray for him; as in the verse following the text, the Apostle says, "Brethren, pray for us." Is it the business of your minister to watch for your souls, with such indefatigable assiduity, you easily see how necessary it is that you do what you can to strengthen him in this work. That you administer to his temporal wants, that he may give himself wholly to these things. The great backwardness among people in general with respect to this matter at present, has an unfavourable aspect. "Who goeth a warfare any time at his own charges? Who planteth a vineyard, and eateth not of the fruit thereof? or who feedeth a flock, and eateth not of the milk of the flock." I Cor. 9:7.

Doubtless this man is sent here for the rise and fall of many in this place. We hope he will be used as a mean of leading some to Christ; while on the other hand, we even tremble at the thought, he may fit others for a more aggravated condemnation. Take heed how you hear.

A few words to the Assembly in general, will close the subject.

What has been said about the character and work of gospel ministers, shews us at once that it is a matter in which we are all deeply interested. The greater part of the people present, I expect to see no more, until I meet them at that day, which has been the main subject of the foregoing discourse. With respect to the characters of the people present, we can say but little about them; only this we may observe, *they are all dying creatures*, hastening to the grave, and to judgment! There must we meet you,—there an account of this day's work will come up to view,—there each one must give account concerning the right discharge of the work assigned him! The preacher must give account, and you that hear also. Let me say to such as are yet in their sins, and proclaim it from this part of the wall of Zion. That the enemy of your souls is at hand,—that destruction awaits you. Oh! flee! flee! to Christ Jesus; bow to his sovereignty; know this, that except you are born again, and become new creatures, in the dispositions of your mind, you cannot be saved. Shall ministers watch and pray for your souls night and day, and you pay no attention to them? Since they are so valuable, having such a relation to God, did men regard divine glory, they would regard their souls, as being designed to exhibit it. Be instructed, then, to delay no longer, but by repentance toward God, and faith in the Lord Jesus Christ, make peace with him, before you are summoned before his awful bar. Let me bear testimony against a practice too common on such occasions as this: Many people think it a time for carnal mirth and dissipation, than which nothing can be more provoking to God, nor inconsistent with that day, and strict account that such an occasion tends to excite in the mind. May all, both ministers and people, be exhorted to diligence in their work, that finally we

53

may adopt the language of the blessed Apostle,—"As also ye have acknowledged us in part, that we are your rejoicing, even as ye also are ours in the day of the Lord Jesus." Amen.

The Important Concerns of Ministers and the People of Their Charge

This funeral sermon is rare; there are only two known copies, at Brown and Howard Universities. It was printed in Rutland.

———

The important concerns of ministers and the people of their charge at the day of judgment; illustrated in a sermon, delivered at Rutland, Orange Society, at the interment of the Rev. Abraham Carpenter, their worthy pastor.

1 Thess. ii., 19.—"For what is our hope, or joy, or crown of rejoicing? Are not even ye in the presence of our Lord Jesus Christ at his coming?"

The second coming of Christ is a source of peculiar joy and consolation to the people of God; it is a day in which their hopes and expectations will be fully answered. Tribulation attends the good man while in this life; the scenes of divine Providence are mysterious, and many things unaccountable and insignificant without a day of judgment; they will then be explained and adjusted, to the joy and admiration of all who love Christ's appearing. Many of the events that take place in this life stand in a solemn relation to the judgment day, and none more so than the gospel ministry; hence it is that the attention of the true servants of Christ is so much taken up with a future state. St. Paul, being detained from the church at Thessalonica, sends this epistle as a token of his love and respect to them; in which he anticipates that blessed period when he should meet them at the bar of Christ, which would afford such joy and satisfaction as to more than compensate for all their sorrow, more especially for his being prevented a personal interview with those to whom he wrote. *"For what is our hope, or joy, or crown of rejoicing? Are not even ye in the presence of our Lord Jesus Christ at his coming?"* We have two very important ideas suggested in the words. One is, that ministers and their people must meet each other at the day of judgment. The second is, that although ministers are often separated from their hearers in this life, yet the people of God among whom a pious preacher finishes his work will be a cause or crown of peculiar joy and satisfaction at the second coming of Christ.

With respect to the first point, we may observe, to give us a striking contrast between this and the coming world, we are in the present state subject to many vicissitudes.

What changes are taking place in empires, states, societies, and families! In nothing is this more observable than in matters relating to ministers and the people of their charge. A persecuting spirit, that prevailed in the apostolic age, was often a means of parting friends, and especially of driving preachers from churches. The same cause has had influence in every age of the church; but if religious societies are so happy as to escape such a calamity, yet it pleases the Great Head of the church, in his sovereign wisdom, to separate ministers and their people by death; this gives feeling to a pious preacher, and in some degree has influence in every sermon he delivers. That all mankind will be collected before the bar of Christ, to see the great and intricate affairs of the universe adjusted, is a plain dictate of reason and Scripture; but that many will meet there as having mutual concerns with each other, is evident. More especially ministers and the people once committed to their charge doubtless will appear in some sense as distinct societies, as having particular and personal matters to attend to. This supposes that they will have a knowledge of each other; for without this, the purposes of their meeting in such a manner could not be answered. How far this will extend, or by what means it will be conveyed, is too curious to inquire. It seems, unless we are able by some means to distinguish those from others with whom we have been intimate in this life, the designs of a future judgment will in some measure be frustrated. The great end of that day is to illustrate divine truth, or make that appear conspicuous to created intelligence. To effect this, God will make use of mankind as instruments; this is the method he takes in this life, and doubtless it will be most eligible in the world to come. For our acquaintance to be summoned as witnesses for or against us at this court, will perhaps be the best means to administer conviction. In this way the great God can speak in language easy for finite creatures to understand. One design of the world being divided into distinct societies and communities, is doubtless to prepare matters for the day of judgment. The relations between ministers and people is such as renders them capable of saying much about each other; in this way the justice and mercy of God will be illustrated, Divine proceedings vindicated, and every mouth stopped. It is our conduct in this life that will direct Divine proceeding towards us at the final judgment; that the equity of God's administrations may appear, 'tis necessary that our characters be clearly investigated. The salvation and damnation of many souls will be through the instrumentality of faithful and unfaithful watchmen; this is an idea contained in the charge God gave to Ezekiel, 32d chapter. It will be necessary that the motives by which ministers have been influenced in their work be brought out to view; for without sincerity of heart they can never execute their office with any degree of true faithfulness, and are a high affront to God, and a vile imposition on the people.

At the day of judgment the *doctrines* with which a minister has entertained his hearers must be examined. However doctrinal preaching may be discarded by many, and such words as *metaphysical, abstruse*, etc., are often made use of to obstruct free and candid inquiry; yet it is evident that one great end of the gospel ministry is to disseminate right sentiments; hence it is that Paul so often exhorts Timothy to take heed to his *doctrine*. Sound doctrine, as well as good practice, is necessary to constitute the Christian character: "Whosoever transgresseth, and abideth not in the *doctrine* of Christ, hath not God."—2 John, 9.

A careful inquiry will be made whether an empty parade of learning, elegance of style, etc., have been the main things with which a people have been entertained, tending only to gratify vain curiosity, and to fix the attention of the hearers on the speaker. This made St. Paul contemn such a mode of preaching, and determine not to know any thing save Jesus Christ, and him crucified, 1 Cor. ii., 2. Whether vague, equivocal expressions have been used to convey, or rather to obscure the truths of the gospel, by which any thing and almost every thing may be understood. This is causing the trumpet to give an uncertain sound, and has no tendency to impress or give feeling to the mind, as is the case with the words of the wise, being as *goads* and *nails*, Eccle. xii., 11. Whether to please men has had greater influence in our composing and delivering our sermons than the glory of God and the good of souls. People will be examined at the bar of Christ whether they have not been dealt plainly with; been told their characters and danger; that they are wholly opposed to God, destitute of every thing that is holy or morally good; that they are by nature under the curse of God's law, exposed every moment to endless woe; that they are hopeless and helpless in themselves; the necessity of the renewing influences of the spirit; the nature of their impotence, that it consists in an evil heart; that therefore they are altogether inexcusable, and are criminal in proportion to the degree of their inability; that nothing short of repentance towards God and faith in the Lord Jesus Christ is the immediate duty of all that hear the gospel.

Ministers and their people must meet before the judgment-seat of Christ, to give an account whether the true character of God has in any good measure been investigated; as a sin-hating and sin-revenging God.

Without this the character of God is kept out of sight, people left in the dark, and are not able to determine whether they love or hate the true God.

It must be known whether people have had the character and work of the Redeemer set before them; the design of his sufferings, the efficacy of his blood, and the necessity of our union to him. The manner in which divine truth has been delivered will be a matter worthy of serious examination at that day; whether with that earnestness and fervour becoming the vast importance and solemnity of gospel truth, tending to affect the mind. The deportment or examples of ministers among their people will be closely attended to; their private visits, exhortations, and reproofs, holy desires and wrestlings for the souls of their hearers, will not escape public notice; the improvement that people have made of such advantages will be brought into public view.

How often people have attended on the ministration of the word, and the manner how, will be matters of serious concern at the judgment day. Those excuses that men make for neglecting public worship will be weighed in a just scale. Whether people have so far contributed to the temporal support of their ministers as to enable them to devote themselves to the service of Christ; or, by too great neglect, have not obstructed the gospel, robbed God, wounded their own souls.

It will be useful that the *time* of a minister's continuance among a people be known, as it will serve to set the characters of gospel despisers in a true point of light. That ministers and the people of their charge will meet each other at the bar of Christ, is suggested in my text, and in other parts of the sacred writings. It has already been observed that in this way truth will appear conspicuous, and the conduct of God will be vindicated, and the designs of a judgment day in the best manner answered. It may further be observed, that the matters relating to the gospel ministry are of such magnitude that it appears important that they be attended to; they concern a judgment day and an eternal state. When ministers and people meet in the house of God, it is an acknowledgment that they believe in a future state of retribution, and is a sort of appeal to the day of judgment. The influence of a faithful or unfaithful minister is such as to affect unborn ages; it will commonly determine the sentiments and characters of their successors, and in this way they may be doing good or evil after they are dead, and even to the second coming of Christ. That God's hatred towards false teachers, and against those who choose them, together with their criminality, may appear, it will be necessary that these matters be laid open at the tribunal of Christ. As a proof of the matter under consideration, I may only add, that there always has been an important controversy, in a greater or less degree, between ministers and part of their people; it is so with faithful preachers and some of their hearers; wicked men oppose the doctrines they preach, and will not be convinced. Unfaithful preachers have advocates and opposers; the dispute involved the character of Christ; it cannot be settled in this world. How necessary that ministers and people meet at the great day, to have the matter decided, the doctrines of Christ vindicated, and the characters of ministers or people exonerated.

II. Another important idea contained in the text is, that the church or people of God among whom a faithful minister finishes his work, will be a cause or crown of peculiar joy or rejoicing at the coming of Christ. It will be matter of great satisfaction to sit down with Abraham, Isaac, and Jacob, and other saints at that day; but the Scriptures represent that godly ministers will derive peculiar joy from the pious part of their congregations, Dan. xii., 3; 2 Cor. i., 14; Phil. ii., 16. Reflecting on past providences will be a source of great joy at the day of judgment; and as many things have taken place between a minister and his people in which they are more particularly conversant and interested, when they come to be explained it will afford special joy and admiration; as they have been companions in tribulations, so now it is likely they will be in a more peculiar sense copartners in joy, and help each other in magnifying the Lord for special favours, and displays of divine power and grace on their behalf.

The prayers and struggles of pious teachers have been for Zion in general, and for those over whom the Holy Ghost has made them overseers in particular. Now God will give their hearers who have been converted through their instrumentality as a kind of reward and fruit of their travail or labour. When it appears that God has made use of the true ministers of Christ for the conversion of some of the souls once committed to their charge, it will excite wonder, joy, and humility in the minds of pious teachers, that God should deign to honour them as instruments of such glorious work, by which they will be led to adore sovereign grace and condescending love. As it is often through the painful labours of Christ's servants that souls are brought home to God, doubtless he will approve of such virtues by conferring signal honours on those who have turned many to righteousness, who will shine as stars for ever and ever.

Pious people will give such account of their faithful teachers as will meet with the approbation of God, which will be expressed by that heavenly plaudit, "Well done, good and faithful servant!" Their mutual accounts will be given up with joy, and not with grief, Hebrews xiii., 17. The hopes and expectations of such ministers are great, as the apostle suggests in the text—For what is our hope, or joy, or crown of rejoicing? are not even ye? etc. He speaks of it as the earnest hope and expectation of all Christ's ministers, by calling it *our* hope. They reflect with pleasure on the approaching happy moment, and when it comes it will greatly gratify their holy desires.

That it will be possible to hold equal communion with all the saints, especially at one time, in the invisible world, perhaps is not admissable. It appears that the wicked who have been associates in sin here will be companions of torments hereafter, Luke xvi., 28.

They are to be gathered like the standing corn, and to be bound in *bundles* to burn. It is more than possible that the righteous who have lived together in this life, will have a more intimate access to each other in the world to come.

If it will be useful for them to meet in some sense as distinct societies, perhaps it will subserve the interest of the universe that they in a degree continue so. It is the character of the true church of Christ that they treat his ministers with respect in this life, accounting them as the ministers of Christ and stewards of the mysteries of God, 1 Cor. iv., 1. They will help them in their work, 2 Cor. i, 11. God will in the great day reward people for such kindness; as hereby they express their love to Christ, Matt. xxv., 40. This will gratify the benevolent feelings of Christ's servants; at the same time fill them with holy admiration and deep humility, that what has been done to such poor sinful creatures should be taken notice of.

Ministers and the people of their charge will assist each other, and be united in bringing a verdict against the wicked and impenitent among whom they lived while on earth. The saints are to judge the world, 1 Cor. vi., 2. One way by which they will do this will doubtless be to declare before angels and men what they know about them, or their conduct in this life. An attachment to divine justice will make this delightful work. Ministers must declare what and how they have preached to them, and the bad improvement they have made of the gospel, so far as it has come under their observation; how they have despised and mocked the messengers of the Lord, condemned his word and ordinances. Pious hearers can witness to the same things, and in this way the mutual testimony of godly ministers and people will be strengthened and supported, and Divine proceedings against impenitent sinners vindicated. Thus the church will be a crown of joy to her faithful pastor.

Improvement

1. We may infer from this subject that the gospel ministry is of God, and that we ought to seek its welfare, and use suitable exertions for its support.

Doth Scripture and reason dictate that it is of so much importance, especially as it relates to a judgment day, we may conclude that God would not do without it, and we may see Divine wisdom and goodness in the institution. Nothing more conducive of Divine glory, and salutary to men, than the preaching of the gospel. Without these glad tidings are proclaimed, the incarnation of Christ is vain. Nothing but opposition to God, and disregard to his glory, will make men indifferent to the preaching of the gospel. A rejection of Christ and his ministers has commonly vice and open profanity for its inseparable companions. The opposition that the impenitent part of mankind have made to the servants of Christ, has doubtless in some measure had its rise from a consciousness that they must meet them at the bar of Christ, to their disadvantage.

We may conclude, that, since the gospel ministry is so very useful, it will be continued to the end of the world.

2. When a faithful minister is taken away, it ought seriously to be regarded. But few ways perhaps that God shows greater displeasure against a people than in calling his ambassadors home. By this he threatens to put

an end to his treaty of peace, and become irreconcilable. It may sometimes be the case that God has no more chosen or elect ones among them. When Paul and Barnabas were preaching at Antioch, as many as were *ordained* to eternal life believed, then they departed, Acts xiii. All the encouragement for a minister to preach among a people, so far as the salvation of souls ought to be a motive, is the doctrine of election. After the death of a faithful minister there is less hope of a people.

We may further observe, when it is considered that we are to meet them no more in the house of God, to hear them declare unto us the words of reconciliation; but our next interview will be at the tribunal of Christ, to hear them testify for or against us, how affecting the consideration! It is more solemn to die than if we had never been favoured with the gospel ministry. People, whether they hear or forbear, shall know, to their joy or sorrow, that there hath been a prophet among them, Ezek. ii., 5.

3. The subject affords direction how ministers should preach, and how a people ought to hear, viz., with death and judgment in view. It is this that makes preaching and hearing a serious matter, and renders the house of God so very solemn. We must soon meet before the bar of Christ, and perhaps before the next Sabbath, to have our sermons and our hearing examined by Him who is infinite in knowledge, and is present in every congregation. Did we always consider these things, it would tend to abolish that coldness, drowsiness, and indifference, that too often attend the ministers of the gospel, and that formal spirit which is too apparent among hearers. How would it check that levity of mind and disorderly behaviour that presumptuous creatures often indulge in the house of God. *How dreadful is this place!*—is a reflection suitable on all occasions, and more especially when we meet for public devotion.

4. The surviving widow and children will for a moment suffer the word of exhortation. Are not you in some sense his hope and joy? Was it not a reflection that tended to smooth the rugged road through death, that he should meet you before the bar of Christ, and that you would be a crown of rejoicing in that day? If ministers and people are to meet each other before the tribunal of Christ, as having special business together, then we may conclude that this will be the case with particular families, such as husbands and wives, parents and children; you can say much about each other upon that occasion, having for so long a time composed one family on earth.

You, who are this day called to mourn, must give an account how you have improved his public and more private admonitions; and especially this providence. The present occasion, however solemn, will appear more so at the great day. Consider, that although he is gone to return no more, yet God, the source of consolation, ever lives. His promises are always new to the widow and fatherless. That God who gave has taken him away. But still he lives in another state, and is more useful to the universe than he could be in this world. God's people always die in the best time, manner, and place. You have only time to take up the body and bury it, set your houses in order, and follow him. Manifest your love to the deceased by preparing to meet him, and make his heart glad in the day of the Lord Jesus. Contemplate the rectitude of divine government, and a future world, and be still.

Let the children remember, that to have a pious faithful parent taken away is an unspeakable loss. Your father has done much for your bodies, but we trust more for your soul; never, never forget his prayers and admonitions. Can you, dare you meet him at the bar of Christ in impenitence? Should this be the case, instead of those endearing and parental caresses that you have received from him in this life, he will join with the Judge of all in saying, *Depart!* He will declare what he has done for you, and condemn you. Let your mother experience that tender regard and kind assistance, during her short continuance with you, as becomes dutiful, obedient children. Make her heart glad by a holy life, and let your father live daily before her eyes in your pious examples.

Let me say a word to the church and congregation in this place. Dear friends, I am not a stranger to these mournful sensations that the present melancholy providence tends to inspire. I trust I am a hearty mourner with you, and am a sharer in your loss.

By the foregoing observations you have reason to conclude that you have lost a faithful minister.

You can't forget those solemn and affectionate warnings that he has given you from the desk, nor those pious examples he has set before you. He has preached his last sermon. Your next meeting must be before the tribunal of Christ, where those sermons you have heard him deliver in this life will come to view, and the improvement you have made of them. Will you, my brethren, be his crown of rejoicing in that day? If you were his hope and joy in this life, you doubtless are still. It is with satisfaction we trust that he this moment looks forward to that day, when he expects to see this the dear people once committed to his charge; and doubtless he hopes to meet some of you as crowns of rejoicing. Oh! do not disappoint the hope and expectations of your reverend pastor. Manifest your love to him by imitating his holy examples, and by having those heavenly instructions that he so often inculcated always in remembrance; and by preparing to give him joy in the day of the Lord Jesus. Examine what improvement you have made of the gospel ministry while you had it; and whether too great inattention has not had influence in its being removed. Have you ever experienced the power and efficacy of the gospel upon your own souls? Have you by the Holy Spirit been formed into the moral likeness of the blessed God, and into the image of his son Jesus? Or have you been contented with the mere form of godliness? Have you not, through sloth and unbelief, neglected attending on the preaching of the gospel during the residence of your pastor among you? Oh! what account will such gospel despisers have to give another day! Consider, I entreat you, how dreadful it will be to have these things brought into view when you come to meet your minister, who was once, and perhaps is now, an eyewitness of your conduct, and will testify against you to your everlasting condemnation!

Your minister, though dead, now speaketh. He preaches a most solemn lecture to us all this day on mortality.

You will, as it were, hear his voice when you look on the place of public worship, where he and you so often attended—when you look on his grave, which is here among you—and when you look to the second coming of Christ. Think often of that day. Let the Sabbath, and worship of God, be still dear unto you; and remember him who has spoken unto you the word of God, whose faith follow.

The Influence of Civil Government on Religion

Haynes' ardent Federalism led him to make quasi-political addresses despite the risk of alienating members of his congregation. This was published in Rutland in 1798.

―――

The Influence of Civil Government on Religion. A Sermon Delivered at Rutland, West Parish, September 4, 1798. At the Annual Freemen's Meeting.

At a legal town meeting, holden at Rutland, on the first Tuesday of September, 1798. VOTED, That the Selectmen of this town be requested in the name of the town, to return their thanks to the Rev. LEMUEL HAYNES, for his christian and patriotic discourse, this day delivered, and request a copy for the press.

NATHAN OSGOOD *Town Clerk*.

The Author is not insensible of the reproach to which the following publication may subject him, at a time of so great civil dissension; and has consented to have it appear abroad with a degree of reluctance. However, as all view it a detraction of their liberty, when they are not allowed with honesty and candor to speak their own sentiments: he presumes it will be a sufficient defence against any imputations from those who may differ with him in opinion.

Psalm xi. 3.
If the foundations be destroyed, what shall the righteous do?

King David was raised up on high, the anointed of the God of Jacob, and the sweet psalmist of Israel. In various ways did he give evidence that he was a man of virtue and religion. His attachment to the commonwealth of Israel, and engagedness to support the laws and dignity of his country, were conspicuous ornaments in his character. Amidst the base inventions of designing men, to enervate the bands of government, assume the reins, and disseminate discord among the people, animated with a holy regard to the rights of God and men, rendered him invincible to every rival. He could hear his competitors say as in verse first, *Flee as a bird to your mountain*; and behold the *wicked bend their bow, and make ready their arrow upon the string*, without abandoning his country's cause, or wantonly trifling with the liberties of men. *If the foundations be destroyed, what shall the righteous do?* is a reflection worthy the king of Israel in a time of public calamity. By *foundations*, is generally thought to mean the civil laws or government of Israel, these were invaded, and threatened to be destroyed by proud and factious men, which David in the text considered as a violent attack upon religion and the good man's cause. If the laws and authority of the land are trampled upon, what shall the righteous do? Intimating that their religious interest would greatly suffer thereby.

> "If government be once destroy'd,
>   (That firm foundation of our peace)
> And violence makes justice void,
>   Where shall the righteous seek redress?"

The influence of civil government upon religion and morality, and their connection, is a matter to which our candid attention is called on the present occasion. That God is able to support his cause in the world without the intervention of legislative authority, and that they have no connexion, is a sentiment warmly advocated by many; and indeed none can dispute them, without calling in question the power of Omnipotence: but whether it be agreeable to the established constitution of heaven, in ordinary cases, to support religion without civil authority, or whether it be not favorable to virtue, is the inquiry. That God is able to appoint state officers without people's meeting to give their suffrages, is what God has done, and has natural power to do; but none will infer from thence, that such appointment actually will take place without public exertions.

1. Civil government was *appointed* by God to regulate the affairs of men. Israel of old received laws, both of a civil and religious nature, from the great Legislator of the universe. This is evident to all who are acquainted with sacred or profane history. *He removeth kings, and setteth up kings*, Dan. ii. 21. *Thou shalt in any wise set him king over thee whom the Lord thy God shall choose*, Deut. xvii. 15. St. Paul, to enforce obedience to magistracy, points to the origin of civil power, Rom. xiii. The powers that be are *ordained of God*. Whosoever, therefore, resisteth the power, resisteth the *ordinance of God.*—For he is the minister of God to thee for good. Every appointment of the Deity is favorable to religion, and conducive thereto, as there is no other object worthy [of] divine attention; to suppose otherwise would be an impious reflection on the character of God.

[2.] When we consider the obvious end for which civil government was instituted, it is easy to see that it is designed as a support to virtue. To suppress vice and immorality—to defend men's lives, religion and properties, are the essential constituents of a good government.

The wickedness of the human heart is so great, that it needs every restraint. To oppose the impetuous torrent of iniquity; to humanize the soul, and to conduct men in the way of felicity, are objects to which the laws of God and those which are commonly called the laws of men, do mutually point. Without our lives and interests are defended, how can we practice piety? Human laws, as well as divine, do in a sense respect the heart. The criminal is punished for his enormities, by the hand of the civil magistrate, because they are considered as flowing from a bad heart. To say that an institution tends to maintain order, justice, and the rights of men, or that it is favorable to religion, are expressions synonimous. Although the government of a commonwealth has a particular and a more immediate respect to the temporal interests of men, yet there is a higher object to which they stand related, and that renders them important.

3. Further light will be cast on the subject by attending to the qualifications and work of the civil magistrate, as given in the word of God, from whence we derive the institution. The character required in any profession, will at once determine the end and design of it. The God of Israel said, the Rock of Israel spake to me, He that ruleth over men *must be just*, ruling in the *fear of God*, II Sam. xxiii. 3. The character of a statesman is drawn by the pen of unerring wisdom, Deut. xvii. And it shall be when he sitteth upon the throne of his kingdom, that he shall write him a copy of this law in a book, out of that which is before the priests the

Levites. And it shall be with him, and he shall read therein all the days of his life; that he may learn to fear the Lord his God, to keep all the words of this law, and these statutes, to do them: that his heart be not lifted up above his brethren, and that he turn not aside from the commandment, to the right hand or to the left. "The Hebrews have recorded thus, When the king sitteth upon the throne of his kingdom, he is to write him the book of the law for himself, beside the one which is left him by his father, etc. If his father has left him none, or if that be lost, he is to write him two books of the law, the one he is to reserve in his house, for so he is commanded. The other is not to depart from before him. If he go out to war, it goeth with him; if he sit in judgment, it is to be with him, etc. Maimony treat. of Kings." See Ainsworth's annotation. This book contained what is commonly called the law of Moses, giving directions about civil and religious affairs. This shews that the lawyer should concern himself with the sacred oracles, and that his profession is favorable to religion. St. Paul further informs us, That rulers are not a terror to good works, but to the evil. Wilt thou then not be afraid of the power? do that which is good, and thou shalt have praise of the same. For he is the minister of God to thee for good. But if thou do that which is evil, be afraid; for he beareth not the sword in vain: for he is the minister of God, a revenger to execute wrath, upon him that doeth evil. Rom. xiii—The design of civil government is in the best manner answered when kings are nursing fathers, and queens nursing mothers to the church of God, Isaiah xlix. 23.

4. Were we to compare those countries and places where wholesome laws exist, and are executed, with those that are without them, we shall find the contrast striking.—Where there are no laws, no subordination, there licentiousness and barbarity hold their empire, and like a malignant fever diffuse their baneful influence without restraint. Every one that is acquainted with sacred or other histories, knows the propriety of the remark. Were we to advert to our own experience, we have the clearest conviction. Is it not the case in general, that a contempt of the good laws of the land, and impiety are inseparable companions?

We have recent demonstration, that civil authority is in some sense, the basis of religion, and have too much reason to adopt the language in the text, *If the foundations be destroyed, what shall the righteous do!* It is far from my intention to appear in the habit of a partizan, or to stimulate dissension on an occasion like this, while I point you to the unprecedented conduct of a foreign power, as witness to the truth of the topic under consideration. To exaggerate matters I have no inclination, nor to wound the tender feelings of humanity by a tedious detail of French enormities. To pursue their lawless ravages would be to trace the cruel exploits of a blood thirsty Hannibal, or merciless strides of an imperious Alexander. Near twenty villages in Germany have become a sacrifice to the vengeance of a more than savage army. Switzerland, Geneva, (the latter, a place remarkable for their religion and good order) have fallen victims to their cruelties. The soothing words, *liberty* and *equality*, were so dear to us, that we were hoping that true republicanism was their object, and were almost decoyed into their wretched embraces; but they leave not the least traces of it behind them. It is evidently their design, to exterminate order and religion out of the universe, banquet on stolen property, give rules to the world, and so become the tyrants of the earth.

"Ecclesiastics, of every description, and particularly the professors of both sexes, (says a late German writer) seem to be the chief objects of republican malevolence, immorality and cruelty; in which the soldiers were led on and encouraged by their officers." That an abolition of religion is an object of French insanity is too evident to be disputed; hence it is that they are inimical to civil authority, as they view it favorable to morality. We cannot mistake them, when we consider their contempt of the Holy Scriptures, their atheistical decisions, and their more than beastly conduct. Libertinism, and not republicanism, is most certainly their object. It is an inquiry worthy of attention, whether the few years revolution in France has not done more towards promoting infidelity, deism, and all manner of licentiousness, than half a century before. The near connection of religion with wholesome laws, or civil authority, is doubtless an ostensible reason why the latter is so much the object of resentment. The contempt that these states have met with from the French Directory, in their not receiving our Envoys: their insolent and enormous demands on our property—their blind and deceitful intrigues—their lawless depredations on our commerce at sea, are sufficient to shew that it is not peace, liberty and good order they are after, but to make themselves sole arbiters of the world. Many have been caressed with the fascinating yell, *Long live the republican!*—and opened their gates to the French army, but have too late found their tender mercies to be cruelty, and themselves in the hands of a plundering banditti. What outrages have been committed on the persons of old and young! Wives and daughters abused in the presence of their husbands and parents.—Those in sacred orders, notwithstanding their age, illness and profession, dragged from their beds, their houses pillaged, and they have been the chief objects of spite and detestation. Let many villages of Swabia, in Germany, witness to the truth of this observation. Such are the sad effects of no law, no order, no religion; and if the foundations be destroyed, what shall the righteous do?

The candor and patience of this audience are requested, while a few reflections are deduced from the preceding observations.

1. It is undoubtedly our duty to become acquainted with the laws of the land. That by which the commonwealth of Israel was governed, was to be well studied by their statesmen, Deut. xvii. Especially those who are to be representatives of the people, should well understand the laws of their country: those then of the profession are not disqualified to sit in the seat of government, by virtue of their knowledge in state policy. It is the design of civil government to secure the rights of men, which should be held sacred; it being so nearly connected with religion, renders it important.—It is a subject to which we ought to pay attention, that we may be in a capacity to pursue the best measures to promote it. It is a remark, not without foundation, that they who make the widest mouths against divine revelation, are commonly those who know the least about it, and form their opinion on popular cant. Whether this is not often the case with many who set up against the good laws of the state, is a matter worthy of inquiry. He that can arraign and condemn the constitution and laws of his country, without information, and will judge of a matter before he hears it, in the view of Solomon forfeits the character of a wise man.

2. Is there such a connection between civil and religious order, then we ought to support the former, would we prove ourselves friends to the latter. Indeed he that can oppose and destroy the good laws of his country, his religious character is greatly to be suspected.—He that loves religion, will value and prize that which tends to its support, and feels the influence of the idea in the text, *If the foundations be destroyed, what shall the righteous do?* It is really the character of a good man, that he affords his influence, his property, yea his life in the defence of his country, if called for. We should most chearfully impart our substance for the support of the laws of the land, and strengthen the hands of the legislature when they are endeavoring to adopt good measures for raising a revenue. Many are complaining, that the wages of the State officers are too high; were I to attempt a decision on this point, perhaps I should appear contemptible, as being destitute of christian modesty and self-diffidence.—That men who leave their families and devote their time and talents in their country's cause, ought to have a

compensation, is agreed on all hands,—what is an adequate reward, is difficult for those who live several hundred miles from the seat of government to determine; an honest man under such a disadvantage would feel a delicacy in determining, lest he might do injustice to his neighbor. He would not view that man qualified to be a representative of the people that would be exorbitant in his demands; and rather choose to refer it to the members on the spot, who are the best judges of their own expences and retrenchments. The common labourer thinks it an infringement on his liberty, if his wages are to be determined by him who hires him. Should we set up office to vendue, and make *low wages* the test of our elections, this would be an impious trifling with the sacred rights of men, an insult on the importance and dignity of government; in this way men of an ignorant, low and mercenary spirit, would creep into the seats of preferment.

Our blessed Lord has taught us, by precept and example, to respect civil government, and to render tribute to Caesar. We have the same sentiments enjoined by St. Paul, Rom xiii, "Whoever therefore resisteth the power, shall receive to themselves damnation. Wherefore ye must needs be subject, not only for wrath, but also for conscience sake. For this cause *pay you tribute* also; for they are God's ministers, attending continually upon this very thing. *Render therefore to all their dues*."

3. How absurd to discard the book, commonly called the Holy Scriptures, and yet be advocates for good civil government! They are so coincident and congenial in their nature and tendency, that it is really a doubt whether a man can, upon right principles, be an honest advocate for one, whose heart rises against the other. Hence it is, that those who have been votaries for religion, have generally been friendly to good civil authority. *Thou shalt love the Lord thy God with all thine heart, and thy neighbor as thyself*, is an epitome of the whole Bible system. He that is acquainted with the laws of the land, will see that they mostly point to this great object, and are a sort of comment on, or copy of the sacred oracles. A contempt of the Holy Scriptures, domination, anarchy, and immorality are inseparable companions.

It is, truly, strange to see men of genius and education plead for the good laws of their country, and yet unfriendly to divine revelation; They have certainly a reciprocal reflection on each other, and their influence in a great measure stand and fall together.

Would we be hearty friends to government, let us value and conform to the written word of God, that our conduct may not appear glaringly inconsistent and contradictory.

4. We infer, That it is suitable for the ministers of the gospel to enforce obedience to the laws of the state. In this way they discover a laudable regard for the rights and properties of their hearers, plead for religion, and espouse the cause of their divine master.

Many think that state policy is a subject out of the sphere of Christ's ministers, that they ought to seek the peace and good will of their people, by avoiding such matters; but he that cannot sacrifice his own reputation, his living, yea, his own life in the cause of religion, and the good of his country, has forfeited his character as a faithful ambassador of the Prince of Peace.

Paul was far from commending such clerical prudence as some plead for, Tit. iii. Put them in mind to be subject to principalities and powers, to obey magistrates, to be ready to every good work, to speak evil of no man.

5. We may learn, Why there are so many *sedition acts* in the Bible, since religion and good government are so nearly connected. One we have, Eccle. x. 20, *Curse not the king, no, not in thy thought.* Another we have, Exod. xxii. 28. *Thou shalt not revile the Gods, nor curse the ruler of thy people.* We have the same law repeated in another section of God's word, Acts xxv. 5, *Thou shalt not speak evil of the ruler of thy people.* Compare Rom. xiii. The Apostle gives us direction how to escape the terrors of such laws, verse 3. *Do that which is good, and thou shalt have praise of the same.* When scandalous libels are cast at men in private life, they will have recourse to law for satisfaction: when ministers of state are wickedly impeached, why should the libeller go with impunity? is not the crime enhanced by the dignity of the whole commonwealth? Shall the character of a chief magistrate, or of a whole country, be of less or of no more importance than a man in a private capacity? Can men think their liberties retrenched, when they cannot vent their spite and false invectives against civil rulers without detection? May we not as well cry out, *Aristocracy!—Tyranny!—*and *Oppression!* because we cannot commit the most daring outrage on the person, character and property of our neighbor, without being plagued with the molesting hand of civil authority? From such kind of liberty, good Lord deliver us! (Should it be said, that those precepts, that particularly respect our duty to rulers, are rendered unnecessary by those general laws that prohibit *bearing false witness against our neighbor*, and that enjoin decent behaviour toward all mankind, etc. We may observe That wickedly to impeach men who are intrusted with affairs of the commonwealth, is an insult cast upon the political body, tending to enervate the bands of government. If satisfaction is given to the magistrate only in a private capacity, this does not retrieve the character of

the state, which has a right to enact and execute laws, with a more particular relation to itself, tending to support its own dignity and importance.)

6. The subject sets before us the importance of the present occasion. Since it is so necessary to maintain civil government; our lives, liberties and religion, in a sense, depend upon it. Men should be appointed who are friendly to religion and morality, by which they will be peculiarly attached to the good and wholesome laws of their country, on account of the benign influence they have on practical godliness. Men of wisdom and understanding, of force and stability, who will enforce the laws of the land by precept and example; who will not bear the sword in vain, but be a terror to evil doers, and a praise to them who do well. These are qualifications pointed out in the word of God, and ought to be sought for. Diffidence, in an ecclesiastical and civil minister, is a distinguishing ornament. The magnitude of the object will cause the good statesman to recoil at the thought in language similar to that of the chief magistrate of Israel, I Kings, iii. "And now, O Lord my God, thou hast made me king instead of David my father: and I am but a little child: I know not how to go out or come in. Give therefore thy servant an understanding heart, to judge thy people, that I may discern between good and bad: for who is able to judge this thy so great a people?" He that would thrust himself into office, is a selfish man: is seeking his own, not the public good. Confidence in public opinion will dispose a man to acquiesce in their decisions about himself, unbiassed by fulsome flattery or bribery. He that would hire his neighbor to give him his suffrage, is to be suspected as an enemy of his country, and unfit to be intrusted with its important concerns. He has already declared that he values his own judgment about himself above all others, and will perhaps have the same sentiments in every thing in which he is called to act.

The true philanthropist wants the support of his country unsolicited, by which he is encouraged to undertake in its cause, and not from proud, selfish, or pecuniary motives. The dignity, modesty, and goodness of his mind, will render him incapable of holding himself up to view as a candidate for office.

Should the question be asked, How shall we know the man of virtue and patriotism? The answer is obvious, and rationally decided by unerring wisdom, *By their fruit ye shall know them.*

We infer the integrity of a *Washington*, and an *Adams*, from the invincible attachment they have manifested to the rights of men, through a long series of events, when they had it in their power to sell their country and accumulate millions to themselves. To suppose such men, who have risked their lives, their all, in the cause of freedom for many years, should in the last stage of life turn traitors, when they would have nothing to promise themselves but endless disgrace, confronts every dictate of reason and experience. Perhaps it is not possible for the human mind to have a firmer basis for confidence; and to impeach such characters, without better foundation than ever has appeared, to me, at least appears disingenuous, and argues a jealousy more cruel than the grave.

Who can reflect on the fatigue, vexation, and hazard to which a WASHINGTON has been exposed in espousing the contested rights of his country, and not feel a sort of indignation to hear his character villified and impeached without a cause? Are these the returns he is to receive from ungrateful countrymen!—It is true men are not to be idolized, but when we consider them as instruments qualified and raised up by God for great and peculiar service to mankind, it is undoubtedly our duty to love, honor and respect them.

If I am not mistaken, we live in a day when our liberties are invaded, and the rights of men challenged beyond what we ever experienced, and that under the soothing titles of *Republicanism*, *Democracy*, etc. These are precious names if well understood; but when they are speciously substituted in the room of *libertinism* and *licentiousness*, they make us sick.

Our internal dissensions have an unfavorable aspect, and give pain to the human breast: by these things we lay ourselves open to foreign invasions, and augment taxation. Union and firmness in our country's cause becomes us at such a day as this—It is not a time for empty compliment; effeminate cowardice; nor for temporizing, when our all lies at stake. Our enemies wish us to delay, and debate, and flatter, that they may make themselves masters of all our property at sea.

There is no harm for the freeborn sons of America to tell Frenchmen, That we will not give up our rights unless our lives go with them; that they were bought at the expence of too much blood and treasure to be trifled with.

That the very ghosts of our brethren, who bled in their country's cause, would haunt our imaginations?—That we treat with contempt the insolent demands of a Talleyrand, aided by a sly intriguing Directory, who would wrest millions from our pockets to enslave us.—We may tell them in the most decisive unequivocal language, without loss of time, That we have a right to choose our own Envoys, maintain our own neutrality, without the dictates of French despotism. Have we any evidence that the French nation are really seeking peace with us, while they refuse to treat with our Ambassadors, such as we send to accomplish the desirable object? while they thrust the dagger at our heart? destroy our lives and property at every opportunity? May we not pertinently adopt the language of Jehu to Joram, II. Kings, ix. 22. And it came to pass when Joram saw Jehu, that he said, Is it peace, Jehu? and he answered, What peace, so long as the whoredoms of thy mother Jezebel, and her witchcrafts are so many?

Do they wish for peace, let them come with the olive branch in their hand, and make us restitution for the millions of our property that they have wantonly destroyed; and be ashamed for the innocent blood that they have mingled with the ocean, which calls for vengeance on both sides of the Atlantic. Then heaven-born peace shall erect her laurels on our shores, and gladden the heart of every free-born son of America.

Let us rise in the defence of our country, and shudder at the thought of a French invasion; viewing the last drop of our blood too small a sacrifice to be withheld when our rights, our religion, yea, our all lie at the stake. It is not the design of this discourse to obstruct a free and candid examination into political proceedings: this is a priviledge belonging to every man, and no one has a right to take it from him.

It is a matter worthy of serious inquiry, whether our present constitution and government have not the essential vestiges of *free republicanism*, according to the true meaning of the term. Does it not originate in the free suffrages of the people; who have it in their power to appoint to, and depose from office? Is it an infringement of our liberties to subject to the decision of the majority? True freedom does not consist in every man's doing as he thinks fit, or following the dictates of unruly passions; but in submitting to the easy yoke of good regulations, and in being under the restraints of wholesome laws.

We should do well to examine whether we do not too much despise and undervalue the civil government and independence that God by remarkable interpositions or providence has put into our hands. Whether our uneasiness under it, has not provoked Omnipotence to threaten our liberties, by letting loose a foreign power upon us. Let us learn to prize and support the good and wholesome laws of our land, that heaven may be at peace with us.

But few, if any will own themselves advocates for French measures; but I hope it will give no offence to those who of late appear unfriendly to our present civil administrations, if they are earnestly intreated to inquire, whether they are not *practically* espousing their cause, however good their intentions may be. That our foreign enemies consider them in this point of light, we have the clearest evidence, and are thereby encouraged to preserve in their lawless depredations.

We have heard that it is the character of the good man to be subject to higher powers. That civil authority ought to be opposed when it becomes tyrannical, and oppressive, is agreed on all hands. We should all do well to examine the motives by which we are actuated, perhaps they are selfish. It is sometimes a proud haughty disposition that sets men against government, and a thirst to get themselves into the chair. This made Absalom so dissatisfied with the government of Israel, and caused him to disseminate dissensions among them, II. Sam. xv. 4. *Absalom said, moreover, Oh that I were made judge in the land, that every man which hath any suit or cause might come unto me, and I would do them justice.*

On the whole, let us in all these things view the hand of a superintending Providence, that ruleth over the nations of the earth, and disposeth of all events, both in the natural and moral world, so as to accomplish the best good of the universe; will cause even the wrath of man to praise him, and the remainder will restrain.

Let us repent of our sins, that are the cause of God's controversy with us, and obtain reconciliation with him through the mediation of Jesus Christ. Let us seek after a holy union of sentiment and affection in religion, and this will tend to unite us in other things, and especially in that which is in some sense the barrier and support of it. The question would then become serious and general. If the foundations be destroyed what shall the righteous do? Let us support and execute the good laws of our land, and endeavor to strengthen the hands of them who rule well. Let no root of bitterness spring up and trouble us, for while the mind is under the influence of prejudice and passion we cannot attend to any subject to advantage. We should exercise a spirit of love and forbearance towards those who differ from us, and endeavor to restore them in the spirit of meekness. May we all remember, that whatever zeal or attachment we may seem to manifest towards civil institutions; yet if we are not in our hearts and lives in some good measure reconciled to the law and government of God, we shall finally be placed with the workers of iniquity.

The Nature and Importance of True Republicanism

Haynes' status as a veteran of the Revolution made him a particularly appropriate choice to deliver this anniversary address, in which he did not hesitate from commenting on the political situation of the day. The address was published in Rutland in 1801.

———

The Nature and Importance of True Republicanism: with a Few Suggestions Favorable to Independence. A Discourse, Delivered at Rutland, (Vermont,) The Fourth of July, 1801.—It Being the 25th Anniversary of American Independence.

"But ye shall not be so: but he that is greatest among you, let him be as the younger; and he that is chief, as he that doth serve."

Luke 22:26

The occasion of these words was a dispute among the disciples of Christ about superiority, as may be seen by attending to ver. 24th; And there was also a strife among them, which of them should be accounted the greatest. They had imbibed a strange notion that the Saviour was about to emancipate the Jews from the Roman yoke, and to restore their civil rights. Elated with the delusive prospect, they began to contend for posts of honor, and who should have the pre-eminence in the new establishment. The insatiable thirst in mankind for preference has appeared in every age, and been a fruitful source of many evils. Our blessed Lord, to manifest his detestation against such haughty ambition, points his disciples to the gentile world, ver. 25th: "And he said unto them, The Kings of the Gentiles exercise lordship over them; and they that exercise authority upon them are called benefactors." Plainly suggesting, that for them to seek for posts of honor under the specious garb of sanctity, was symbolizing with the heathen, and acting perfectly inconsistent with the nature of that kingdom, he came to introduce; the lineaments of which are concisely drawn in my text: "But ye shall not be so: but he that is greatest among you let him be as the younger, and he that is chief as he that doth serve."—

In which words we have the nature, and design of a free government, epitomised, by the unerring hand of wisdom. Liberty and equality are words very familiar at the present day, and may possibly be abused. That there ought to be a kind of subordination among men, none will dispute; and that it is beneficial to society, is equally obvious. A veneration for parents, difference [deference] to the aged, and respect to officers both in church and state, are matters taught us in the word of God. The idea is implied in my text; a proud ambitious aspiring temper was what Christ went to discard. To be greatest was the design of the disciples, without a generous regard to the community at large; to get into office was the great object: blind to the interest of the commonwealth, the importance of the matter did not come up to view; but in a heedless manner they would thrust themselves forward, only to be called great. If from such selfish motives men crowd themselves into office, a similar administration may well be expected. It is of singular importance to ascertain the true criterion of greatness. When a man distinguishes himself by a proper regard for the general good, he is then worthy the name; he rises to eminence, and commands a kind of veneration from all around him.—This is that true dignity the blessed Jesus taught among men, and that shone conspicuous in his life. *He that is greatest among you let him be as the younger; and he that is chief, as he that doth serve.* Plainly suggesting, that it is the design of the appointment to office, to serve the public, and is the only test of true greatness.

The nature and design of a republican government;—Its peculiar Importance;—Together with a few observations favorable to independence, will very briefly be attended to on the present occasion.

I. Some of the features of a free government will be drawn. The word is so common among men, that it may be thought a definition is scarcely necessary; however, as people have annexed different ideas to it, a small attention to the matter may not be impertinent. The propensity of the human mind has such a preponderancy to evil, that it is more than possible it has proved a stimulus to vice; and so our liberty becomes a cloke of licentiousness. That some have carried the point so far, as to break through every barrier of restraint, we have painful evidence: While others, to avoid this extreme, have fallen on *Charybdis*, and refused that liberty wherewith Christ has made them free.

It has been thought by some, that to secure the rights of conscience is a very important fruit in a free government, and the essential part of it; such ideas are so vague and indefinite, as to cast but little light on the subject: men can make conscience of almost any thing to carry a point. The scriptures speak of a *feared* and *defiled* conscience. How often is this noble light in man obscured and rendered more than useless, through the prevalence of a corrupt heart, and the light in us becomes total darkness? In this way many will plead exemption from duty, and make a loud outcry against civil injunctions that would enforce their obligations thereto. When the dictates of conscience invade the rights and well-being of society, they are not to be gratified. When it becomes evident that a man is cloaking some malicious design against his neighbor or the commonwealth, under the sanctity of religion, it is quite suitable that he be impeded by the hand of the civil magistrate. The ideas then that we ought to connect with Independence, Republicanism, Liberty, etc., will admit of a very simple definition. By attending to the end, or design of it, we have the thing itself. It is to defend and secure the natural rights of men. By this expression is meant, those privileges, whether civil or sacred, that the God of nature hath given us—To know what this charter comprises, we are to view them in their relation to society at large: When they are congenial with this object, we ought most cheerfully to fall in with the design, and view ourselves as breathing the very spirit and life of true liberty. This is that noble independence and republicanism taught in my text. Every deviation from this text, is inconsistent with true liberty, and ought to meet with some kind of obstruction from civil authority.

That I have not erred in the above description is evident, from the magnitude of the object proposed, viz. the *general good*: therefore most salutary to men, and only worthy of divine approbation.—It is true, men may disagree as to what will conduce to the general good, and so human laws be very imperfect. That the public voice is to decide on the subject, must be granted. Yet there may be so great a defection in a kingdom or commonwealth, as to vindicate the minor in withdrawing; but so long as we remain connected with a society, I feel no way but to submit, without an attack on the rights of men, and the principle of true liberty, unless where the real rights of conscience are evidently invaded.

Our beneficent creator has furnished us with moral and natural endowments, and they according to common sense, are our own; if so we have a right to use them in every way wherein we make no encroachments on the equal rights of our neighbor.—Others can have no demand on us for what they never gave or for which we are in no sense indebted to them. Every attack of this nature ought to be opposed with the same laudable zeal and abhorrence as if it had been made on our lives. As we stand related to God, it is true we are not our own, yet he allows us this prerogative to exert all our faculties, in behalf of the general good.—The laws of the commonwealth are to defend mankind in the peaceable possession of these invaluable blessings, which equally belong unto all men as their birthright.—As civil regulations respect the community, and all are equally interested in them, we at once argue their origin, viz. from the people at large. This is that genuine republicanism that we ought most earnestly to contend for, and is the very foundation of true independence; the excellency, and importance of which, will in the next place be considered.

The benign influence of such a constitution and government, comprised in the above remarks, may be clearly deduced from the considerations, that it is falling in with the divine plan, and coincident with the laws of nature. These rights were given to men by the author of our being, as the best antidote against faction; to meliorate the troubles of life, and to cement mankind in the strictest bonds of friendship and society:—Those who oppose such a form of government, would invert the order of nature, and the constitution of heaven, and destroy the beauty and harmony of the natural and moral worlds.

The troubles incident to men, have their origin from this source; nor can the body politic enjoy peace, symmetry and tranquility, until it resumes its order; but like a dislocated bone, will diffuse convulsion and pain through every member. The natural body is in health and prosperity so long as its constituted laws have their free operation; but when obstructed, sickness and death are inevitable.

It may further be observed, that a free republican government has the preference to all others, in that it tends to destroy those distinctions among men that ought never to exist. "All men are born equally free and independent & have certain inherent and unalienable rights," to use the language of our own constitution, which coincides with the holy oracles, Acts 17:26. The more this can be maintained the nearer it answers the original perfect draught. If God saw such a state of society was most favorable to men, it ought still to be maintained. The distinctions only to be reprobated are such as have no true merit in them, but are merely nominal, such as birth, riches, empty titles, etc.—These were the things contended for by the disciples of Jesus, which he discards in the text; they would be great without goodness or without serving the public. Palm upon an aspiring mortal the flattering titles of King, Prince, Lord, etc. merely because he was born under a more splendid roof or lay in a softer cradle, than his neighbor, has more gold in his chest, and his farm is wider at both ends, or what thro' mistake has a higher parentage, he will at once forget the only test of true greatness, and only value himself on his being able to tyrannize over others, and can look down on his own species with contempt. This at once throws the balance of power into the wrong scale and enervates the bands of society. This has been the fruitful source of domination and blood-shed which has denominated this world an aceldama; this has kept Europe at war with little cessation for more than nine centuries; and its influence has been felt in the happy climes of North America.—Blessed be God! the bloody flag could not be established on our shores; and while others are falling victims to the hard and cruel hand of tyranny, we enjoy peace, far from the din of war, and the hideous habitations of cruel oppressors.

There cannot be a greater source of evil to mankind than to imbibe wrong sentiments about true greatness.—In a land like ours, where the people are free and view each other as brethren engaged in one common cause, virtue and philanthropy will be considered as the true criterions of distinction.—He will be esteemed great who is servant of all, who is willing to devote his talents to the public good. These are the prominent features of a free, republican government, and should attach us to our present constitution.

Again, A free, independent administration, like ours, is very friendly to knowledge and instruction; it expands the human mind, and gives it a thirst after improvement. The amazing progress that these states have made in useful arts and science, of almost every kind, during the twenty five years of our independence, will justify the present remark; perhaps no history will be read to better advantage.—When men are made to believe that true dignity consists in outward parade and pompous titles, they forget the thing itself, and the greater part of the community view the other as unattainable, they look up to others as above them, and forget to think for themselves, nor retain their own importance in the scale of being. Hence, under a monarchal government, people are commonly ignorant; they know but little more than to bow to despots, and crouch to them for a piece of bread.

The propriety of this idea will appear strikingly evident by pointing you to the poor Africans, among us. What has reduced them to their present pitiful, abject state? Is it any distinction that the God of nature hath made in their formation? Nay—but being subjected to slavery, by the cruel hands of oppressors, they have been taught to view themselves as a rank of beings far below others, which has suppressed, in a degree, every principle of manhood, and so they become despised, ignorant, and licentious. This shews the effects of despotism, and should fill us with the utmost detestation against every attack on the rights of men: while we cherish and diffuse, with a laudable ambition, that heaven-born liberty wherewith Christ hath made us free. Should we compare those countries, where tyrants are gorged with human blood, to the far more peaceful regions of North America, the contrast would appear striking.

On the whole, does it not appear that a land of liberty is favourable to peace, happiness, virtue and religion, and should be held sacred by mankind?

In the last place—A few directions were promised, as necessary means to secure, or maintain our liberties and independence. The fate of the once noble republic of Rome, and many others: What took place in the interregnum of eleven years and four months in England, between the reigns of Charles First and Second, may shew that 'tis more than possible that such a precious diamond may lose its lustre, and undergo a total extinction. The present unhappy divisions among us, do not wear the most favourable aspects, as to this matter.

In the first place—It is quite necessary that people well understand the true *nature* of republicanism and independence; that they import something noble and excellent; nothing vain and licentious, but what is promotive of order, virtue and morality.—The state of mankind, is such, that they cannot live without law: break down this barrier, and our case at once becomes alarming. It is nothing strange, if through the perverseness of human nature, our system has been misunderstood, as falling in with the lusts of men, and favorable to a dissolute life: than which nothing can be more subversive of the scheme. That even in regenerated France, there has been something of this nature, is too evident.—We should always keep in mind that a true republican is one who wishes well to the good constitution and laws of the commonwealth, is ready to lend his heart, his sword and his property for their support; gives merit its proper place; respects magistrates, according as they appear to regard the happiness of society, and seeks the general good.—He is peaceable and quiet under an wholesome administration; but anarchy and confusion are of all things most detestable, while he grows better under the benign influence of good government. It is very common for people to expect too much from such a system, and cannot in any degree be satisfied without a perfect administration. This is not to be expected in this degenerate world; Therefore some imperfections in those who serve the public, must be dispensed with.—This is an idea of peculiar importance in a republican government like ours, where civil officers are so directly amenable to the people. Let it be remembered, that true independence has religion, regularity, and a veneration for good order for its objects.

When a minor comes of age, and is no longer under tutors and governors, it is too often the case, that he forgets all kinds of subordination, and sinks into dissipation and vice, and is at last shut up in a bastile, or becomes a prisoner at Newgate.

2. Would a people maintain their independence, the wholesome laws of the commonwealth ought to be faithfully executed. It is generally expected that a republic breathes kindness, tenderness or benevolence. From the merciless hand of tyranny, there is a natural, and easy transition to a state of extreme moderation:—Whatever laws are enacted, they lose all their importance without a regard to their sanctions.—They must be firmly and faithfully executed, or at once they fall into contempt, the bands of society are broken down, and destruction becomes inevitable.

3. The neutrality of these states ought to be held sacred; not only because it is so earnestly recommended in the legacy of him whose name is still precious to every true American, I mean the immortal WASHINGTON; but because it also comports with the plain dictates of reason.—"Leave off contention before it be meddled with," was the advice of one of the wisest princes; the infection is dangerous; by it we shall be apt to imbibe the ferocity of warriors, become inhuman, and involve ourselves in the general faction. Let us stand & behold other nations at war, with emotions of pity; while to us the laurel of peace sits regent on the throne and sweetens every enjoyment. That we have hitherto been preserved from taking an active part in foreign contentions, demands a tribute of thanks to him, who has raised up instruments and blessed their judicious endeavors.—Let us be what these words import, FREE AND INDEPENDENT STATES.

4. As a further means to maintain our rights and immunities, we should beware of discord among ourselves. That a kingdom divided against itself cannot stand, is a divine maxim, and confirmed by a long experience. Union in every society is essential to its existence.—Every thing of a petulant and party spirit ought carefully to be avoided.—Candid discussion is useful in every community; while bitterness, invective and enthusiasm, only prejudice the heart and blind the understanding. How often have public occasions, that otherwise might have proved profitable, been rendered more than useless for want of that prudence, moderation and friendship that should always distinguish a free people.—That the unhappy divisions among us, have been greatly stimulated by such means, we have painful evidence. That the press can plead exemption from such an imputation, cannot be admitted.

Foreign powers envy our tranquility, they abhor republicanism; as by it their craft is in danger. They wish in every possible way to separate us, that we may fall an easy prey to their pride and avarice. Next to maintaining our independence, let us cultivate a laudable union among ourselves and this will render us invincible to every rival.

5. Might I be endulged a little, I would say, that education and the diffusion of useful knowledge, is very favorable to a free government. Oppression and usurpation hold their empires where ignorance and darkness spread their sable domain. Let people be well instructed, let them read the history of kings, and know the rights of men, and it will be difficult to make them believe that the names, King, Lord, Sovereign, Prince, Viscount, and such childish trumpery, ought to command their purse, their property, and liberty; but that goodness, virtue or benevolence, are things that demand veneration.

6. The end and design of government, which is to secure the natural rights of men, suggests another idea of importance as necessary to support our present Constitution, viz. That such men be appointed to office whose characters comport with it.—If to preserve our lives and property, and to defend the public from every encroachment, are the great objects of civil government, then men of a philanthropic spirit, who will naturally care for mankind, ought only to occupy places of public betrustment. He that would wish to become consequential in any other way, only in seeking the good of his neighbor, is dangerous to society.—"But ye shall not be so;" says my text, "but he that is greatest among you, let him be as the younger, and he that is chief, as he that doth serve."—The end of the appointment is to serve our generation by the will of God; then men of a narrow selfish, mercenary

spirit should forever be excluded from posts of preferment. The fawning sycophant, who is seeking promotion only to gratify his pride and ambition, will if an opportunity presents, sell his country for less than thirty pieces of silver.

The sentiment now inculcating receives abundant energy from the oracles of divine truth, and should ever be held sacred.

7. In a word, it would be an unpardonable error should I forget to mention that which after all is the great and only source of felicity, peace and prosperity among men, I mean religion. A republican government has its basis in this. Can we form a more noble idea of piety and Christianity than what is comprised in the words benevolence and true patriotism. To love God and one another, and to seek the happiness and good of the universe, involves every thing that is great, noble, virtuous and excellent. Selfishness enervates every social band and endearment, sets men at variance, and is the source of every evil. Vice debases and weakens the human mind; and is to the body politic what sickness is to the natural constitution. No sooner did Sampson trespass on the rules of religion & morality, than he became a weak, menial slave, and did grind in the prison house. Pride, dissipation and impiety, have crumbled empires in the dust, and buried their names in everlasting oblivion. A sacred regard to holy institutions is necessary to secure the divine favour and protection, and to maintain the order of society. Those words of inspiration cannot too often be repeated, and are worthy to be written in indelible characters on the fleshly tables of our hearts: "Righteousness exalteth a nation; but sin is a reproach to any people."

But to draw towards a close.

A review of this subject may tend to inspire our breasts with the magnitude and importance of our independence, which is the design of the present appointment to commemorate.

Hail! happy era! that broke the galling yoke, and taught the free-born sons of Columbia to assert their birth-rights. This auspicious day, never, never to be forgotten, will be held in the highest veneration to generations yet unborn. This is the day that fair liberty purified the once contaminated regions of North America, and illuminated our country with its exhilerating beams!—This is the day, fatal to tyrants; its influence will extend to the remotest corners of the globe, and tell the groaning sons of despots that they may be free.—This is the day that will form a surprising and important epoch in the annals of history, and be viewed with pleasing astonishment to remotest ages. It cannot be expected that the rising generation can form a competent estimate of that legacy, transmitted to them by noble ancestors: they were not on the stage when calamity, war and death spread desolation through our bleeding country; yet they will find such vestiges of zeal for liberty, and for the contested rights of their country, as will be more glorious and significant than the pyramids of Egypt.—We trust they will never forget to hold these things sacred, and convey them inviolate to posterity.—May America ever retain her dignity, and grow in esteem on the true basis of merit;—be a scourge to tyrants, a retreat for the oppressed—May her civil, military, and religious operations, ever conspire to promote peace, piety and prosperity, and introduce those happy days, when the danger of war shall be too remote to disturb our repose, or wound the tender feelings of the soul. Nothing can be more detrimental to religion than tyranny and oppression, or to that kingdom the blessed Jesus came into the world to set up, which gave rise to the caution in the text, "But ye shall not be so; but he that is great among you shall be as the younger, and he that is chief, as he that doth serve." May we not almost predict that this will be the blissful region that will introduce the golden age, or peaceful kingdom, that shall break in pieces all the haughty empires of the world and so America become the glory of the whole earth. The prospect grows upon our imagination and fills the soul with anticipating joy!—Oppression, tyranny and domination are the mystical Euphrates, that must be dried up that the beams of this rising morning may illuminate our globe. The veteran sons of Vermont, should not be the last to espouse the rights of men as her zeal shone conspicuous at an early period. The present flourishing situation of this state, its population, and commerce, are truly surprising; should she be as distinguished for her peace, virtue and morality, she will soon become a star of no small magnitude in the revolution. These sentiments are not suggested to stimulate pride and vain ambition, but to that noble spirit adverted to in my text, which is the highest ornament of human nature on earth, and renders us fit subjects for the entertainments of heaven.

Our independence was purchased at a dear rate: more than an hundred thousand fell in the important struggle.—The sweet, the delicious draught, that this day cheers our spirits, is the price of blood. The disconsolate widow, the bereaved parent, and the weeping orphan, can still relate the mournful disaster. To buy our freedom, the generous warrior has forsaken the inviting charms of domestic life, has distinguished himself in the field of battle, & become a victim to the king of terrors. Many of our once ruddy youth have fallen in the inhospitable desart, and been a prey to savage barbarity. How many have breathed out their souls beneath some lofty oak, or more humble shrub, without a friend to witness the agonizing groan, or soothe the convulsions of nature! The tributary tear should trickle down our cheek, while the detail of woe accosts our imagination!—The situation of our country before independence was proclaimed, was such that nothing but a preference of liberty to life itself, could give rise to the declaration. We were comparatively small;—Our troops undisciplined, and unaccustomed to the hardships of war; our military stores scarcely sufficient for a single combat; a formidable enemy to oppose, whose arms had commonly proved victorious; we had also intestine foes, who were ready to betray us, etc. May we not say with the utmost propriety, "If it had not been the Lord who was on our side, when men rose up against us:—then they had swallowed us up quick, when their wrath was kindled against us."—Those advocates for liberty, whose names are this day precious, and thro' whose instrumentality our independence is established, derived all their skill, prowess and zeal from that almighty being, who directs all the affairs of men. Nothing short of a kind of miraculous interposition has brought us hitherto.—With the warmest emotions of heart, let us erect an altar of praise to him who is the author of our independence, and to whom we are still to look for its support.

Let us never forget the remarkable divine goodness towards us in the times of distress. Many of you can remember those days of tribulation, being driven from your habitations, & were disturbed with the frightful haunts of blood-thirsty savages, through the silent watches of the night! Our lives, our all hung in suspense; but the Lord, who is the scourge of tyrants, the friend of liberty, hath done great things for us whereof we are glad. Let us raise up tribute of thanks to our great benefactor, and offer the most unfeigned gratitude on the altar of praise. May that exalted name, the Lord Jehovah, animate our souls, to whose paternal benignity we owe our present dignity, that we may never be blind to his holy government, thro' the glare of prosperity. On occasions like this, we are too apt to forget this object, and tarnish our laurels by immoderate indulgence. To cultivate peace, friendship and freedom, is falling in with the nature of the appointment. Would we maintain our independence, let us secure the patronage of him from whence it derived its existence, and who has distinguished America by most signal displays of goodness and power. To be impatient under a constitution like ours, and not be ready to use every laudable endeavour on all proper occasions to defend it, argue an unpardonable supineness. Explore every corner of the globe for an equal asylum, tired in the fruitless chase, you would most eagerly seek the refreshing shades of happy Columbia. Still it is a land of improvement; we are not to conclude that the fair tree of liberty hath reached its highest zenith; may we not add to its lustre by every new and valuable acquisition: But we should keep in mind the principles and end of government: That it is to curb the passions of men; to suppress vice and immorality; to build up society, and to establish religion in the world. What encouragement in such a land as this, for men to seek for greatness on the true basis of merit, or to rise in the scale of being by serving their country, or by devoting their talents to the general good? On the other hand, those who would climb up any other way, will be accounted thieves and robbers. To shun the shoals of despotism on the one hand, and the rocks of anarchy on the other, requires skill, prudence and moderation. A candid, careful and impartial vigilance, under the auspices of heaven, will be our sure and constant protection.

Should the FOURTH OF JULY be ever promotive of peace, friendship and religion, the word INDEPENDENCE will have a commanding influence, and be more durable than pillars of marble.

Divine Decrees

This sermon, published in Rutland in 1805, includes the first listing of Haynes' M.A., an honorary degree conferred by Middlebury College in 1804. The sermon was reprinted in Utica in 1810.

———

Divine Decrees, an Encouragement to the Use of Means. A Sermon Delivered at Granville, (N.Y.) June 25, 1805, before the Evangelical Society, instituted for the purpose of aiding pious and needy young men in acquiring education for the work of the Gospel ministry.

By faith, Moses, when he was born, was hid three months of his parents, because they saw he was a proper child; and they were not afraid of the King's commandments.

Hebrews 11:23

The children of Israel having been in Egypt about one hundred and thirty-four years, the time drew near when God intended their deliverance, which took place eighty years after the birth of Moses. The whole time of their sojourning there was two hundred and fifteen years.

God, in accomplishing his most holy purposes, makes use of means, and those that are in the best manner calculated to exhibit his wisdom, power and goodness; such as to blind mortals do not appear to be adapted to the end designed.—What human sagacity could have thought that the wickedness of Joseph's brethren was to fulfil a prediction to Abraham, one hundred and eighty-four years before, (Gen. 15:13) or to bring the Israelites into Egypt? That the cruel edict of Pharoah to destroy the Hebrew male children, should be introductory to the emancipation of the chosen tribes, according to divine promise three hundred and forty-two years before? Moses was born at a time most unlikely to be an instrument to effect the above purpose, it being after the children were devoted to death. Aaron, the elder, and the rest of the family were passed by.

Men are naturally blind to divine government; and as this is the great source of happiness and consolation to the people of God, it seems suitable that he should so work that we may plainly see and acknowledge the operations of his hand. Pharoah's wicked design to destroy the Church of God, was made greatly subservient to its deliverance. Moses is qualified for the important work through the instrumentality of those who were the greatest enemies to it. History informs us, that some of the Seers of Egypt had intimated that a great man was to be raised up from among the Hebrews about this time, who was to be their deliverer, which gave rise to the tyrannical edict of the Egyptian court. Josephus relates that the parents of Moses were informed by divine revelation some way, that this child was designed by God as the deliverer of the children of Israel from their bondage, which is also intimated in my text. They saw something in his looks, perhaps, or by some other means, were made to put confidence in God, that he would preserve him from devoted destruction. They saw he was a *proper child; fair in the sight of God*—as the words are in the original. The conduct of the parents, in consequence of the heavenly vision, is truly remarkable. Their faith was strong, so as to exclude distrust in God, and fear of the King's commandment.

To collect your minds to a general point, I would propose the following observation, viz. That, although pious people believe and confide in the unalterable purpose and providence of God to bring about all events, yet they will diligently use such means as God requires, and that tend to their accomplishment.

It is proposed to shew,

I. That all things are brought about by the fixed purpose and providence of God.

II. That the people of God do believe and trust in his absolute government.

III. Yet they are diligent in the use of such means that are appointed, and necessary to accomplish events.

That there are events constantly transpiring, both in the natural and moral worlds, all allow. That they are the effects of cause is equally evident. 'Tis certain that they had a beginning, and so not self-existent; for there could be nothing in them to operate as the cause of their being before they had any. As nothing can begin to exist without God, so it cannot *continue* without him. 'Tis impossible for Deity to communicate or impart independence to any; this is peculiar to himself; and it would imply the grossest absurdity and contradiction to suppose it of any other being. 'Tis certain that men do not create, or bring about events, only as instruments in the hand of God. Many of them we have no idea about before they take place; and they depend on so many minute circumstances, that we can discover no kind of connexion between the means and the end; so that we can have no design in the matter. Joseph could not discover, while he was telling his dreams, that it was to be the means of saving the house of Israel from perishing in a time of famine, and of bringing them into Egypt. Pharoah had no design of bringing them out, by passing the cruel edict against the Hebrew children, or by educating Moses. Things are daily taking place contrary to the designs and exertions of man; and they are often defeated in their anxious expectations.

The preservation of the Church amidst such a series of fiery calamities, must certainly be the good will of Him that dwelt in the bush.

That all things depend on God for their existence is a sentiment abundantly taught in the word of God. Rom. 11:36. "For of him, and through him, are *all things*." I Cor. 8:6. "But to us there is but one God, the Father, of *whom are all things*, and we in him; and one Lord, Jesus Christ, by *whom are all things*, and we by him." II Cor. 5:18.—"*All things are of God*." Even the wickedness of men is effected or brought about by the agency or providence of God; such as sending Joseph into Egypt, and the crucifixion of Christ. God brought the Israelites out of Egypt by an high hand, and a stretched out arm, by means of wicked instruments.

Not only events of great, but those of less magnitude, are ascribed to God; even the falling of a sparrow, or a hair of our head. It is difficult for us to distinguish between great and small events; there is not a superfluous link in the whole chain; they all depend on each other. It was necessary that Moses should be born at that time; that the careful parents should lodge him in the flags, by the side of the river, at such a place; that Thermuses, Pharoah's daughter, should come to such a place to wash; that her eye should be fixed on the spot, and discover something amidst the thicket; that her curiosity should excite her to have it fetched; that little Moses should weep, and excite female compassion; that he should fall into the hands of a tender mother, etc. These things are beyond the wisdom of mortals; and are parts of the ways of the Almighty.

If, then, God effects or brings about all events, he has design or volition agreeably to Eph. 1:11. "Who worketh all things after the *counsel of his own will*." There is no other way by which the Deity can give existence to things; he is incapable of what is called accidental events; and it is by the effective acts of his will, that he creates, or causes things to exist. Besides, could he work without design, he would not be virtuous or praise-worthy. Indeed, were there any possible events that could take place without God, it might be very difficult for us to find out which they were; and to be in a capacity always to comply with that holy injunction. Prov. 3:6. "In all thy ways acknowledge him." As all things are the effect of divine volition, design or decree, the purposes of God must be eternal and unchangeable. God is incapable of any new design; this would suppose him to increase in knowledge, or that he is growing wiser, and by extending our views back, his knowledge would decrease; admit this, then there was a time when he knew nothing at all.—There can be no alteration in the mind of the Deity, as nothing new can come up to his view, as a ground of such mutation. God eternally saw the propriety of all things taking place just as they do, and has adopted the best possible plan. Some are unwilling to acknowledge the absolute and unlimited providence and agency of God in the production of all things, especially with respect to the existence of moral evil, that it implies wickedness in Jehovah; as though there must be the same in the cause as in the effect: should this be admitted, we must deny God in the greater parts of creation and providence. Would men learn to distinguish between events in their own nature, and the good to which they are made subservient, it would relieve them of many difficulties. However wicked Pharoah was in devoting the Hebrew children to death, yet good was effected thereby, and the hand of God shone conspicuous. (All will allow that God *permitted* or *suffered* sin to take place; But if, on the whole, it is not promotive or made subservient to the highest possible good, then he cannot be vindicated in *permitting* it to be; but if it is best that sin should have existence, why cannot the divine Character be cleared in *causing* it to take place? Some, to relieve themselves of difficulties, suppose sin to be merely negative, consisting in the want of holiness; But can this be criminal only as implying positive exercises of hatred to God? Should I tell my neighbor who stands by me, that the pen with which I now write is crooked—should he reprove me for my impertinence and deficiency of language, and say I had not declared the thing as it is; for it *wants straitness*, should I gain much philosophical instruction by the remark?) If it be inconsistent with moral rectitude to stir up and employ wicked instruments, as best calculated to bring about his purposes, then the hand of God is not to be seen or acknowledged in sending Joseph into Egypt, and in bringing Israel out, in the destruction of the Babylonish empire, or in the crucifixion of Christ.

II. The people of God do believe, and confide in his absolute government.

It is allowed that the really pious men through want of instruction, and not well understanding all the terms that are made use of to express divine government, appear to oppose it: improper terms may be used on the subject; yet all that love God, will love his holy character. It is not to be supposed, but what there may be much remaining even in the children of God that is not reconciled to his decrees—they are sanctified, but in part; yet, so far as they fear, love, and serve God, they will acknowledge his government. That which distinguishes the righteous from the wicked is, the one loves God, the other hates him. To love God is to be pleased and delighted with his character, as exhibited in his word and works. As the whole of God's moral perfections consist in design, so that will be the principal objects of the Christian's love and joy. The reason why the wicked are so much opposed to the decrees of God, is because they give us so clear a discovery of him. As the moral perfections of God constitute his holiness or goodness, so it is the great object of virtuous affection. The natural perfections of the Deity are no further desirable than they are promotive of goodness. The feet of those are beautiful to the Saints, that bring such good tidings, "THY GOD REIGNETH," Is. 52:7. Zion was glad when she heard that God reigned, and called upon all to rejoice on the occasion, Ps. 97. We find that it has always been the practice of the people of God to acknowledge him: therefore it is that they attend to the external duties of religion, such as the public worship of God, prayer, and praise, by which they express their belief and love of a superintending providence. This was the object of the faith of those mentioned in my text. They had a firm belief in divine purposes concerning Moses, so as to exclude all fear of the King's commandment. The righteous view, and hold communion with God in his works, and repair to his absolute government in times of distress, as their only hiding place; Ps. 27. It was God's immutable promises and designs that supported Noah, Abraham, Isaac, Jacob, Moses, David and all God's people in all ages of the world—God has appointed the Lord Jesus Christ to be King on his holy hill of Zion, and has laid the government on his shoulders; the pious are his obedient subjects; and it is their duty to submit to him. They are to have the *mind* of Christ, as they would not forfeit their interest in him; Rom. 8:9. Rejoicing in the absolute dominion and agency of God was an important trait in his character; Luke 10:21. "In that hour, Jesus rejoiced in spirit, and said, I thank thee, O Father, Lord of heaven and earth, that thou hast hid these things from the wise and prudent, and hast revealed them unto babes: even so, Father, for so it seemed good in thy sight."

That the inspired writers were friendly to, and put their trust in the unchangeable purposes, power and wisdom of God, is evident to all that are acquainted with the holy Scriptures. It was in the view of this that they could have rational ground of support and success in their exertions in the cause of God; this has been the great source of consolation to the Church in all ages of the world, and will be to the second coming of Christ.

III. Although the people of God believe and confide in Divine Providence, or unchangeable purposes of God, yet they will be diligent in the use of such means as are necessary to accomplish events.

This idea is remarkably illustrated in the conduct of the parents of Moses, alluded to in the text; they hid him three months. Their care was excited by the full trust they had in God that he designed him for some important work.—Their faith was so great, as to exclude all doubt but what God would take care of the child, and fulfil his own purpose, in spite of all the designs of the enemy: *"They were not afraid of the King's commandment."* They did not fear to exert themselves to the utmost for the preservation of the child, nor that their measures would not be successful. He was doubtless secreted, and removed from place to place, to elude the search of the enemy. An ark was invented for the security of the helpless infant; every seam carefully secured, with slime and pitch, that the babe might have a dry and safe asylum. It is carried to the river side; deposited among the flags—an unlikely place to be found. She chose a place where the swelling of the Nile would not be likely to carry it away. The ark was not committed to the foaming waters, to be exposed to the voracious monsters of the deep; but as much care was exercised as though the life of the child wholly depended on their vigilance. Miriam, the sister of Moses, must lie in ambush at a suitable distance, to watch every disaster; and often to run and sooth the cries of the solitary infant. But "Moses was not safer when King in Jeshurun, encompassed with the thousands of Israel—was not safer in the mount with God—is not safer within the walls of the new Jerusalem, than in the flags" (Dr. Hunter).

The same spirit of vigilance shone conspicuously among all the people of God in all ages of the world. God revealed unto Abraham his unalterable designs concerning him and his posterity; and yet how diligent was he in using such means as tended to bring the events to pass. By faith he went out. By faith he sojourned in the land of promise, etc. The conduct of Isaac, Jacob, Moses, David, and the prophets, illustrate the same sentiment. Paul, in Acts 27. is a striking instance of the truth now under consideration. When it was revealed to him, that God's purpose was to save all in the ship, yet his diligence in the use of such means as tended to their preservation, exceeded all the mariners. He was evidently encouraged by the purpose of God revealed; yea without means, he tells them plainly, they *cannot be saved*.—No preacher ever held up the decrees of God more clearly, and more frequently than Paul; and none of the Apostles were more laborious; he labored more abundantly than they all; I. Corin. 15:10. We derive similar ideas from the doctrines and examples of him who spake as never man spake. The purposes of God with respect to the deliverance of the Jews from the Babylonish captivity, stirred up the saints to prayer; Dan. 9:2. The certainty of the incarnation of Christ, excited Old Testament Saints to prayer for the accomplishment of it; and this is what God greatly approved. The parents of Moses have a place in the sacred canon—whose faith is highly applauded.

2. Faith, in divine purposes, will excite the people of God to the diligent use of means; as he has appointed them as instruments, by which he will accomplish his designs; and has commanded them to be workers together with him: indeed, without the exertions of men, it is impossible that they should take place. God revealed to Abraham, that his seed should go down into Egypt, and at such a time be delivered; but this supposed a series of second causes, all dependent on the first cause; without them the event could not take place. One was the edict of Pharoah to destroy the male infants of the Hebrews; that Moses should be born and hid three months; that he should be educated at the expense of the King of Egypt; that the Egyptians should be visited with ten plagues, etc. I might with propriety make the same remark with respect to the deliverance of Israel from the Babylonish captivity, and the birth and death of Christ. The people of God consider themselves as active instruments to bring about his holy designs; and are, in a good degree, cured of that unreasonable temper of mind, that will deduce unnatural consequences from certain promises, in order to gratify a licentious conduct.

3. The truly pious are pleased with the absolute decrees of God—as what will promote the greatest possible good. If it is desirable that all God's counsels should stand, then it must be pleasing to saints to be in the use of

such means as tend to bring them to pass—without which they cannot exist; this makes them *cheerful* in the service of God; as they are seeking the same glorious ultimate object with him. Jachobed, and her husband, doubtless understood that God, by this remarkable child, designed the deliverance of the Church from the iron furnace, which was an animating object; all they did in fitting him for this work, afforded satisfaction.—Although the children of God cannot always see the connexion between means and end, yet they put such confidence in the Divine Being, as delights their souls in persevering in the path of duty—believing that God will effect the greatest good by it.

4. The friends of God delight in *expressing* their obedience to him. The use of means afford them opportunity to glorify God, and commend him to others. If love and obedience are delightful exercises to the saints, then to express them will be pleasing. As God cannot exhibit any true virtue, or moral excellence, without pursuing a plan, so neither can we, unless we regard his will and interest, and are workers together with him.

5. The humble Christian will feel his own weakness and insufficiency to do anything of himself, and will see that all his sufficiency is of God, and his faith and hope will rest on his power and providence to do all; which will be a motive to diligence. This will be the foundation of his trust, and will excite him to "work out his own salvation, with fear and trembling; knowing that it is *God that worketh in him*, both to will and to do of his good pleasure," Phil. 2:12, 13. This supported the parents of Moses amidst all their care about him, and by which "they were not afraid of the King's commandment."

6. Christians will very diligently attend to means, as they will see much to be done. Wherever they turn their eyes, they will behold work laid out for them; and it is criminal to stand idle in the market-place. The good man will see enough to employ his head, his heart, his hands, and his temporal interest, in the service of God. The reason that so many can find but little to do for God, is on account of a slothful and indolent heart, that refuses to labor.

Improvement

1. The doctrine of the decrees of God, or his absolute government, is a powerful motive to morality and religion.—This idea is abundantly held up in the holy Scriptures. Eccl. 52:14. "I know that whatsoever God doth, it shall be forever: nothing can be put to it, nor any thing taken from it; and

God doth it that men should *fear* before him." The same thing is declared in Ps. 33. Men are there exhorted to fear and reverence God, from the consideration that [sic] "that the counsel of the Lord standeth forever; and the thoughts of his heart to all generations." Compare Job 33:13. and on. The absolute dominion of Jehovah is the object and foundation of all true morality; and to withhold this doctrine, or to preach contrary to it, is highly immoral—tending to cherish looseness of sentiment and conduct. Ministers, therefore, are far from falling in with the true dictates of prudence and religion, by keeping back this doctrine, or by explaining it away by vague and indefinite expressions.

2. The agency and government of God is perfectly consistent with the liberty and freedom of men, and with their being the subjects of blame and praise; so that it does not exclude moral good and evil from the system. *That* cannot destroy virtue that is the very essence or foundation of it; nor vice that greatly enhances it. The reason why the wicked must be slain before the face of God is because they oppose his holy government or plan; Luke 19:14. That the providence and agency of God does not destroy our freedom, and so not our criminality, is evident from universal experience. Even Pharoah and Balaam, though very wicked men, own it; Ex. 9:27; Num. 22:34. If the unchangeable purposes of God destroy human liberty, it will more effect the morality and freedom of the Deity; as he fully sees all things unalterably fixed, and many events he cannot bring about without our agency or instrumentality, any more than we can without his. It is highly absurd to suppose that an agent can have no freedom in prosecuting a wise, holy, and unalterable plan.

That events are constantly taking place, all will allow; and when they come to exist, we know that it was always certain that they would. To say that it was ever possible that they should not come to pass, is as contradictory as to say they have no existence now. It makes no difference as to all things that do take place, as to their fixedness, or certainty, whether we admit that they were decreed or not: so that the liberties of men would be equally effected on any other hypothesis.

3. It argues no imperfection in the Deity that he cannot execute his designs without the intervention of second causes. God exercises no less power than if he used no means; he takes such ways to execute his decrees that are wisest and best, and can take no other. Creatures are to take nothing to themselves. "Neither is he that planteth any thing, neither he that watereth; but God who giveth the increase;["] I Cor. 3:7.

If it is desirable that the purposes of God should be executed; then it is suitable we use such means as he has appointed. This sets human exertions in a very important point of light.

4. Those who live unholy, vicious lives, have not a proper belief of the great doctrines of grace, or the immutable decrees of God. Men, it is true, will try to accommodate them to their lusts, as they do all the doctrines of the Bible; but no man was ever influenced to licentiousness from a true love and faith in these sentiments: so that the doctrines themselves, nor those who preach them, are accountable for the bad use that is made of them; but the corrupt and vicious tempers of men. Review the characters of those who have been advocates for divine government, and you will find that it had a holy and practical influence on all their conduct.

5. We infer the perfect safety of the Church, and in what view it is so. It is founded on the immutable purposes and providence of God. Not all the evil designs of Pharoah and his wicked courters, could destroy the chosen tribes. Every exertion to prevent their increase was made; heavy burdens were imposed; they were denied wholesome food. It was not uncommon for them, says a Jewish historian, to faint and die under the cruel hands of their task-masters; and they were often denied a burial. But the more they afflicted them, the more they multiplied and grew; "And they were grieved because of the children of Israel;" Exod. 1:12. An attempt to frustrate the divine purpose was subservient to its accomplishment. The wrath of men and devils will praise God. All the good promised to Israel, so many ages before, was brought about, and not one thing failed. These things afford comfort and consolation to the people of God, while they are truly alarming and confounding to the enemies of the church.

6. The subject, so far illustrated sets the design of the Institution to which our attention is particularly called, on the present occasion, in an important point of light. It is to aid pious and needy young men in acquiring Education for the GOSPEL MINISTRY. A remarkable spirit of zeal and liberality in the cause of God has been excited in the minds of the pious, in various parts of the Christian world. Missionaries have been sent out among the heathen, and to our new settlements; and their labors have been crowned with abundant success. People, while watering, have been watered themselves. The conversion of thousands, I believe, has been the effect of these benevolent exertions. The desert and the solitary wilderness have been made to blossom as the rose. Recent instances of the trophies of divine grace, in some parts of Africa, have made glad the city of our God.—The friends of

Christ on both sides of the Atlantic, have united in this glorious cause; but much still remains to be done.

PEOPLE, within our reach, are perishing for lack of spiritual food. The harvest is great—but the laborers are comparatively few. The number of those qualified to carry the bread of life to the dying, are inadequate. Our missionary exertions must be greatly impeded, unless pious, ingenious and learned men be found to engage in the service. Our Evangelical Society virtually embraces the same object of those commonly called Missionary Societies—as necessary and subservient thereto. Whatever funds are raised, unless proper preachers can be obtained, they cannot be rendered useful. That a competent degree of literary acquirements are necessary and indispensable in those who engage in ministerial labors, none will deny, who have the importance of the work on their minds. The patronage of those who love God and the Souls of men, is earnestly solicited. We hope you will not withhold that pecuniary aid which the urgency of the case requires.

I stand here this day, my friends and brethren, to plead for thousands of poor perishing, dying fellow mortals, who need the bread of life; whose cries and distresses call for compassion, beyond the groaning Israelites. Who, that knows the love of God, and the terrors of eternal death, but longs to run to their relief! Satan, the potent and imperious prince of darkness, has long since issued his cruel and bloody edict against the Church of God, to destroy and exterminate it from the earth.

We stand this day to plead the cause of that Jesus, who sits upon the holy hill of Zion, with pardon in his hands, and whose delight is with the sons of men; and who is now calling for your assistance. We plead the promises and predictions of God's word, that may encourage your hope and trust. Be not afraid of the haughty mandate of the prince of darkness, for it shall be made to subserve the interest of Christ's kingdom—God requires exertions as much as he did for the preservation of Moses, or the deliverance of Israel out of Egypt. It is sacrificing the cause of God, and the immortal Souls of men to withhold. Is there not an impropriety in our bearing the name of christians unless the love of Christ constrains us? Is it not an important trait in the characters of the godly, that they *took joyfully the spoiling of their goods*? That they *suffered the loss of all things, that they might win Christ*, and save Souls? What illustrious examples of benevolence do we find in the word of God; especially in the blessed Savior of the world? *That though he was rich, yet for our sake he became poor, that we, through his poverty, might be rich*. Can there be a more delightful employment, this side heaven, than to wrest Souls from the jaws of death and hell, and to send the blessed news of salvation to a perishing world.

To promote the felicity of the universe is the happiness of the redeemed in glory; and this spirit, among Christians, is heaven begun on earth. If your hearts do not glow with holy affection towards perishing sinners, by which you are disposed to do something for their relief, you have reason to fear and tremble, that you have no inheritance among the Saints in light.

The design of our institution is far from being new: God's people have, in all ages, in a measure drank into the same spirit. That angel of a man, Doctor Doddridge, in describing objects of Christian benevolence and liberality, observes, "I would particularly recommend to you the very important and noble charity of assisting young persons of genius and piety with what is necessary to support the expence of their education for the ministry, in a proper course of grammatical or academical studies." Consider that you are God's Stewards, and that all your property belongs to him, and you are to use it in his service. That he can easily make up if he sees fit, what your liberality imparts: and if you "Cast your bread upon the waters; for you shall find it after many days;" Ecc. 11:1. If we withhold, shall we not rob God, and incur his righteous displeasure? who will soon call us to give an account of our stewardships! Remember the maxim of the wise man, "There is that scattereth, and yet increaseth; and there is that witholdeth more than meet, but it tendeth to poverty," Proverbs 11:24. Since this spirit of liberality has shone so conspicuous in many parts of the Christian world, I think we have had manifest tokens of divine approbation. God has poured out his spirit in such copious effusions as to make it obvious that it is "An odour of a sweet smell, a sacrifice acceptable, well-pleasing to God." Let us not be weary in well-doing, for we shall yet reap a more plentiful harvest, if we faint not.

If we delight in giving, God will delight in rewarding. "Bring ye all the tithes into the Store house—and prove me now herewith, saith the Lord of Hosts, if I will not open you the windows of heaven, and pour you out a blessing, that there shall not be room enough to receive it;" Mal. 3:10. We may make a profession of religion—tell much of our regard for God; but words, as one observes, are *cheap things*, and are by no means the test of our sincerity. How many of this character are to be found; who when objects of charity are presented, that call for a pittance of their store, like the young miser in the gospel, go away sorrowful, having large possessions?

My Christian friends and brethren, you will be far from pleading exemption from duty by having recourse to the reasonings of a licentious world—"That if God has determined all things, our endeavors are unnecessary"—this, I trust, has been sufficiently reprobated in the foregoing discourse, as betraying an unbelief of the doctrine by which you profess to be influenced, and that you are governed by carnal principles. Consider that you are the only ones that will heartily engage in this cause; "For out of Zion shall go forth the law, and the word of the Lord from Jerusalem;" Is. 2:3.

Perhaps the conversion of every Soul is the effect of the Church's travail and exertions. Are there not thousands at the present day, that are casting in their mites, and in this way, sending a morsel of the bread of life to starving, perishing Souls? Surely it is a rich and valuable Treasury, that will refund an infinite and eternal reward, to all true adventurers. What if by distinguishing yourselves, by withholding, you should not be admitted to their society hereafter, nor taste of the rewards of the righteous?

The Institution for which I am now pleading cannot fail of attracting your attention, if we only consider the extensive nature of the object. It is that by which we may do good after we are dead. It is but a moment that we have in this present life to stretch out the benevolent hand to the distressed, or to pluck them from devouring flames. To act with reference to this life only, is too contracted for a Soul that has been ENLARGED. With what beauty and elegance is this sentiment illustrated by the Apostle Peter, in his second Epistle, 1 ch. 15 ver. "Moreover, I will endeavor that you may be able, after my decease, to have these things always in remembrance." It will be a tree of righteousness, that will spring up over your grave, diffusing divine fragrance—bringing forth fruit, till time shall be no more. Will it not afford unspeakable delight, should we ever arrive in the fields of immortal bliss, to meet with thousands, who through our instrumentality, were saved from endless perdition! What admiring thought of divine mercy and condescension would it excite, that God should make use of such poor despicable instruments for the salvation of souls! God will deign to take notice of it, and declare it before the assembled universe, and bestow an eternal reward of grace, even for giving a cup of cold water, in the name of a disciple. They who shall be instrumental of turning many to righteousness, shall shine as the stars forever and ever. The blessing of many that were ready to perish, shall come upon you; and thousands yet unborn may give glory to God.

How many among us are reaping the blessed effects of the pious exertions of God's people while on earth? The vigilance of Moses, Oh, how amply rewarded! The faith and care of his parents will never be forgotten, through ceaseless ages.

It is with pleasure that we often converse with people on the occasion of their first awakening; and hear them relate it was by reading a Flavel, a Hopkins, an Edwards, or a Janaway, etc. Do any of us hope that we have become friends of God; and shall, through astonishing grace, be admitted to the rewards of the righteous; doubtless it was in answer to the pious exertions of some who now sleep in the dust. Is it not a debt justly due from us to them, and the best requital we can make them for their beneficence, to do all we can for the salvation of others?

The Institution before us looks forward to heathen nations, and we may be among the number of those who shall introduce the glorious days of the MESSIAH, when "the earth shall be full of the knowledge of God." Should we refuse to comply with the present call of divine providence, and withhold our hand from contributing, will not those who are perishing for lack of provisions, rise up in judgment, and condemn us at the bar of Christ! The reproof of a Hottentot as lately related in a missionary publication, cannot but give feelings to a Christian. Upon becoming acquainted with salvation, she thus exclaims, "What a pity, what a sin it is, that you Europeans, who have for so many years enjoyed in great abundance the heavenly bread, should keep it all to yourselves, and not spare one little crum[b] to the millions of poor heathen! Adding, You may depend upon it, you should not have the less for yourselves, by giving some to them; but the Lord Jesus would bless you, and give you the more." She also observed that, "Could we but conceive fully of the miserable situation of the Hottentots, we would certainly feel more compassion."

We earnestly solicit the aid of all who have the least love to the Redeemer, and to the Souls of men; yea, all that have natural affections. You must do violence to the dictates of common compassion and humanity to withhold your assistance ye that are strangers to God, remember, that it is more blessed to give than to receive. We wish you to put in with us—we wish you the reward of the liberal. It is true, that unless love to God and the souls of men directs you, your services, however great, will be but *vain oblations*, and displeasing to the Most High, though your interest devoted may be the occasion of the salvation of thousands yet unborn. It will be so with the professors of religion, if the glory of God is not their object; they will lose their reward. There is as much propriety in calling on the wicked to engage in this duty as in any other. You are under obligations to repent, to love God, and to express it in all those ways he has appointed and commanded.

Could we persuade young men and young women, instead of spending time and property in carnal dissipation, to turn their attention to the object before us, of what service might they be to the interest of Zion while on the earth! The people of God, your pious parents, yea, God himself, would pronounce you GREATLY BELOVED. Would it not afford consolation in death, to reflect, that the time, talents, and property given you by your Creator, instead of their being consumed in a ball room, or around the card-table, have been devoted to God? O! that you would seriously think on that divine injunction and promise, Matt. 6:33. "Seek ye first the kingdom of heaven and its righteousness, and all these things shall be added unto you;" and Luke 16:10. "Make to yourselves friends of the mammon of unrighteousness; that when ye fail, they may receive you into everlasting habitations.["]

It is with pleasure I relate, and to their honor be it mentioned, that some even among our young women, we would hope prompted by a holy zeal for God, whose circumstances are far from being affluent, have engaged to contribute some thing yearly to our Society. May it excite many to follow their laudable example. There is no external duty that is spoken of in Scripture, that is so evidential of our love to God, as imparting a portion to the necessities of the souls and bodies of men. It will be publicly held up at the day of Judgment, as a test of the sincerity of the righteous—"For I was an hungry, and YE GAVE ME MEAT." Let none plead their inability to administer. Cannot you look round, and see many ways by which you may retrench your expences without any real injury to yourselves or families, and spare a little for the Lord? Should we throw in only two mites, like the widow in the gospel, like her we should meet divine approbation.—"For if there be first a willing mind, it is accepted according to what a man hath, and not according to what he hath not." II Corin. 8:12.

A single cent, truly devoted to God, by faith and prayer may issue in the conversion of thousands. The circumstances of hiding Moses—the building the ark—the weeping of the babe, etc. were apparently trifling events; yet connected with infinite consequences. The deliverance of millions from bondage—the preservation or being of a Church depended upon them.

"I cannot believe," says Chrysostem, "that he has ever tasted the sweets of religion, that has no tender concern for the salvation of others."

But after all, since the success of our endeavors depends on the blessing of heaven, we earnestly intreat the prayers of God's people of every denomination, that he would bless the Institution—increase its funds—make those faithful, and instrumental of turning many to righteousness, to whom aid may be imparted—that it may more abundantly flourish after we are dead—and the whole world be filled with the glory of God: AMEN.

Universal Salvation

Haynes' most famous sermon appeared in over seventy editions and was reprinted as late as 1865. The text here is taken from the manuscript which appears to be the setting copy; it is held by the Schomburg Center for Research in Black Culture.

––––––

Universal Salvation: A Very Ancient Doctrine; With Some Account of the Life and Character of Its Author. A Sermon. Delivered at Rutland, West Parish, in the Year 1805.

Preface

There is no greater folly than for men to express anger and resentment because their religious sentiments are attacked. If their characters are impeached by their own creed, they only are to blame.

All that the antagonists can say, cannot make falsehood truth, nor truth, falsehood. The following discourse was delivered at Rutland, Vt., June, 1805, immediately after hearing Mr. Ballou, an Universal Preacher, zealously exhibit his sentiments. The author had been repeatedly solicited to hear and dispute with the above Preacher: and had been charged with dishonesty and cowardice for refusing. He felt that some kind of testimony, in opposition to what he calls error, ought to be made; and has been urged to let the same appear in print. But whether, on the whole, it is for the interest of truth, is left to the judgment of the candid.

A Sermon

Genesis 3, 4, And the serpent said unto the woman, ye shall not surely die.

The holy scriptures are a peculiar fund of instruction. They inform us of the origin of creation; of the primitive state of man; of his fall, or apostacy from God. It appears that he was placed in the garden of Eden, with full liberty to regale himself with all the delicious fruits that were to be found, except what grew on one tree—if he eat of that, that he should surely die, was the declaration of the Most High.

Happy were the human pair amidst this delightful Paradise, until a certain preacher, in his journey, came that way, and disturbed their peace and tranquility, by endeavoring to reverse the prohibition of the Almighty; as in our text, ye shall not surely die.

> She pluck'd, she ate,
> Earth felt the wound; nature from her seat,
> Sighing through all her works, gave signs of woe,
> That all was lost.
>   Milton

We may attend,—To the character of the preacher; to the doctrines inculcated; to the hearer addressed; to the medium or instrument of the preaching.

I. As to the preacher, I shall observe, he has many names given him in the sacred writings; the most common is the devil. That it was he that disturbed the felicity of our first parents, is evident from 2 Cor. 11:3, and many other passages of Scripture. He was once an angel of light and knew better than to preach such doctrine; he did violence to his own reason.—But to be a little more particular, let it be observed:

1. He is an old preacher. He lived above one thousand seven hundred years before Abraham; above two thousand four hundred and thirty years before Moses; four thousand and four years before Christ. It is now five thousand eight hundred and nine years since he commenced preaching. By this time he must have acquired great skill in the art.

2. He is a very cunning, artful preacher. When Elymas the sorcerer, came to turn away people from the faith, he is said to be full of all subtlety, and

a child of the devil, not only because he was an enemy to all righteousness, but on account of his carnal cunning and craftiness.

3. He is a very laborious, unwearied preacher. He has been in the ministry almost six thousand years; and yet his zeal has not in the least abated. The apostle Peter compares him to a roaring lion, walking about seeking whom he may devour. When God inquired of this persevering preacher, Job 2:2, From whence camest thou? He answered the Lord, and said, From going to and fro in the earth, and from walking up and down in it. He is far from being circumscribed within the narrow limits of parish, state, or continental lines; but his haunt and travel is very large and extensive.

4. He is a heterogeneous preacher, if I may so express myself. He makes use of a Bible when he holds forth, as in his sermon to our Saviour; Matt. 4:6. He mixes truth with error, in order to make it go well, or to carry his point.

5. He is a very presumptuous preacher. Notwithstanding God had declared, in the most plain and positive terms, Thou shalt surely die, or In dying, thou shalt die, yet this audacious wretch had the impudence to confront omnipotence, and says ye shall not surely die!

6. He is a very successful preacher. He draws a great number after him. No preacher can command hearers like him. He was successful with our first parents, with the old world. Noah once preached to those spirits who are now in the prison of hell; and told them from God, that they should surely die; but this preacher came along and declared the contrary, ye shall not surely die. The greater part it seems believed him and went to destruction. So it was with Sodom and Gomorrah. Lot preached to them; the substance of which was, up, get ye out of this place, for the Lord will destroy this city. Gen. 19:14. But this old declaimer told them, no danger, no danger, ye shall not surely die. To which they generally gave heed, and Lot seemed to them as one who mocked; they believed the universal preacher, and were consumed. Agreeably to the declaration of the apostle Jude, Sodom and Gomorrah and the cities about them, suffering the vengeance of eternal fire.

II. Let us attend to the doctrine inculcated by this preacher; ye shall not surely die. Bold assertion! without a single argument to support it. The death contained in the threatening was doubtless eternal death,—as nothing but this would express God's feelings towards sin, or render an infinite atonement necessary. To suppose it to be spiritual death, is to blend crime and punishment together; to suppose temporal death to be the curse of the law, then believers are not delivered from it, according to Gal. 3:13. What Satan meant to preach, was that there is no hell, and that the wages of sin is not death, but eternal life.

III. We shall now take notice of the hearer addressed by the preacher. This we have in the text, And the serpent said unto the woman, etc. That Eve had not so much experience as Adam, is evident; and so was not equally able to withstand temptation. This doubtless was the reason why the devil chose her, with whom he might hope to be successful. Doubtless he took a time when she was separated from her husband.

That this preacher has had the greatest success in the dark and ignorant parts of the earth, is evident: his kingdom is a kingdom of darkness. He is a great enemy to light. St. Paul gives us some account of him in his day, 2 Tim. 3:6. For of this sort are they which creep into houses, and lead captive silly women, laden with sin led away with divers lusts. The same apostle observes, Rom. 16:17, 18. Now I beseech you, brethren, mark them which cause divisions and offences, contrary to the doctrine which ye have learned, and avoid them. For they that are such serve not the Lord Jesus Christ, but their own belly; and by good words and fair speeches deceive the simple.

IV. The instrument or medium made use of by the preacher will now be considered. This we have in the text: And the serpent said etc. But how came the devil to preach through the serpent?

1. To save his own character, and the better to carry his point. Had the devil come to our first parents personally and unmasked, they would have more easily seen the deception. The reality of a future punishment is at times so clearly impressed on the human mind, that even Satan is constrained to own that there is a hell; altho' at other times he denies it. He does not wish to have it known that he is a liar; therefore he conceals himself, that he may the better accomplish his designs, and save his own character.

2. The devil is an enemy to all good, to all happiness and excellence. He is opposed to the felicity of the brutes. He took delight in tormenting the swine. The serpent, before he set up preaching Universal Salvation, was a cunning, beautiful, and happy creature; but now his glory is departed; for the Lord said unto the serpent, because thou hast done this, thou art cursed above all cattle, and above every beast of the field, upon thy belly shalt thou go, and dust shalt thou eat all the days of thy life. There is therefore, a kind of duplicate cunning in the matter, Satan gets the preacher and hearers also.

And is not this triumphant flattery,
And more than simple conquest in the foe?

Young

3. Another reason why Satan employs instruments in his service is, because his empire is large and he cannot be every where himself.

4. He has a large number at his command, that love and approve of his work, delight in building up his kingdom, and stand ready to go at his call.

Inferences

1. The devil is not dead, but still lives; and is able to preach as well as ever, ye shall not surely die.

2. Universal Salvation is no new fangled scheme, but can boast of great antiquity.

3. See a reason why it ought to be rejected, because it is an ancient devilish doctrine.

4. See one reason why it is that Satan is such an enemy to the Bible, and to all who preach the gospel, because of that injunction, And he said unto them, go ye into all the world, and preach the gospel to every creature. He that believeth and is baptized shall be saved; but he that believeth not shall be damned.

5. See whence it was that Satan exerted himself so much to convince our first parents that there was no hell; because the denunciation of the Almighty was true, and he was afraid they would continue in the belief of it. Was there no truth in future punishment, or was it only a temporary evil, Satan would not be so busy, in trying to convince men that there is none. It is his nature and his element to lie. When he speaketh a lie, he speaketh of his own; for he is a liar, and the father of it.

6. We infer that ministers should not be proud of their preaching. If they preach the true gospel, they only, in substance, repeat Christ's sermons; if they preach ye shall not surely die, they only make use of the devil's old notes, that he delivered almost six thousand years ago.

7. It is probable that the doctrine of Universal Salvation will still prevail, since this preacher is yet alive, and not in the least superannuated; and every effort against him only enrages him more and more, and excites him to new inventions and exertions to build up his cause.

To close the subject: As the author of the foregoing discourse has confined himself wholly to the character of Satan, he trusts no one will feel himself personally injured by this short sermon: But should any imbibe a degree of friendship for this aged divine, and think that I have not treated this Universal Preacher with that respect and veneration which he justly deserves, let them be so kind as to point it out, and I will most cheerfully retract; for it has ever been a maxim with me, render unto all their dues.

The following Hymn, taken from the Theological Magazine, was repeated after the delivery of the preceding discourse.

A late writer in favor of Universal Salvation, having closed his piece with these lines of Pope's Messiah:

> The seas shall waste, the skies in smoke decay,
> Rocks fall to dust, and mountains melt away;
> But fix'd his word, his saving pow'r remains,
> Thy realm forever lasts, thy own Messiah reigns.

His antagonist made the following addition to them:

Universalism Indeed.

> "When seas shall waste, and skies in smoke decay,
> Rocks fall to dust, and mountains melt away;
> In adamantine chains shall death be bound,
> And hell's grim tyrant feel th' eternal wound."

> But all his children reach fair Eden's shore,
> Not e'er to see their father Satan more.
> The tot'ring drunkard shall to glory reel,
> And common strumpets endless pleasure feel.

> Blest are the haughty who despise the poor,
> For they're entitled to the heav'nly store:
> Blest all who laugh and scoff at truth divine,
> For bold revilers endless glories shine.

Blest are the clam'rous and contentious crew,
To them eternal rest and peace is due:
Blest all who hunger and who thirst to find,
A chance to plunder and to cheat mankind,

Such die in peace—for God to them has giv'n,
To be unjust on earth, and go to Heav'n:
Blest is the wretch whose bowels never move,
With gen'rous pity or with tender love;
He shall find mercy from the God above.

Blest all who seek to wrangle or to fight,
Such mount from seas of blood to worlds of light:
Go riot, drink, and every ill pursue,
For joys eternal are reserv'd for you;

Fear not to sin, till death shall close your eyes;
Live as you please, yours is th' immortal prise.
Old serpent hail! thou mad'st a just reply
To mother Eve, "ye shall not surely die!"

But reader stop! and in God's holy fear,
With sacred truth, these tenets first compare;
Our Saviour's sermon on the mount peruse—
Read with attention, and the bane refuse!

The Death
of Job Swift

Job Swift (1743-1804), a graduate of Yale with an honorary doctorate from Williams, was minister in Bennington for many years and something of a patriarch among Vermont's Congregational clergy. Haynes preached this sermon at Swift's death and it was included in *Discourses on Religious Subjects*, a collection of Swift's sermons published in Middlebury in 1805.

Swift was particularly kindly in his relationship with Haynes. At gatherings of ministers in homes with limited accommodations, Swift always quickly volunteered to share a bed with Haynes to preclude any possible incident of discrimination.

———

The Death of the Rev. Job Swift

"And the time of departure is at hand."

II Tim. 4:6

Among the many sources of evil to men, there are few more hurtful than their inattention to future scenes: this subjects them to unavoidable troubles here, and endless sorrow hereafter. Men are generally disposed to crowd eternal realities from them, and put far away the evil day. Having the last week heard of the sudden death of the Rev. Dr. Swift, which I consider, speaking after the manner of men, a greater loss to the church than could have taken place in the death of a single individual in this state; and having lately had so agreeable an interview with him, it has fixed my mind so intensely on eternal realities that I found some difficulty in turning my attention on any other subject.

If ever the sentiment in my text was proclaimed in powerful and significant language, it is in this alarming dispensation of Divine providence. *The time of my departure is at hand.*

St. Paul wrote this epistle after his last confinement at Rome, about nine years after the former, and a little before his death, as intimated in the text. Although the exact time of our death is fixed by the unalterable purpose of God, Job 7:1; 14:5, yet this moment to us is uncertain. We are not to suppose that Paul understood this; but by what he could discern by the conduct and temper of his enemies, he concluded that his exit was near. *Analuseoos*, which is rendered departure, signifies "to return home; to weigh or loose anchor; to change our place. It is a metaphor taken from mariners, importing the sailing from one port to another. Death is, as it were, the unfolding the net, or breaking open the prison door by which the soul was before detained in a kind of thraldom."—*See Leigh's Critica Sacra*. Paul expected to live in a future state, and that death was not an eternal sleep, but that a crown of glory awaited him beyond the grave. That we ought to live in the constant expectation of death, is the point to which our attention is particularly called on the present occasion.

The *nature* and *importance* of the duty will be considered. There are many people who, though they have the clearest intimations that they must die, yet do not expect it. Every age of the world affords us painful examples of the truth of this observation. Death often comes and finds us sleeping. Many no doubt will go into eternity within one hour, that have no expectation of dying for years yet to come. Some of you who are now present will doubtless die within a few weeks, who are not looking for such an event. Many of you have more worldly schemes already laid out than you can accomplish to the day of your death. Follow men to their death-bed, and you will generally find that death is an unwelcome and unexpected messenger. Who those are that live in the expectation of death, is a question of serious importance.

People who expect to die will have their thoughts much on the subject, as one who is about to remove to a great distance will think and converse much about the matter. Job called the grave his house, and made his bed in the darkness; and said to corruption, Thou art my father, and to the worm, Thou art my mother and my sister. The man who considers that the time of his departure is at hand, will not be much elated with sublunary objects. Of whatever importance they may be to others, yet to him they are of little consequence, as he is just ready to leave them. I Cor. 7:29, 30, 31. "But this

I say, brethren, the time is short. It remaineth, that both they that have wives be as though they had none; and they that weep, as though they wept not; and they that rejoice, as though they rejoiced not; and they that buy, as though they possessed not; and they that use this world, as not abusing it; for the fashion of this world passeth away." Neither prosperity nor adversity will much affect him who expects every hour to come to the end of his journey, or close his eyes on things below.

The man who expects soon to remove, will have his mind much taken up with the country to which he is going. He will inquire about it, and form as much acquaintance with it as possible; he will attend to the geography of it, and will have it much in his conversation; will wish to know how it is like to fare with him when he arrives there. The dying man, who acts in character, will read the word of God—that informs us about eternal things;—will endeavour to obtain a knowledge of the heavenly state—of its laws, inhabitants, and employments. He will look upon the things that are not seen—that are eternal. I Cor. 4:18. And his conversation will be in heaven. Phil. 3:20.

A man that adopts the sentiment in my text will set immediately about the work of preparation for death,—will, without any delay, set his house in order. Being struck with a sense of the shortness and uncertainty of life, he will summon every faculty of his soul to the most vigorous exertion in this great work; will do with his might what his hand findeth to do: he will not put off that work until to-morrow that should be attended to to-day, since he knows not what a day may bring forth. He will pay a diligent attention to the means of grace. Prayer, reading, meditation, and attending religious institutions, will be matters of serious importance. When men are apprehensive that they are drawing near the eternal world, they commonly have very different views of many external duties that they despise in days of health. Visits from ministers and pious friends, prayer and religious conversation, now appear valuable. The man that really expects soon to die, like Paul in the text, will be solemn, serious, and honest; will not trifle with sacred things; but will act in view of a judgment to come.

Farther: They who are properly looking out for death, look upon it as an event to which they are exposed at any time, at any place, or on any occasion, at home or abroad; and they will endeavour not to engage in any work inconsistent with being called immediately before the bar of Christ. A willingness to depart out of time, and to land on the shores of immortality, comports with the nature of the duty under consideration. With what holy and ecstatic joy does the apostle, in the chapter and verse from which our text is selected, anticipate the approaching moment of his departure. "For I am now ready to be offered, and the time of my departure is at hand. I have fought a good fight, I have finished my course, I have kept the faith. Henceforth there is laid up for me a crown of righteousness, which the Lord, the righteous judge, shall give me at that day; and not to me only, but unto all them also that love his appearing." In a word: to live as expectants of death, is to do the work of every day in the day; that we faithfully discharge the duties we owe to God, to ourselves, and fellow-creatures; that we live in the daily exercise of Christian graces, and persevere in holy obedience, in a constant dependance on the mercy of God through Jesus Christ. We are now to attend to the importance of the duty, or the propriety of our living in the constant expectation of death.

We argue from Divine injunctions. How constantly and forcibly is the sentiment enjoined in the word of God.—"*Watch therefore. Be ye also ready. Let your loins be girded about, and your lights burning,*" etc.; are the repeated admonitions of him who spake as never man spake. To live in the constant expectation of death, is falling in with the dictates of the written word of God—and with the examples of the people of God, who attained to eminent degrees of piety. They considered themselves as strangers and pilgrims on the earth—that their days were as a shadow—and that the time is short. The dispensations of Divine providence illustrate the same idea, that the time of our departure is at hand, and call for correspondent deportment. The history of mankind—the repeated instances of death within our own observation—point us to the grave, and proclaim, with united voice, that "There is but a step between us and death." Men of every character, station, age, and relation in life, are daily falling victims to the king of terrors, and leave us this kind of admonition, that the time of our departure is at hand.

If we were to look round at the various instruments of death, we learn the propriety of constant watchfulness. Almost every thing we behold is armed with deadly weapons, and ready to destroy: even when we think we are fleeing from the enemy, we often run into the arms of death. The feeble and delicate state of our bodies loudly proclaims our approaching dissolution. The pains and infirmities which have already racked this earthly house of our tabernacle, show us that it cannot be long before it will crumble and fall. When I turn my eyes around on this congregation, I behold evident signatures of death in every countenance, which speak the language in the text, *The time of my departure is at hand.*

Suitably to imbibe this sentiment would have a happy influence on us in every department of life—on ministers and people, parents and children, friends and neighbours. We should lay hold of every opportunity to admonish, reprove, and instruct. Did we consider on all occasions that it is more than possible that we are giving our last and dying advice, would it not make a great alteration as to the *manner* of our addresses? Keeping death at too great a distance tends to make us cold and indifferent about the things of religion. It is often the occasion of that foolish jesting and levity, in which we are too prone to indulge; this renders our visits among our friends so very barren, and turns our conversation on subjects of no importance. Were it constantly sounding in our ears, *The time of my departure is at hand!* it would have a salutary influence on our conduct, and others would derive unspeakable advantage from it. I might further add, as an incentive to the duty under consideration, that to live in the constant expectation of death is the only way to be prepared for it, and obtain a victory over it. The reason that this enemy breaks in upon us with such terror and surprise is, because we do not watch, or keep awake. When our blessed Lord calls upon us to watch, he takes the metaphor from the sentinels that stand on guard, or on the watch-tower. The word signifies to *keep awake.* If we view death at a great distance, and so fall asleep, should he come at such a moment, we fall an easy prey to the king of terrors. On the other hand, do we stand looking for and hastening to the coming of the Lord, with our loins girded about, and our lights burning, that when Christ shall come and knock, we may open immediately—we shall have the blessedness of those servants whom the Lord when he cometh shall find so doing. This no doubt supported our reverend father whom God has lately called home; he could say, amid the agonies of dissolving nature, "Death has no terrors to me." This account I lately had from one living in the family at the time of the doctor's death. His usual calmness and fortitude of mind shone conspicuous in his last moments, and astonished spectators. In a word, the magnitude and importance of death, judgment, and eternity, should command the utmost attention, watchfulness, and circumspection.

The subject, thus far illustrated, suggests a number of thoughts, which, if pursued by way of improvement, would afford us useful instruction.

In the first place, it is natural to observe, that it is very probable that there are many people that will never be saved. They are on the very borders of the grave—they have but a few moments to live—and yet have done nothing to prepare for death—and have no disposition to do any thing. The work is great—and they are fully determined to do nothing by way of preparation. This no doubt is the case with many present.

We may further observe, that there is but a little difference between men's outward circumstances; between the rich or the poor, the old and the young: death will, in a moment or two, lay all on a level. There is but a very little difference between the dead and the living,—only a single step.

We are taught once more by a review of this subject, that all disputes about religion will soon subside. 'Tis vain for men to spend their time in warm and angry contentions about matters that will be decided in a single moment. "The time of our departure is at hand."

How ministers are to preach, and how people are to hear, and how all ought to conduct, in every place and on all occasions, are easily deducible from the preceding discourse, viz., In the constant view of death and the eternal world. The sound should always be in our ears, "The time of my departure is at hand!" and should have a commanding influence on all our behaviour.

We should, by this subject, be led to examine ourselves, and take a review of our past life, since we are soon to leave this world, and our endless happiness or misery depends on the manner in which we improve the present life. Blessed are all those who can adopt the language of the dying apostle, "I have fought a good fight, I have finished my course, I have kept the faith," etc.

In a particular manner we ought to be excited to the utmost diligence in religion, since our time is so short, and since the sentiment is so powerfully inculcated by the deaths of others with whom we yesterday conversed.

The recent instance of mortality speaks with too much energy to be disregarded. Perhaps scarcely ever was there a death in which we were more interested, or one in which God could have manifested equal displeasure against us. If so important and virtuous a character could not be exempted, but must be called away suddenly in the midst of his usefulness, may we not with propriety every day be looking out for death? The situation in which God in his providence had lately placed Dr. Swift, and the remarkable success that attended his ministerial labours among the people where he resided, afforded pleasing prospects, and promised a long continuance; but, in a moment, our expectations are frustrated by Him who destroyeth the hope of man. The preacher has not the vanity to suppose that a commendation from him would add much weight to a character so well established among all who were acquainted with him. I have often thought, and repeatedly mentioned in private conversation, that I never saw the description of a gospel minister, as given in the word of God, so illustrated and exemplified by any person as in the life and character of Dr. Swift.

Few ever attained a more thorough acquaintance with divinity, or were so capable of opening the mysteries of the gospel. He appeared always ready to solve difficult passages in the Scripture and questions in theology. I believe numbers in the ministry are ready to acknowledge that many important ideas on this subject they have obtained through his instrumentality. Affability, Christian zeal, and firmness in the fundamental principles of religion, were distinguishing traits in his character. These things I thought shone more conspicuous in him than usual at our last meeting. His benevolence and hospitality often astonished those who came under his roof. Those who had taste for plain, instructive, experimental preaching, greatly admired his public performances. His attachment to, and exertions in, the missionary interest were great: I have often thought to the prejudice of his health, especially of late. About the last conversation I had with him was on the subject of missions. He requested me to go to a place at some distance to preach, as he had given the people previous encouragement. I told him I was pre-engaged—he replied, "It will not do to neglect them, I must go myself." But few churches in this state, on this side of the mountain, but owe much of their present prosperity, under God, to Dr. Swift. Perhaps no man was more approved, and more useful in ecclesiastical councils than he. In our associations, where he always presided, he was truly a burning and a shining light. But, however hard to realize the thought, he is gone! Heaven has so decreed! and it becomes blind mortals to submit. Oh! let us be thankful to God that we have enjoyed him so long! Let us call to mind, and rightly improve, the advantages with which we have been favoured, and endeavour to imbibe that temper, and imitate those virtues, that dwelt so richly in him. Oh, that a double portion of his spirit might rest upon all the ministers of Christ! That those, especially in this state, to whom he has been so kind a father and benefactor, would consider how loudly God, by this providence, calls us to engagedness in his cause—knowing that the time of our departure is at hand. Let us learn to put our trust in that God who is able to take care of his church without us, or those who are more eminent in gifts and grace, and who worketh all things according to the counsel of his own will. *Amen.*

October 28, 1804

An Entertaining Controversy

This pamphlet consisted of a reprint of Haynes' *Universal Salvation* followed by Hosea Ballou's rejoinder and Haynes' reply. It was published in Rutland in 1807 and reprinted in Middlebury in 1828.

———

An Epistle, to the Rev. Lemuel Haynes, containing a brief Reply to his Sermon delivered at West-Rutland, June, 1805, designed to refute the Doctrine of Universal Salvation. By Hosea Ballou, Preacher of that much despised Gospel.

"If they have called the master of the house Beelzebub, how much more shall they call them of his household."

Jesus Christ

Barnard, April 22, 1806

Rev. Sir,—The design of this epistle is to inform you and the public, how I viewed your conduct, at the time you delivered the sermon to which I now reply; and what I think concerning said sermon, and its general complexion. As to your conduct, when I was with you, in your desk, I must say, (as many of your own parish and others have said) it was the most unchristian-like behaviour I ever saw in one who professed to preach Christ and his salvation.

The sermon which I delivered at that time, in your hearing, was uniformly like its subject, which is *love*: see I John 4:10, 11. The main doctrine contended for, was the great love wherewith God loved us, while we were aliens from him by wicked works; the exhibition of that love through Christ, and the propriety of our loving one another, as a rational duty arising from the manifestation of God's love to us. In this sermon, sir, you heard nothing spoken corrosively against any name, or denomination of professors. You, your parishioners, and gentlemen from other towns, who were present, must bear me record, that I treated my subject fairly, and my hearers with respect. Think, then, how great was my astonishment, and the confusion of the people, on hearing the discourse which you delivered at the close of mine.—A discourse fraught with *low cunning* and *spirited satire*, and delivered with an *aspect* perfectly suited to the subject. It was so extraordinary for its indecency, I greatly marvelled that there was a single individual in the world, who professed the religion of the meek and lowly Saviour, that could be guilty of such an infringement on the principles of the *christian* and the *gentleman*.

Your discourse, sir, has fallen into my hands, through the medium of the press, which is a second astonishment to me, as well as to others who first heard it. Why you should be willing to appear in print, as you do, and must appear to every candid mind, who reads your sermon, is more than I can account for.

It sometimes happens among men, that those of respectability, who, generally speaking, walk uprightly as men ought to walk, may on some certain occasion, render themselves indecorous, by speaking unadvisedly with their lips. But it is a rare instance indeed, and one which we might hope never would happen, for a good man deliberately to persist in such glaring abuse as appears in the sermon alluded to.

You say at the close of your discourse, that, as you have confined yourself wholly to the character of Satan, you trust no one will feel personally injured, etc. You may depend, sir, that I do not view the *injury* as done to myself, though every person of discernment must see that your design was personal. The injury done by your sermon is of that nature which ought to cause all good men serious reflections. For a man who has received public and solemn ordination to the pastoral care and charge of a parish, who ought to be a pattern of piety and good works, a pattern of meekness and charity, who ought to be tender hearted and pitiful, having compassion on those whom he views to be ignorant and out of the way, to treat another who professes to believe in, and worship the same God, hopes for salvation by the same Saviour; who has received the above mentioned solemn injunctions to feed the sheep and lambs of Christ, and who, through grace, has been enabled to support a moral character, to the acceptance of his numerous friends, with that *unfriendly*, *injudicious*, and *unchristianlike* communication, ought to wound the feelings of all the friends of truth. The injury, sir, is done to that cause, of which, you and I, and every other professor of religion, ought always to be careful. But as for myself, it is a small thing for me to be judged by men, or of men's judgment. I will now begin my reply, observing,

On your *title* page, you say, *universal salvation* is a very ancient doctrine, to which I am agreed; believing it to be as much older than any other doctrine which opposes it, as truth is older than the inventions and traditions of men: But you have made a very capital mistake, in describing the character of its author; however, it is the same mistake which has been made by many since the christian apostacy, which is, really mistaking the character of the devil for that of the Almighty. This I will make appear, by an easy argument.

The true character of God is that of universal goodness, and that of the devil is evil in all of its operations. Now, sir, if *universal salvation* from all *sin* and *misery* be a natural production of an *evil principle*, the natural production of a *contrary principle* would be *universal damnation* in *sin* and *misery*. But if salvation from sin be the work of God, it ought not to be ascribed to the devil, because it is done universally. It would seem, that ideas of *limited* goodness, applied to the Deity, might possibly be borne with by the enemies of Universalism; but if a doctrine of *universal* goodness be exhibited, *the devil of course must be its author!* Nothing can be plainer than the mistake which divines have made in this matter.

Agreeably to the above mistake, you go on and take your text from the words of the devil; and though I shall be able to prove your discourse inconsistent with itself, yet I do not think that harms it any, as to its agreement with the spirit of him who first spoke the words from which you preached.

I ought not to pass over your preface, without observing two particulars.

1st. You say, "There is no greater folly, than for a man to express *anger* and *resentment* because his religious sentiments are attacked." Did you mean this as an acknowledgement for the *anger* and *resentment* which you manifested on the occasion which you embraced to discover to me, and others, your deadly hatred of Universalism? If this be your meaning, you ought not to be excused for the neglect of particular application; if this be not your meaning, you are more unpardonable still.

2d. You say, you had been repeatedly solicited to hear, and dispute with me, and had been charged with *dishonesty* and *cowardice* for refusing. Did you do right, sir, not to inform your readers who it was that thus *solicited*,

123

and charged you with *dishonesty*? Did you mean to intimate that I had done these indecent things? You know you have no reason to believe I ever saw you until the day you gave me all the knowledge of yourself which I have ever obtained personally. If it were some of your own parish who charged you with *dishonesty*, it must have been some one who thus knew your *want* of *rectitude*, or by whom you certainly ought not to have consented to be influenced. If your parish all have such implicit confidence in you, that they would prefer scandal to themselves, rather than render you accountable for your random shots of slander, you may possibly still go on with impunity.

In these remarks my language is full severe; however, I hope the reader will consider it within the bounds of faithful rebuke.

There *happened* to be a *little sentiment* in your sermon, and *that little* on a subject which I think I have reason to believe the clergy are generally in the wrong. This sentiment was one principal reason of my making this reply, as I have wanted to find an antagonist on that point.

You say, on page 11th, "The death contained in the threatening was doubtless *eternal death*." Will you contend that man died an eternal death *in the day of transgression*? If he did, he certainly has not been alive since; no, nor will he ever be again. If you say he did not die an *eternal death in the day of transgression*, you make out that what the serpent said to the woman was true.

On page 10th you say, "This audacious wretch had the impudence to confront Omnipotence, and say, Ye shall *not* surely die." And why did you not add, that, notwithstanding his impudence, he was in the right, according to orthodox divinity, and then quoted your authors?

Can any mortal be so blind as not to see, that if the Almighty threatened man with an *eternal death* in the day of his transgression, and a serpent told him, that would not be the case, and man sinned in violation of the prohibition, and still lived afterwards, the serpent was in the right, and the Creator in the wrong? How can you call the serpent an audacious wretch for speaking the truth? It surprises me, that a person, who professes to love God and hate the serpent, should take the pains that you do to prove the serpent's word is more to be depended on than the Almighty's.

I do not know but your readers, in general, may be confounded with the profundity of your argument on *eternal death*, and the serpent's intention in his preaching; truly there is something very curious in it. You go on, page 11, from the assertion, that *eternal death* was meant in the threatening, and argue, saying, "as *nothing* but this would express God's feelings towards sin, or render an *infinite* atonement necessary." In order for you to be duly prepared to make these assertions, you ought at least to possess a complete knowledge of the whole nature of sin, cause and consequences, and all the *feelings* (as your term is) of God towards it, and also the fulness of his wisdom and knowledge, or you could not, with any propriety, have limited the *Holy One of Israel*, to that *one single point*. You speak of an infinite atonement. Wherever an atonement is necessary, it is to satisfy the dissatisfied; and an *infinite dissatisfaction* must exist, in order to require an *infinite atonement*. To say, that any being in the universe ever was *infinitely dissatisfied*, and then to talk of the mode of satisfying such a being, would, in my opinion, betray great inconsistency, and a large share of ignorance, or something worse.

You argue further, on the same subject, saying, "To suppose it to be *spiritual death*, is to blend *crime* and *punishment* together." This observation, it seems, you thought was sufficient argument to prove, that the *death* intended was not a *spiritual death*. But, before there can be any force in your reasoning, it must be made to appear, that the death, which according to the word of God, man actually died in the day of transgression, was the ministration of a *penal* law. If both Scripture and reason fail you on this point, not only your argument, in this particular, will appear groundless, but many other ideas, being connected with the error, must inevitably fail. You must see to this, unless you think your readers are willing to take your word.

You further say, "To suppose *temporal death* to be the *curse* of the law, then believers are not delivered from it, according to Gal. 3:13." Here your argument goes to prove, that there is such a thing as being *delivered* from that death which man was to die in the day of transgression. If you mean, that this deliverance may be so affected, that those delivered never taste of that death, all the force of your argument is to prove the *possibility* of what the serpent said being true. If you mean to argue the possibility of a deliverance from that death, after man had partaken of it, by a resurrection, you deny the absolute *eternity* of the *death*. Go which way you will, sir, you are snared and taken in your own craftiness.

You further say, "What Satan *meant* to preach, was, that there is no hell, and that the wages of sin is not death, but eternal life." Here I must say, you are possessed of the most retentive memory of any person I ever heard of, or else you are the most extraordinary conjurer the earth ever produced. Either you must have existed, in some sort of an animal, in the days of Adam, and have been conversant with the serpent, who, perhaps in

125

confidence, told you his whole plan and meaning, and, by the laws of transmigration, you have come to be what you are now, and retain all those things in perfect memory, or you must have made the discovery by conjuring.

Perhaps you may say I do not treat this subject with that christian candor which I contend for. To which I answer, I know of no way, to shew to you and others, the glaring absurdities contained in your sermon, without making its author appear to disadvantage.

When a professed minister of the gospel undertakes to tell what a serpent *meant*, who talked almost six thousand years ago, in order to make a certain doctrine appear ridiculous, against which, he is unable to bring any Scripture evidence, he ought not to complain, if he sees his ridicule justly falling on his own head.

Did you, sir, ever meet with the idea in any of the Universalian authors, that the *wages of sin is eternal life*? If you never did, do you believe that you ought to be looked upon as an honest man, when you endeavor to represent such an idea? Do you expect to be treated with that respect, to which the gentleman is entitled, while you studiously represent the *devil* as an *universal preacher*, in order to stigmatize those with whom you dare not contend, on fair and open ground? Will your low cunning support you long in the estimation of enlightened people? Have you not already practised this mischief of misrepresentation to your damage in your own parish? How far abroad do you wish to have yourself known to be a person who can so easily descend to unjust measures to carry a bad design into effect?

Sir, I profess to believe and preach universal salvation from all sin and moral death; and I glory in the belief and labor, notwithstanding all you and the rest of the enemies of the doctrine have said, or can say. But I do not believe that the *wages of sin is eternal life*; I thank God that his gift, through Jesus Christ our Lord, is even to *those to whom sin has proved death*; to which truth, all God's holy prophets have borne testimony. Jesus preached the same doctrine. The apostles were faithful in its propagation, and all real christians and good men, in all ages, have fervently prayed for its accomplishment. All this I am ready to prove, and I pledge myself to do it, whenever I may be called on to that effect by a regular antagonist. I have already published a *treatise* on *atonement*, in which I have inserted many arguments in favor of *universal holiness* and *happiness*, which I believe unanswerable; however, should any one attack that work and prove my arguments erroneous, I will disavow them to the public.

On page 9th, you speak of the devil, as not being confined to parish, state, or continent, etc. By this, I suppose you mean to stigmatize those, who, faithful to their Master's command, "Go ye, therefore, into all the world, and preach the gospel to every creature," comply with the same to the utmost of their abilities. Ah! sir, do you consider how far your satire extends? Will you represent all those who enter your parish to preach Christ and him crucified, to be the servants of the devil? Go on then, and meet the certain consequences.

Although I believe in the final salvation of all men, yet I as fully believe, that all unrighteousness of men will receive a due recompense of reward. And should you persist in your present line of conduct a little longer, I do not think you will believe the consequences of sin to be altogether in another world.

On page 13th, inference 3d, you say, "See a reason why it ought to be rejected, because it is an *ancient devilish doctrine*." You will not contend, that Universalism ought to be rejected merely because it is an ancient doctrine? It is true, God preached it when he promised, that the seed of the woman should bruise the serpent's head; he preached it, by the bow of the cloud, to Noah; he preached it by promise to Abraham, saying, "In thy seed, shall all nations of the earth be blessed;" he preached it to Isaac and Jacob, by confirming the same promise to them; he preached it by the law and figurative priesthood given to Israel by Moses; he preached it by the mouth of all his holy prophets, who testified of the restitution of all things, through the glorious mediation of the promised Shiloh: But because it was preached so long ago, do you think it ought to be rejected?

You say it is a *devilish doctrine*! Harsh, inconsiderate expression! Is that doctrine which argues the destruction of the devil and his works, a *devilish doctrine*? Is the doctrine, which argues *universal reconciliation* through Christ, a *devilish doctrine*? O, may God forgive you this folly, and lay not this sin to your charge!

Must I believe you ignorant of the testimony of scripture, in support of the two points above hinted? Then read Heb. 2:24. "Forasmuch then, as the children are partakers of flesh and blood, he also himself took part of the same, that through death, he might *destroy* him that had the power of death, that is the *devil*." Also, I John 3:8. "For this purpose, the Son of God was manifested, that he might *destroy* the *works* of the *devil*." By these quotations, it is plain, that the object of Christ in his mission, was to destroy the *devil* and his *works*. See also, Eph. 1:10. "That in the dispensation of the fulness of times, he might gather together in one, *all things in Christ*, both which are in heaven, and which are on earth, even in him." Also, Col. 1:20.—"And (having made peace by the blood of his cross) by him to reconcile *all things* unto himself; by him, I say, whether they be things in earth, or things in heaven." These, and a multitude of scriptures more, read plainly to prove *that true*, which you are pleased to call *devilish doctrine*.

Page 14th, inference 7th, you say, "It is probable that the doctrine of universal salvation will still prevail," etc. To which I reply, "If this counsel, or this work be of man, it will come to nought; but if it be of God, ye cannot overthrow it."

A few observations on that *obscene poem*, which you had the indecency not only to read in public at the close of your sermon, but also to insert in your pamphlet, will not be deemed improper. The burden of this poem is to convey an idea that Universalists suppose all manner of vile characters will be received to the enjoyment of everlasting happiness, without being cleansed from moral defilement. I will not pretend to say, that such characters as yourself may not have caused some very uninformed persons to believe, that Universalists held to such absurdities; But I do not believe you have that idea yourself; and why you should wish to deceive, you must be accountable.

When Jesus said unto the thief on the cross, "This day shalt thou be with me in paradise," must we rationally infer, that Jesus meant there should be a *thief* with him hereafter in heaven? Yes, with as much propriety as you have indicated all you have by that poem.

I close with a word of advice.

Rev. Sir—If you view me an enemy to mankind in general, and to yourself in particular, yet good advice can do you no harm; but providing you profit by it, and practice accordingly, it will be just as good from me, as from any other person in the world. However, I can say, in the fear of God, that I am not an enemy to you, or to any other person. I sincerely wish all men holiness of heart, and happiness in the same; and I can truly say, also, did I believe, that at last you would not find favor in the Lord, my soul would be filled with inexpressible sorrow! I not only wish you happiness in the world to come, but I wish you may enjoy it here; and so conduct, as to live in good agreement with the people of your charge, and in good repute among your acquaintance. Agreeably to this desire, sir, I give you the following advice:

Cast off all your prejudice towards those denominations who differ from you in sentiment, or opinion; treat them all as you are willing to be treated by them; never be so cruel as to misrepresent their tenets, in order to cause people to dislike them; be honest with all men; use no underhanded means to prosecute your designs; let all your conduct stand in the fair and open sunshine of *truth*. When your conscience dictates to defend your sentiments, be *cautious* that you contend fairly and honorably, and treat your antagonist as a brother, and not with disrespect. Study humility, and by example teach it to others. Search the scriptures impartially, never endeavoring to cause them to bend to this or that system of divinity; rather yield your tenets to the word of God, than endeavor to cause that immutable word, which cannot be broken, to bend to your peculiarities of sentiment.

If you see cause to enter farther into a correspondence with me, and answer this epistle, do be so good as to give me no occasion to use such severity as has been necessary in this; which if you are careful to observe, I will treat the subject of controversy with all the candor that I am master; and in every instance, will be,

Sir, Your humble servant, for Christ's sake,

HOSEA BALLOU.

Rev. Lemuel Haynes

A Letter to the Rev. Hosea Ballou: being a Reply to his Epistle to the Author; or, his attempt to vindicate the Old Universal Preacher.

Rev. Sir,—You may, perhaps, think it strange that I have so long neglected answering your epistle, and that my inattention is a mark of disrespect. It is not more than two or three weeks since I have had time to give it only a cursory reading. Should you think that there are things in these remarks inconsistent with christian sobriety, you will turn to Prov. 26:5, which passage has had peculiar influence and repeatedly dictated the following strictures.

In your first page you charge me with calling the master of your house Beelzebub, together with his household. I have examined the sermon and find no such title applied to him or his household. So that I plead *not guilty*.

You tell us that the design of your epistle is to inform me, and the public, how you viewed my conduct at the time I delivered the sermon, about which you seem to be so much agitated. You say, "It was the most unchristian-like behavior I ever saw in one who professed to preach Christ and his salvation; and that some of my own parish and others have said the same." Possibly you might think so, and some others might think so,—and myself and many others think very different, and what of all that? there is nothing proved; it comes to this, you and I, and other people will think just as we please. However should the matter terminate according to the decision of my own parish, as you call them, you may be very jealous that it would not be agreeable to your wishes. But what kind of advantage it would be to the public to have us inform them what we think of each other, I cannot conceive; I have real doubts should we bring it all out to view, whether we, or others would derive much advantage by the exhibition.

You go on to tell us that the sermon you delivered at that time was a lovely thing, or, "like its subject—*love*;" to prove it, you have directed us to your text; that it was I John 4:10, 11. If preachers were to determine the merit and worth of their own discourses, perhaps we should have but few bad sermons. Quoting your text would have proved the point, if it was always certain that if a man has a lovely text he has a lovely sermon; there are exceptions to this rule. Many of your hearers had a very different idea of your performance, from what you represent in your epistle.

You proceed further to extol the discourse—that there was nothing "*corrosive* against any name or denomination of professors." Let me here observe, that had you treated my name, or the names of any denomination of men, with contempt, and let another name alone, you would never have heard from me; but, sir, let me tell you, that there is a name which is *above every other name*; this is a name in comparison of which, your name and my name is of little worth. If I am not mistaken, this name was treated by you with the utmost contempt, as well as all such as have a real veneration for it. By this time I believe you have my ideas of your sermon, and of your conduct, and it may be our ends are equally answered.

You call my discourse "fraught with *low cunning*." Sir, when you will shew the difference between *low* cunning and *high* cunning, perhaps I shall be able to determine to which of these cunnings your answer to such a piece belongs.—You express great astonishment, and seem to be filled with two great wonders; the one is, that I should ever deliver such a discourse, and that it should ever come to you through the medium of the press, this is a *second* astonishment, and that it should be done *deliberately*. Sir, the piece has gone through several editions, some of them with my approbation; which may lead you on to a third, fourth, fifth, or sixth wonder. I hope you will never be led to *"wonder and perish."*

You observe, "every person of discernment must see that your design was personal." But how came they to find out my design, or who was intended? it could be only by comparing the doctrine of the old preacher with others. If men of *discernment* could see a likeness between that and yours, I can see no ground of complaint, unless it be, that there are persons of *discernment* in the world, who are able to judge right. Had you found any thing said about the character and preaching of that old declaimer contrary to truth, you ought to have pointed it out; or if there is no similarity between his sermon and yours, you should have shewed it and then persons of *discernment* would have been undeceived.

You tell us, page 3, that your moral character is good. Sir, as you know more about it than any body else, and are under peculiar advantages to recommend it; being destitute of prejudice and prepossession, I have no disposition to call your assertion in question.

You cannot help repeating that my conduct is *unfriendly, injudicious, unchristian-like,*—inconsistent with *meekness, piety, good works*, with *solemn ordination*, with *feeding the lambs of Christ, injurous to the cause of Christ*, and *wounding the feelings of all the friends of truth*. Sir, men have very different views about the *cause of God, piety, good works*, the *friends of truth, feeding the lambs of Christ*, etc. I have my doubts whether such a group of hard censorious expressions, just now adverted to, is perfectly consistent with pure benevolence, or attachment to the cause of god; with *meekness* with *solemn injunction*, etc. I would observe, "Every person of discernment," will see that your intention was to prejudice the minds of your readers, to prepare them for your remarks, in pertinency with your object. You immediately add, "I will now begin my reply."

I have no doubt at all but the discourse you complain of, and my conduct at the time of delivery, tended to injure what some may call the *cause of God*, to *cut* or *wound* the *feelings* of some, and did not afford such *food* as many are hungering after. I can see no injury done to the cause of God in giving the devil his due, or in calling him a universal preacher, if he was one. Or how any person's *"feelings"* need be *"wounded,"* unless they approve the doctrine, or can make it appear that he has repented, and given up the sentiments.

You proceed to correct a very capital error that myself and many others have made; we have "really mistaken the character of the devil for that of the Almighty." Wretched mistake! Oh, fatal delusion! that Satan should have the services of the church for so many ages; that so many should suffer and die to his glory; trusting to him to support them in death, and all their hope beyond the grave! How thankful should we be for so remarkable a light, to illuminate our dark world, and correct the fatal delusion! Generations passed away, will lament the tardy rising of this cheering star, while posterity yet unborn will hail its exhilarating beams!

We will now attend to your "Easy Argument."

"If universal salvation from all sin and misery be a natural production of an evil principle, the natural production of a contrary principle would be universal damnation in sin and misery; but if salvation from sin be the work of God, it ought not to be ascribed to the devil, because it is done universally."

Sir, did the devil mean in the declaration "Ye shall *not* surely die," to produce universal holiness or happiness? or has the effect actually took place? You think the saying could not come from the devil, because there is evil in all his operations, and so could not produce good. True—yet he could promise good. But let men and devils preach universal salvation from all sin and misery in their way to eternity—it never will produce the effect, nor will they give the least evidence that this is their design. Satan meant to lie to our first parents, and encourage sin and misery, which is the natural tendency of his doctrine.

To suppose Satan, or any other being, aims at universal holiness and happiness, by encouraging men in sin, or disobedience, is highly preposterous. You say, "A contrary principle would be universal damnation in sin and misery." If there be any meaning in your assertion, it is this—That for God to give law to his creatures, and to threaten them with death in case of disobedience, tends to produce "universal damnation in sin and misery." We have mistaken the character of the devil for that of the Almighty. *The soul that sinneth it shall die. The wages of sin is death.* This is the language of Satan, and exhibits his character—"*Thou shalt not surely die.*" "*You shall have peace, though you walk in the imagination of your own heart.*" This, according to your statement, is the language of the Almighty. Thus you have corrected a very capital mistake, that myself, and *many since the christian apostacy*, have heedlessly ran into. Not only will students in theology derive particular advantage by your improvement, but legislators will feel themselves much interested in the discovery: it will save them from annexing penalties, or sanctions to laws, as they tend to encourage *universal damnation in sin and misery.*

You pretend to be at a loss how to understand or apply this expression in the preface to my sermon, viz: "There is no greater folly than for a man to express anger and resentment because his religious sentiments are attacked." Sir, I have no doubt but you perfectly understand me; yet I much scruple whether you have made the application as you ought: had it been the case, it would greatly have altered the complexion of your epistle. So long as you can remember that uncommon and imperious resentment that marred your conduct, on hearing my sermon about the Old Preacher, you will never hesitate about the matter, to which the above remark has a more particular reference.

You go on to exculpate yourself from boasting that I was a coward, and dare not dispute with you; but why should you plead not guilty before you was charged with it? I scruple whether your argument to exonerate yourself is much to the purpose. You say you never saw me before; but is there no way that a man may use menacing language about another without seeing him? If you will call on me, I will endeavor to produce documents of a challenge from you since our meeting, though we had no personal interview.

Please to examine, also, the 8th page of your epistle. I will pay only a moment's attention to the method you take to prove me to be a man dishonest, and destitute of rectitude, or paying too much regard to slander. Your words are, "If it were some of your own parish who thus charged you with dishonesty, it must have been someone who knew your want of rectitude; or by whom you certainly ought not to have consented to be influenced." Sir, I think you have corrected as great a mistake among logicians, as divines. This is your reasoning. If a man charge another with dishonesty, it is either true, or if not, he ought not to take notice of it or deny it; but if it is a matter of fact, then he may be influenced by it, and contradict it. This sentiment is a good comment upon your epistle. Should I here add—"That through grace, I have been able to support a good moral character to the acceptance of my numerous friends," I fear it might excite a degree of jealousy in your mind, that I had too soon become an egotist.

You go on and attempt a vindication of the character of the old universal preacher, by observing, that he spoke right according to orthodox divinity. You say, "Will you contend that man died an eternal death in the day of transgression? If he did, he certainly has not been alive since, nor will he ever be again. If you say he did not die an eternal death in the day of transgression, you make out what the serpent said to the woman was true. Can any mortal be so blind as not to see?" etc. Sir, I am one of those blind mortals that firmly believe that the threatening to our first parents was eternal death, and that the audacious wretch told a horrible lie! You say, if I contend that man died an eternal death in the day of transgression, he has not been alive since, or ever will be. Sir, it is true, you reason well. If eternity contains just twenty-four hours, and no more, then nothing has been alive since, nor ever will be. No one ever supposed that the whole threatening of the law was fully executed in the moment or day of man's fall, or ever will be to its full extent on the wicked. The idea is, in dying he should die, or be liable to an eternal death. (We are not to suppose that God meant to tell our first parents, that they should die an eternal death in one day; or that a space of time that had an end, was endless. This is not what the serpent meant to deny. To suppose that in order to have the threatening true, the wicked must suffer until eternity has an end, is impossible; and it would be as far from truth in any period of eternity in this sense as their not dying an eternal death in the first day of his apostacy. The idea is, that they should be exposed to, and deserve an endless duration of penal evil, which in some degree began in the day of transgression. This is what the devil meant to deny.) Eternally dying does not suppose an extinction of being, any more than eternally living. It is certain that man did not die a temporal death completely in the day of transgression. As to spiritual death, we should meet with the same difficulty as in eternal death.—This death consists in sin; but our first parents, nor men in general, have not all their evil exercises in one hour, day, or year; so that it could not be said that this death was executed fully in the day of disobedience. We see then that the declaration of satan was as true, should we consider the threatening in the law temporal or spiritual, as eternal death, since the threatening was inflicted only in a partial manner. If temporal death was the thing threatened in the law, I again observe, that believers are not delivered from the curse of the law, agreeable to Gal. 3:13. You pretend to argue against my proposition, and conclude by saying, "Go which way you will, sir, you are snared and taken in your own craftiness." I own myself to be snared in your intricate reasoning. If any mortal can see the least sense, or pertinency in your observations, doubtless they may profit by it; but I confess I cannot.

The difference between Universalists and others, is not whether all will be saved, or all be damned, which you seem to take for granted in your remarks. Eternal death is the true demerit of sin; and for God to threaten any thing more or less than the crime deserves, is inconsistent with moral rectitude. If the threatening to our first parents was spiritual, and not eternal death, this would suppose God to encourage men to commit one sin to punish another. The whole of spiritual death consists in sin; and when God threatens this as a punishment for the first sin, it must suppose an antecedent crime to precede the first act of rebellion; but this was holiness. To conclude that the second, third, or fourth act of transgression was to testify against foregoing acts of wickedness, or spiritual death, would be for God to bear testimony against one threatening of his law, by another threatening of the law. Is this the common idea of sanction, to law, to threaten the murderer or the thief with further indulgencies in such crimes?

In Gal. 3:13, it is said, "Christ hath redeemed us from the curse of the law, being *made a curse for us*; for it is written, cursed is every one that hangeth on a tree." The idea doubtless is, that he in some sense, bore the curse of the law, in the room of all that believe. Christ did not die a spiritual death—that would have made him a sinner: but he was *hanged on a tree*, endured pain and distress. We are told, Rom. 6:23, that "the wages of sin is death." Death is there the sanction or penalty of the law: If it is spiritual death that is there meant, the reading would be, the wages of sin is sin. Sir, you seem to make a distinction between sin and moral death, page 8th. Your words are, "Sir, I profess to believe and preach universal salvation from all *sin* and *moral death*." I am not able to discern the difference between *sin* and *moral death*, unless the two different words constitute it. You thank God that his "gift through Jesus Christ our Lord is even to those to whom sin has *proved* death." I conclude you mean moral death. Sir, you have made ample provision for those who have sinned, and it has *proved* sin; but those who have sinned, and it did not *prove* sin, you have left without relief.

You suggest, page 3d, that it is a good principle that holds up universal salvation from all sin and misery. You profess to preach universal deliverance from all *misery*. But men cannot be the subjects of universal deliverance from misery, unless they are exposed to it; and they cannot be liable to it unless they are sinners; and they cannot be sinners unless they violate a law. If you preach deliverance from *misery*, it supposes that men are subject to it by the sanction of a law, in consequence of their sin. "In the day thou eatest thereof, thou shalt surely die," was the declaration of God to our first parents. The meaning is, that they were now *exposed* to eternal misery, or penal evil, that began to take place; or that they were under the curse of the law—that was the second death. St. Paul says, that "When the commandment, or law came, sin revived, and I died." That is, he found himself dead: he found himself under the curse of the law, according to the original threatening. We are not to suppose that the whole threatening of the law was executed on our first parents, or on any other transgressor, in one day, or ever can be. There would then be the same objection against man's dying an eternal death, or against the threatening of the law being completely executed in any period of eternity, as there is in its not being fully accomplished in the very day of transgression. ("The threatening expresses two things, viz. the *certainty* of the punishment as infallibly connected with transgression; and that the penalty should follow on *one* or the first act of rebellion. We find much the same language to express one or both of these; and not that the threatening should be immediately *"fully"* executed on the day the crime was committed. Ezek. 33:12, 13. See also, I Kings 2:37. For it shall be that *on the day* that thou goest out, and passest over the brook Kidron, that thou shalt know for certain, that thou shalt surely die. This does not mean that he should die the same day in which he should pass over Kidron; but that he should certainly be put to death for the offence without a further trial."—*Dr. Hopkins' System, Vol.* 1, *p.* 307. Those who wish to see the subject largely and clearly illustrated, are desired to consult the Doctor on the point.) The threatening would admit of a substitute in perfect consistency with divine veracity. When sentence is passed against a criminal, that he must surely die, yet if there can be a way found out that will equally secure the dignity of the commonwealth without his death, all will justify the legislator in pardoning the offender; yet it was proper to say, that in the day of his trial, according to the sanctions of the law, or verdict of the court, he was a dead man. It was the design of God, in threatening our first parents, to secure the honor and dignity of his character and government; and if this can be done as well or better by accepting a substitute, who dare call his truth or veracity into question? We are informed by the sacred pages, that this is the case—that through the Mediator, God can now be just to himself, and the universe, and yet justify him that *believeth* in Jesus.—Rom. 3:26. But such as continue in unbelief, and do not embrace the Mediator, remain in a state of condemnation, and must feel the wages of sin, that is, eternal death.

In page 6th you observe, "In order for you to be duly prepared to make these assertions," (viz. how God feels towards sin,) "you ought at least to possess a complete knowledge of the whole nature of sin, cause and consequences, and all the feelings of God towards it, and also the fulness of his wisdom and knowledge, or you could not, with any propriety, have limited the Holy One of Israel to that single point."—Sir, can we never know that God hates sin, without comprehending all sin, in its *nature* and *consequences*, and the *fulness* and *wisdom* of Deity? If a man must have so much knowledge to know whether God hates sin, I would ask in my turn, how much must one have to deny it? It seems that by some means you have obtained so much information, as to know that God has not an infinite dissatisfaction or hatred towards sin.—I would reply, that God must have an *infinite* hatred towards it, or a *finite* hatred, or no hatred at all.—If God has only a *finite* hatred towards sin, then he is a finite being: Then why are you puzzled to know how I come to judge of the feelings of the Holy One of Israel? Cannot one finite being judge of the feelings of another finite being?—If God has no hatred towards sin, why that compassionate exclamation, page 10, "O, may God forgive you this folly, and lay not this *sin* to your charge."

You admire at my retentive memory in attempting to tell what satan meant to preach almost six thousand years ago. "Either I must exist in some sort of animal in the days of Adam, and been conversant with the serpent, or do it by *transmigration* or *conjuration*."—Sir, did you find out what the serpent did not preach in this way? Is there no other way to obtain ideas? How shall we understand your epistle? we were not with you when you wrote it. Must we understand it by transmigration and conjuration? Was it from these sources that it derived so many new and valuable ideas?

You ask, page 8, "Did you, sir, ever meet with the idea in any of the universalian authors, that the wages of sin is eternal life?" Yes, sir, I think I have, in the first universalian author or preacher. His words are, "Ye shall not surely die. In the day ye eat thereof, then your eyes shall be opened, and ye shall be as gods, knowing good and evil." Now what can be more express? they should have their eyes open, and know good and evil; this surely supposes life; dead people do not have their eyes open, etc.

But you will have it that I mean you, and mean to stigmatize you and others. But, sir, don't be offended; how came you to discern that you was intended? was it done by transmigration or conjuration?

To transmigrate cannot be right
Since 'tis so great an evil;
And he that conjures out of sight
Must conjure with the devil.

In seeing you insist so much that I mean you, and not the old preacher, brought to my mind the following anecdote: As a man was writing to his friend, a bye-stander looked over his shoulder all the time, which led him to conclude in the following manner, "Sir, I should have sent you a much longer epistle, but —— has been all the time looking over my shoulder." The bye-stander exclaimed, " 'Tis false! I have not looked over you, nor do I know a single word you have written!"

You proceed to ask me questions, to which you doubtless expect answers. "Do you expect to be looked upon as an honest man, and to be treated as a gentleman, while you studiously represent the devil as an universal preacher?" Ans. If I never meet with respect, nor am looked upon as an honest man, and have genteel treatment, till I desist from esteeming and representing the devil an universal preacher, I am confident I shall never receive such treatment. I hope never to court genteel treatment, at the expense of divine truth. Should any "person of discernment," view themselves implicated by the sentiment, and have their genteel feelings wounded—who is to blame?

You ask again, "Will your low cunning support you long in the estimation of enlightened people?" Ans. When I receive your definition of high cunning, and low cunning, and who you mean by *enlightened* people, I shall be able to reply.

My querist proceeds, "Have you not already practised this mischief of misrepresentation to your damage in your own parish?" Ans. When the old preacher complains regularly of misrepresentation, and proves the charge, I stand ready, according to former promise to retract, and give the devil his due.

Further you ask, "How far abroad do you wish to have yourself known to be a person who can so easily descend to unjust measures, to carry a bad design into effect?" By *unjust measures*, and *bad design*, I conclude you mean my opposition to the universal preacher. Ans. So far as the old gentleman's ability and influence extends.

Sir, you seem to be full of questions. You ask again, "will you represent all those who enter your parish to preach Christ and him crucified, to be the servants of the devil?" Ans. No sir, none but those who are sent by him, and preach like him, "Ye shall not surely die."

Again, "You will not contend that universalism ought to be rejected merely because it is an ancient doctrine." Ans. No, sir, but because it is a devilish doctrine.

Since it seems so fashionable to ask questions, if it would comport with modesty I would ask a few. How came you to suggest, page 8, that I dare not contend with you on fair ground? Is that the first representation of this kind you have made? If such boasting is natural to you, why do you try to exculpate yourself from any thing of this sort in page 4? Sir, you well remember that when we delivered our sermons, I opened the door for a public discussion: I told you and the congregation my objections against your discourse; I believe the greater part of the people present were of your sentiment; but you wholly neglected to dispute with me. Was not this an offer to meet you on *fair and open ground.*

Some months after, you wrote me a challenge, to appoint a day for a public combat, to choose a committee, or seconds, to see if we fought fairly; I then told you, that I viewed it inconsistent with christian modesty and decency for you to make the challenge, and for me to comply—I am still of the same opinion. Had I complied with your request, and called the people together to hear us debate, I had reason to believe that you would not have engaged in the controversy: as you had utterly refused on a much more favorable opportunity. With what face then can you repeatedly observe, that I "dare not contend with you on fair and open ground?" When you are disposed to repeat the assertion among strangers, please to shew them my written reply to your challenge, and they will find out the truth.

Another question I wish to ask you is, How came you to know so much about the people of *my parish?* You are often mentioning them. You have preached among them a few times, but you are sensible you never saw many of them on such occasions, and it is very possible you never will. If you had left conjuration out of your epistle, I should have many doubts whether you knew much about them.

In page 9th you have the following threats—"Go on then and meet the certain consequences.—And should you persist in your present line of conduct a little longer, I don't think you will believe the consequences of sin to be altogether in another world." Sir, where is your benevolence? Have you forgot your *lovely* sermon, that had nothing "*corrosive?*" Will you torment your fellow-creatures before the time, and fill the mind with forebodings of some dreadful event, nor even suggest what it is—whether it is to consist in *assassination, confiscation, transmigration,* or *conjuration?*

You tell us that universal salvation was preached by God, "when he promised that the seed of the woman should bruise the serpent's head.—He preached it by the bow in the cloud, to Noah.—He preached it by promise to Abraham, saying, In thy seed shall all nations of the earth be blessed.—He preached it to Isaac and Jacob," etc. Here I must say almost in the language of a late writer (Mr. Ballou's Epistle, p. 7, 8), "You are possessed of the most retentive memory of any person I ever heard of, or else you are the most extraordinary conjurer the earth has ever produced.—Either you must have existed in some sort of animal in the days of Adam, Noah, Isaac, and Jacob, etc. who perhaps in confidence to tell you their whole plan and meaning, and by the laws of transmigration you have come to be what you are now, and retain all those things still in perfect memory; or you must have made the discovery by conjuration.—When a professed minister of the gospel undertakes to tell what those meant who talked almost six thousand years ago, in order to establish a certain doctrine, for which he is unable to bring any Scripture evidence, he ought not to complain, if he sees his own ridicule justly falling on his own head."

You have quoted a few texts to prove universal salvation; but have not shewn their pertinency to your point. I shall not, therefore, attend to them. To me they do not appear to approve your doctrine any more than if you had directed us to Num. 22:30.

You observe, that if universalism should still prevail, it will be an evidence that it is true: p. 11. Sir, has not a contrary doctrine prevailed for ages, and does it not continue to do so? Would not your proposition prove too much for you? Could you prove that the doctrine always will prevail, your reasoning, or text, would be in point.

The Poem subjoined to my sermon seems to disturb you on account of its *obscenity*. I have examined every verse, line, word and letter, and I can find nothing that tends to uncleanliness, moral impurity, or licentiousness, unless you esteem the title or subject of the hymn so. I cannot see that in this respect it tends to looseness and impurity, any more than the doctrine in the text, "And the serpent said unto the woman, Ye shall *not* surely die." Is the poem more obscene than this? Let us compare one verse.—

> Fear not to sin till death shall close your eyes,
> Live as you please, yours is th' immortal prize—

>Old Serpent hail! thou mad'st a just reply
>To mother Eve, "Ye shall *not* surely die!"

You say the burden of the poem is to convey an idea that universalists suppose all manner of vile characters will be received to the enjoyment of universal happiness, without being cleansed from moral defilement. Sir, the poem supposes, and I pretend to make others believe, that universalists preach, That if men *lie, murder, steal, commit adultery, KILL THEMSELVES*, etc., yet they will finally escape hell, and be eternally happy. This I own to be the burden of the poem, and this is the burden of universalism; and the doctrine *ought to be a burden*, and *a great burden* to all who love God and the souls of men, because it confronts every dictate of Scripture and common sense. We do not suppose you, or any other preacher, tell people they will go to heaven in their sins: this would be so glaring that even Satan would not preach so; but to tell sinners that they shall all finally be saved from sin and misery, is going contrary to Scripture, and encouraging men in transgression. You add, "I will not pretend to say that such characters as yourself may not have caused some uninformed persons to believe that universalists held to such absurdities: I do not believe you have that idea yourself; and why should you wish to deceive?—You must be accountable." Sir, I would just inquire, if the character you have given me in your epistle be a just one, why did you depart from the rule you prescribe in p. 5, where you reprove me for being influenced by such as do not speak the truth. You say, it is among uninformed persons that I am believed. It appears by your writing that you are not among those uninformed persons. We never had but one personal interview. I preached a short sermon before you which the public are acquainted with. You refused to say a word to me, or answer a single question; yet your information is so great, that you are able to say just what you please. How far your peculiar wisdom and skill (Conjuration) may serve to exculpate you, is not for me to say, as I am ignorant of it.

Nothing can appear more evident, than that the measures you have taken to vindicate the character of the Old Preacher, indicates his cause not to be the best: and that it will need auxiliaries of a very different nature to support it, or it must fall to the ground.

You say you have published a treatise on atonement, which you think is unanswerable.—An encomium from another quarter might have been a little more acceptable. I have read the piece, and have a very different idea of it.

By the leave of Providence, perhaps you and the public will know my mind more fully about it before long.

See that you do not preach for *filthy lucre*: we are very prone to be caught in this snare.—"Good advice can do you no harm."

I close with a word of advice.

Rev. Sir,—You tell me, "in the fear of God that you are not an enemy to me, or any other person,"—that you wish me happiness, etc. But why need you tell me this? I have just been reading your *benevolent* epistle. You say, "Good advice can do me no harm." Sir, I think it *has* not. Perhaps you esteem me a debtor to you for your very friendly admonition, "Good advice can do you no harm." Beware of challenging others to dispute with you, and boasting that they "dare not contend with you on fair and open ground," [epist. p. 8] and that you "want to find an antagonist," [epist. p. 5.] Should you ever be overtaken in this matter, don't deny it—"Good advice can do you no harm." Beware of *pomposity*: we should carry low sails on this tempestuous sea—"Good advice can do you no harm." Learn to distinguish between *benevolence* and *malevolence*, and make no great pretence to the former, unless you are pretty confident you have it, and act it out—"Good advice can do you no harm."

In your next epistle, should you find nothing to employ your pen about but personal invective, and matters that you know nothing of, try according to your promise, to use a little more candor, and not be quite so unmerciful—"Good advice can do you no harm."

Sir, your humble servant,

LEMUEL HAYNES

Rev. Hosea Ballou.
Rutland, March 9th, 1807.

The Presence
of the Lord

The manuscript of this sermon outline is held by The Congregational Library in Boston. It was first edited, titled, and published by Richard Newman in the *Bulletin of the Congregational Library* in 1980. The manuscript is dated Manchester, October 14, 1821, but additional notes suggest it was first preached in Rutland in 1811.

———

"And Cain went out from the presence of the Lord, and dwelt in the land of Nod, on the east side of Eden."

—Gen. 4:16

By the presence of the Lord is sometimes meant his essential presence, from which there is no departing. "Do not I fill heaven and earth? saith the Lord." Jer. 23:24. God is as much in one place as another. Cain could not go out from the Lord in this sense.

By the presence of the Lord is often meant his sensible presence. Jacob said, "Surely the Lord was in this place and I knew it not." Gen. 28:16. There are times and places that God manifests himself more than at other seasons; from this Cain went out, by which he manifested his dislike of God. The point to be illustrated is this, viz., *Sinners don't love to have God with them or be where he is.*

I. A confirmation of this point will be attempted.

II. An inquiry why this is the case will be made.

III. Its folly and criminality will be considered.

I. Cain is called a wicked one, or of that wicked one. I John 3:12. Comp. Jude 1:11.

1. We see this in the first sinners, even Adam and Eve. Gen. 3:8. This is the language of the wicked according to the word of God. Matt. 8:34; Job 21:14; 22:17; Luke 8:28-37. It is a charge often brought against men, that they depart. Jer. 3:20. As a wife treacherously departs from her husband.

2. The wicked shun or withdraw from those places where God is wont to be with his presence, such as [at] reading the word of God, prayer, [and] the worship of God. This was the case with Cain—he went from the place of God's word and public worship, which likely Adam attended and taught, says Ainsworth, [just as the wicked] break the Sabbath appointed to bring us near to God.

3. Sinners take the most direct way to keep God at a distance. They practice such sins as are calculated to make a separation. Is. 29:2. Ps. 5:4—cannot dwell with thee.

4. The way of access to God through a Mediator they do not value, but despise like Cain. Brought no sacrifice for sin.

5. The invitations of the gospel and the means used with the wicked have no influence on them. Yea, they are offended at those measures that are used to bring them to God or cause union. They cannot bear to think of God. Ps. 10:4.

6. The wicked have no sincere desire after God, nor intention to return to him, but go further and further away from God. Is. 1:5. They make no serious inquiry how to return to God, but invent how to increase the distance. Rom. 1:30.

7. The wicked are complaining against God that he is a hard master and that his ways are not equal. Ezek. 18:25; Matt. 25:24.

8. The proneness there is in men to think that God is at a great distance and that he takes no notice of them must originate from the thought that they wish to have it so. Ps. 10:11; Ps. 94:7. God not being with them is a proof.

9. The wicked discard such doctrines that suppose or imply that God is near us, such as his absolute and universal government and our dependence on him.

10. How few deprecate the withdrawment of God's prophet. The wicked discover it on many occasions, yea, under convictions. Acts 7:51. Even in saints, witness Jonah, etc.

II. Why is this the case?

1. Cain was dissatisfied with God for not accepting his offering. Sinners say, if God will not accept such services as we bring, I will bring him none. Cain had no reference to a Mediator in his offering. "If not there is a sin-offering at hand," says Dr. Renirot on verse 7.

2. Sinners are displeased because God accepts others and not them. They charge him with partiality. God made a visible distinction between Cain and Abel. The fire came down on Abel's sacrifice; no doubt this offended Cain.

3. The wicked are dissatisfied with God in the denunciation of his law, that it is too severe. Cain complains that the curse was too severe. Ver. 13. Or too big to be forgiven. So the Greek renders it and Chaldee, says Ainsworth. In him, says this author, may be seen 7 abominations—as many as there are in the heart of man. Prov. 26:25.

1. He sacrificed *without faith*. Heb. 11:4. 2. Was *displeased* with God. 3. *Hearkened* not to God's admonition. 4. Spake *dissembling* to his brother. "Let us go into the field." 5. *Killed* him. 6. *Denied* he knew where he was. 7. *Despaired* and asked not for mercy. See Ains[worth] on the [place?].

4. Sinners are displeased with seeing where God is on account of the company he brings with him. Cain doubtless hated Adam and Eve and the good people called the Sons of God. Lamech, it seems, was [desirous?] of living with them, as some understand that passage. Gen. 4:23, 24.

5. The presence of God does not bring that kind of good they desire, or that is agreeable to their taste, viz., the pleasures and profits of this world.

6. The presence or light of God's law tends to bring their sins to view and to give them torment. This disturbed Cain.

7. The wicked are proud. Ver. 9, 10. Love independence like Cain, who built him a city.

8. Such as have God with them must part with such things that they put much more [value] by than God. Cain called his city after the name of his son Enoch. [Illegible]. Was their Land of Nod.

III. The folly and criminality of Cain and others of his character.

1. It [*i.e.*, escaping from God] is in a sense a vain attempt as to his essential presence (which is the sinner's wish and intent) as well as his sensible [presence]. God was as much in the Land of Nod as where the people of God were in this sense. We may as well attempt to get away from time and eternity.

2. God is the fountain and well-spring of life. Ps. 36:9. It is turning away from the very source of our existence. We cannot live a moment without him. An attempt on soul and body.

3. To go out from the presence of God is deserting all true happiness and comfort.

> The smilings of thy face,
> How amiable they are;
> In heaven to dwell in thine embrace,
> And no where else but there.
> —Watts

4. If we go out from the presence of the Lord, we expose ourselves to all possible misery. Satan takes possession of us. When the Lord left Saul, an evil spirit troubled him. I Sam. 16:14. What a wretched state was Saul in when God departed from him. I Sam. 23:15. Departing from the Lord is spoken of as the source of all evil. "Woe also unto them when I depart from them," was God's declaration to Ephraim. Hos. 9:12.

5. Going out from the presence of [the] Lord has a pernicious influence on others. The conduct of Cain's going out from the presence of the Lord corrupted the old world. Gen. 6:1.

6. Although people take so much pains to get away from God, yet they shall be forced into his presence at death and at judgment. "For we all must appear before the judgment seat of Christ," II Corin. 5:10.

7. To go out from the presence of the Lord is counter-acting the great work of redemption, which was that sinners might be brought nigh by the blood of Christ. Eph. 2:3. It casts contempt on God the Father, Son, and Holy Ghost. The language is that God's company and presence is undesirable and not worthy to be sought. It is contemning God. Ps. 10:13.

Improvement

1. See what distinguishes saints from sinners. The one places his chief delight in having God with him. Ps. 73:25. "Whom have I in heaven but thee?" while the wicked dread nothing more.

2. How vain to look for happiness and felicity while God departs from us. Nothing will do as a substitute.

> Nor earth nor all the skies,
> Can one delight afford;
> No, not a drop of real joy,
> Without thy presence, Lord.
> —Watts

Let sinners despair and return to God. Cain found no comfort in the Land of Nod. A guilty conscience haunted him.

3. Men are voluntary in sinning. Cain *went* out from the presence of the Lord.

4. How hypocritical are the complaints of men that God refuses to save them, when they do nothing to secure the divine presence, but run away from him, like Cain. II Chron. 15:2. "The Lord is with you while ye be with him; and if ye seek him, he will be found of you; but if ye forsake him, he will forsake you."

5. How reasonable that the wicked should be eternally separated from God. They choose it here. They, by their voluntary conduct, lay a foundation for an eternal separation from God in the other world.

6. Sinners must be regenerated in order to go to heaven; the presence of God would be atonement to them, were they to be among the saints in their present state.

7. We may examine ourselves, whether we are prepared for heaven. Do we delight in the presence of God, or are we like Cain? Are those places where God manifests himself precious to us? Do we call them Bethel, the house of God, like Jacob? Gen. 28. Like David? Ps. 24. Are his ordinances sweet?

8. Let us bless God, that although we have gone away from God, yet we may return and find mercy. Your revolt is as unreasonable as was Cain's—and as fatal. You are in danger of being killed, even losing your souls. If you go away from God, you go to hell. This makes hell. Your castles won't save you. Some think Cain only began to build, but did not finish it, that God confounded it. See Ains[worth]. [Illegible]. Need reproof; they desert. John 6:66. You will need Christ's presence in the hour of death at judgment—but you cannot expect it. Learn how to secure it.

Dissimulation Illustrated

George Washington was Haynes' political hero and on his birthday Haynes delivered this political sermon to the Washington Benevolent Society. It was published in Rutland in 1814.

———

Dissimulation Illustrated. A Sermon Delivered at Brandon, Vermont, February 22, 1813, before the Washington Benevolent Society, it being the Anniversary of Gen. Washington's Birth-Day.

"Let love be without dissimulation."

Romans 12:9

Love and hatred are qualities of the mind, and are expressive of all the moral good and evil in the universe. They have their objects, which denominate them virtuous or vicious. That holy love, or affection, comprehends all the duty we owe to God and rational beings, is evident, in that it is all required in the divine law, Matt. 22. Thou shalt love the Lord thy God with all thy heart, and with all thy soul and with all thy mind. The second is like unto it, Thou shalt love thy neighbor as thyself. On these two commandments hang all the law and the prophets. This is illustrative of the holy character of God. God is *love*. I John 4:8. We can discern no moral excellency in any thing else: such as wisdom, power, etc. These without rectitude are dangerous and alarming, according to their strength and magnitude. These powers of mind render Satan emphatically a destroyer, as they capacitate him to do much mischief, being wholly destitute of goodness, or right affection, which distinguishes holy beings from devils. St. Paul declares all other attainments, without love, an empty noise. Charity or love acted out, will be the rule of the divine procedure, at the day of judgment. "I was an hungry, and ye gave me meat." No grace of the spirit can be exercised, without love, such as repentance, faith, or any obedience. That

149

right affection is that which constitutes virtue, is the general understanding of mankind, is evident; therefore it is, that men will make high pretences of love to God and their country, to proclaim their own goodness, and demand respect. The idea is suggested in the text, and through the scriptures, that love is the fulfilling of the law.

Love being the true test or standard of moral excellency, men have engaged in the base and perfidious business of counterfeiting religion, trying to adulterate the true coin, in which they have been too successful. Societies of every description have been formed; specious titles have been appropriated, without much reference to coincidence or propriety. This renders the injunction in the text seasonable and pertinent, *Let love be without dissimulation*. The word *dissimulation*, is the same as hypocrisy, for so the word is rendered according to the original, in many places in the sacred writings. It is supposed in the text, that amidst the many high pretences among men of their love and benevolence, there is danger of dissimulation and hypocrisy.

It will be my business, on the present occasion, in the first place to set before you the propriety and importance of this apostolic injunction.—Secondly, shew when love may be said to be with, and without dissimulation.

That the requirement in the text is peculiarly requisite, is evident from its being so often repeated in the sacred writings. Our love must be sincere, or without dissimulation, because hypocrisy destroys the nature of it; we only make pretence. The word hypocrite signifies a stage player, who exhibits a character not his own. God, the great searcher of hearts, sees all this, and cannot be deceived: therefore love without deceit is that alone that is acceptable in the sight of God. Whatever names we assume; whatever services we perform; whatever zeal we manifest, it is all mockery in the sight of the Almighty, without sincerity of heart. 'Tis a stench in his nostrils, and no more acceptable, than if we slew a man, cut off a dog's neck, offer swine's blood, or bless an idol, Is. 66:3.

2. Love with dissimulation is commonly of no use to society, but often very detrimental. A dissembler is one proud of applause, will advertise himself for office, dazzle the public mind with high pretences, like aspiring Absalom, I Samuel 15. O that I were made judge in the land, that every man which hath any suit or cause, might come unto me, and I would do him justice! Such are not commonly men of the first abilities, who thrust themselves forward into places that do not belong to them, while men of modesty,

talents, and integrity are kept back. As long as matters are congenial, or coincide with their private and selfish views, they may in a degree keep within bounds; but when they go contrary, they will sacrifice a state, yea, a world, to avarice and ambition. Such devotees to applause and hypocrisy will, even when the destinies of their country are at stake, be to a commonwealth what an Arnold was to American freedom, or Robespierre to a French republic.—This shews the propriety of the sacred mandate in the text, Let love be without dissimulation.

3. Mere pretences to religion can afford us no real enjoyment or satisfaction. The selfish man, or dissembler, has to war with his own conscience: his obedience is forced and unnatural: it is with difficulty that he can conceal his own true character, and exhibit another that he hates; is awkward, liable to mistakes; is afraid that others will see the cheat; he is not at home. He is jealous of his neighbor, lest he should have the pre-eminence, and rob him of his stolen goods. He cannot rejoice in the general good; is peevish and fretful under divine government, neither is the love of God or man shed abroad in his heart.

4. It will meet an awful reward at the day of judgment. Such shall have their portion with hypocrites, who are the most natural firebrands of hell, Matt. 24:51. Then will the secrets of men be disclosed; they will be stripped of their false garb and appear in their own; there will be no aping before the tribunal of Christ: it will be fully and publicly known who are, and who are not, friends to God and their country; who are, and who are not, benevolent societies; whether the wars, tumults, and contentions among men are the fruits of benevolent affection; whether the great political noise and bluster among statesmen and others, were the genuine effect of love to God and one another.—That our love be without dissimulation appears to be of the highest importance.

We are now led, secondly, to shew, when love may be said to be with, and without, dissimulation. Let it be observed, that our love derives its moral quality from the object we have in view; as it is a rational affection, it will regard beings according to their magnitude and importance: and as God infinitely exceeds all other existence, he must be supreme in our account. All pretences of love to mankind, and to our country, are vain without this. Benevolence has being for its object; if we love this in a less, certainly we shall in a higher degree. So also, as to complacential love. The scriptures of divine truth abundantly teach us, that all our claims of love to God are vain, if we hate our brother, I John 4:20. Therefore, let our profession of love to

men or to our country be ever so high, while we hate God, the great source
of all existence and happiness, it is highly preposterous, and proves us
destitute of that love, that is without dissimulation. 'Tis not here pretended
but that a man may be useful to his neighbors, and to the commonwealth,
while he is destitute of love to God; yet he has not that affection that the
law requires, or that is enjoined in the text. As state policy is that which
greatly agitates the public mind at the present day, and as it would be in a
measure falling in with the dictates of the present occasion, our principal
inquiry will be in reference to the present convulsion of our public affairs;
whether, amidst the warm zeal, party spirit, war and blood-shed, we can find
much of that love that is without dissimulation. Never was there a day that
men made higher pretences, and it may be there was never less to be
found.—Love that is honest and sincere will incline men to search after
truth: we read of a zeal not according to knowledge. 'Tis not an uncommon
thing to see men bellowing out their passions, with a kind of enthusiastic
delirium, making the highest pretences to patriotism, and offering their
services before they are asked for. They are pertinently described by the
apostle Jude. Clouds without water, carried about of winds; raging waves of
the sea, foaming out their own shame.—Speaking great swelling words,
having men's persons in admiration, because of *advantage*. It was a high
character given to the noble Bereans, Acts 17, that amidst the noise and
tumult of the populace, they searched the scriptures daily, to see whether
those things were so. There are things in a commonwealth that are
particularly under the cognizance of the civil magistrate, that the common
people cannot well investigate; such as raising revenues, and the manner of
their appropriations, etc. Laws that merely affect property; in such cases we
are taught in the sacred oracles, to render unto Caesar the things that are
Caesar's: but when Caesar demands that of me that belongs to God, I
cannot comply. We are not to rob the treasury of heaven to enrich Caesar's
coffers, to assist him in prosecuting a nefarious design against God: this
would be an awful species of dissimulation. The upright honest man will
hold it as his unalienable right to examine into the measures of government,
and bring them to the unerring standard of reason and religion, and will
esteem that man unworthy the name of a republican, or even a Christian, the
moment he relinquishes the sentiment. The 13th chapter of Romans, and
other passages of the sacred writings, are often brought into view, to enforce
unlimited submission to civil authority, and to prevent free and candid
inquiry. Let every soul be subject to the higher powers; for there is no

power but of God: the powers that be are ordained of God. On this passage the ingenious Dr. Macknight has the following remarks, viz. *To the higher powers.* "In other passages, exousias, *powers*, by a common figure, signifies persons possessed of power, or authority. But here, ai exousiai upekontes, *the higher powers*, being distinguished from oi arkontes, *the rulers*, verse 3, must signify, not the persons who possess the supreme authority, but the supreme authority itself, whereby the state is governed; whether that authority be vested in the people, or in the nobles, or in a single person, or be shared among these three orders: in short, the higher powers, denotes that form of government which is established in any country, whatever it may be. This remark deserves attention, because the apostles' reasoning, while it holds good concerning the *form* of government established in a country, it is not true concerning the persons who possess the supreme power, that there is no power but from God; and that he who resisteth the power, resisteth the ordinance of God: for, if the person who possesses the supreme power in any state, exercises it in destroying the fundamental laws, and to the ruin of the people, such a ruler is not from God; is not authorized by him, and *ought to be resisted.*"

To suppose that we are to obey civil magistrates, at the expence of the law of God, and a good conscience, confronts every dictate of reason and religion. St. Paul enjoins obedience to law for conscience sake; but to suppose we are to violate the dictates of a good conscience, and the word of God, for conscience sake, is highly preposterous. Shall the throne of iniquity have fellowship with thee, which frameth mischief by a law? Ps. 94:20. Because Pharoah king of Egypt, issued a law to destroy all the male children of the Hebrews, were the midwives to blame for fearing God, and disregarding the cruel mandate? Or was it right for the people to obey the bloody edict of Herod, to destroy the young children of Bethlehem? Were those to be condemned who refused to worship the image that Nebuchadnezzar set up in the plain of Dura? Or was Daniel reprehensible for disregarding the decree of Darius? Dan. 6. The apostles, in the face of civil authority, propagated the gospel: their answer to civil magistrates was, "Whether it be right in the sight of God to hearken unto you more than unto God, judge ye." God brought destruction on his people of old, because they regarded the laws and acts of their rulers, Hosea 5:11. Ephraim is oppressed and broken in judgment, because he *willingly walked after the commandment.*

When we are called upon by civil authority to engage in war, 'tis the duty of men, if they would not be guilty of blood, to examine the matter for themselves, whether there be just cause of war. The divine command is, *"Thou shalt not kill."* This is a moral precept, and no man with safety can disannul it. Soldiers that are trained up for war from their youth, and are at the beck of cruel despots, have often no better motives than blood-hounds, when let slip, or shaken by the ear: they fight to gratify revenge, obtain a plaudit, or to earn their bread, as a butcher in the yard, or slaughter-house. No war can be carried on, without murder somewhere, and he that don't candidly examine the matter, is not fit to take the field, being highly responsible. To make national honor and dignity to consist in seeking revenge and retaliation, more than the salvation of the lives of our fellow-creatures, is not love without dissimulation. Our divine Lord has taught us to sacrifice things that on the principles of strict justice we may retain, for the sake of peace. Whosoever shall smite thee on thy right cheek, turn to him the other also.—If a man will sue thee at the law, and take away thy coat, let him have thy cloak also.—Whosoever shall compel thee to go a mile, go with him twain. Benevolent affection will dispose men to make a proper estimate, or set a suitable value on things: men's lives are not to be trifled with, or vainly thrown away. People may swagger and pretend great love to their country, expose themselves to fatigue, and the utmost hazzard, but it may be all for temporal emolument: may be willing to sacrifice the lives of many, for the sake of a paltry medal, or school-boy's whistle, to pipe abroad that they have distinguished themselves, and acted their part well in the field of battle, and murdered a thousand men; while the poor disconsolate, bereaved widow, and the hapless orphans, have no place in their affections. If the mere sanction of civil authority, or their declaration of war make it right to enter the hostile field, then when two armies meet, they both are innocent, acting under the direction of their rulers. Should the question be asked, why do these men kill one another? the answer might be, "They fight in the discharge of duty, being ordered by the higher powers, that are not to be resisted." One neighbor and one nation may do another great injury, and yet there be no just ground of war, or shedding of blood.

It is a sentiment perhaps founded on reason and religion, that a *defensive* war only can be vindicated, unless where there is an express command from God, as in the case of Israel's going to war with the nations devoted to destruction. By a *defensive* war I mean, that we have no right to take away our neighbor's life only in the defence of our own. No weapon has been more used and more successful in the days of persecution, than the doctrine of passive obedience and non-resistance. Popes, priests, and cardinals were devoted to this business, and were greatly caressed and rewarded by those in authority.

No one will understand that the preceding observations are made to enervate our obligations to shew suitable respect to civil authority, or magistrates. They are ministers of God to us for good, and ought to be honored and regarded, so long as they act as his viceregents, or rule with propriety; but to suppose that their power is *unbounded*, and must not be opposed, let their measures and edicts be ever so unreasonable, is reviving the old tory spirit that was among us in our old revolutionary war, that we must not rebel against the king, and the government under which we were placed; that they had a right to tax, and dictate to us "in all cases whatsoever." Advocates for such sentiments were called tories. It falls within the sphere of every citizen of the United States, to examine into the causes of the present war with Great Britain; it is a subject of strict morality. The inquiry is vastly important; for should we find no cause for war it might prevent our being guilty of shedding innocent blood, and wantonly sacrificing our own life. But on the contrary, should we find the cause just, it will inspire the warrior with courage and fortitude: being conscious that he is vindicating the cause of God and his country. The man that will shed his neighbor's blood, without serious reflection, and due consideration, is not only destitute of that love without dissimulation, but even of common humanity. The reasons for the present war against Great Britain, are contained in the president's manifesto, and the declaration of a committee on foreign relations, which are before the public. If I understand them, the principal things are, the orders in council—the British stirring up the Indians to destroy us—the attack on the Chesapeake—searching our vessels—impressing our seamen—and the Henry plot.—As to the first, the orders in council, all acknowledge them to be rescinded, and cannot now be a reason for our continuing the war. With respect to the Indians being employed to murder us, the British government have officially denied it, and may demand proof. On this point, our committee observe, "Whether the British government has contributed by *active* measures to excite against us the hostility of the savage tribe, on our frontiers, your committee are not disposed to occupy much time in investigating. Certain indications, of general notoriety, may supply the place of *authentic* documents." Whether these certain indications ought to supply the place of positive proof, or *authentic documents*, in a case of life and death, all have a right to judge. With respect to the attack on the Chesapeake, I consider it a wanton shedding of human blood, and deserves no better name than premeditated murder, which called for the blood of the perpetrators, could such satisfaction be obtained: but was this the act of the British government? I think they have in a degree disapproved it. Perhaps they have not borne all that testimony, against it as they ought; but the president, I have understood, by official testimonies, has settled the matter, having received from the British such satisfaction as he demanded: whether there was a propriety in having this revived and introduced as a cause of war, deserves candid attention.

If recourse is had to another antecedent act of blood-shed, a court of inquiry has been appointed on the subject, according to the laws of nations, and are we not holden to abide the decision? I find this to be the case with the British minister, Mr. Foster, on hearing the conclusion of the court martial, appointed to attend to the affair between Commodore Rodgers and Captain Bingham, he acquiesces in the result; and, if I mistake not, makes no further complaint.

That civil, military, or ecclesiastical courts always decide according to the laws of justice and equity, cannot be admitted: and how can men be competent judges on the subject, unless they attend. It is our duty no doubt to submit, unless maladministration can be proved.

Searching our vessels and impressing our seamen is another thing contained in our declaration of war. That the British government ever pretended that they have a right to impress *our* seamen, I have at present no evidence; if there is any, to me it has never been exhibited. As I understand the matter, they claim a right to their own subjects, especially in times of war, wherever they can find them. No doubt great wrong has been committed on the seas, by unreasonable searches and seizures: our subjects have been taken for theirs, through ignorance, or not being able to distinguish. We have reason to believe, also, that some have been taken by design, which we all disapprove; but will going to war remedy the evil, and drive depravity out of the world? Can it be an effect of love to our country to prosecute war merely for revenge and retaliation? Searches are often made on land as well as water, on our roads, as well as on the highway of nations, where we suspect our property is smuggled or secreted. The officer searches my cellar, my trunk, and my pocket, perhaps he not only takes that which belongs to him, but that also he has no right to; and I may take suitable measures to obtain redress: but the question is, will love without dissimulation dispose me to blow out his brains, or fracture his skull with the end of my whip, loaded with death? It is said many of our people are enslaved by the nation against whom we have declared war. It may be some are, and measures have been proposed by some, who are wishing for a candid investigation of matters, to find out, in some degree, their numbers: but have, by a branch of authority, been repulsed (Massachusetts). If I am not mistaken a demand has been made on the part of our enemies, to make out the number of our impressed seamen, with a promise that they shall be returned. We feel a pity and compassion for our brethren in slavery, and pray for their deliverance and emancipation; but we further inquire, will going to war obtain the object? or is it a crime sufficient to shed blood?

"Our president, (says one) can talk feelingly on the subject of impressment of our seamen. I am glad to have him feel for them. Yet in his own state, Virginia, there were, in the year 1800, no less than three hundred forty-three thousand, seven hundred ninety-six human beings holden in bondage for life!" (Rev. Mr. N. Worcester's fast sermon). I ask, would it be the duty of these slaves to rise and massacre their masters? or for us to advise them to such measures? Partial affection, or distress for some of our fellow-creatures, while others, even under our notice, are wholly disregarded, betrays dissimulation. Another thing mentioned by the committee on foreign relations, is what is called the Henry plot. This is spoken of as exceeding any other thing: their words are, "Another act of still *greater* malignity than any of those which have been brought to your view," etc. This deserves close attention. The fact, as near as I can understand it, is this: It appears, that just before the declaration of war, that a certain John Henry, a man destitute of property and reputation, goes to the seat of government, and has something to tell, with this proviso, that the matter should not be divulged until he has time to escape, lest he be called to an account, or examination, and that he must have a handsome compensation. Government agrees with the proposal. The important secret is this. He informs, that he had been to the governor of Canada, offering his service to attempt a division of the states; that he had made *some* efforts, but was wholly unsuccessful, and the governor would give him nothing for his pains: he would now sell it to the United States for fifty thousand dollars: he is successful, receives his reward, and escapes for his life. On this we remark, that if Henry's story be true, it shews that he and Governor Craig had combined in a wicked, seditious, design, and were highly reprehensible. But we still inquire, is this a sufficient cause of war with Great Britain? I have never seen any colour of evidence to prove that the authority of England had any knowledge of the affair; and even if they had, is it a crime worthy of death, according to the law of God?

I would further observe, that love without dissimulation can see no propriety in punishing by proxy, in the case before us, or in avenging the wrongs of others on the innocent. 'Tis a divine maxim, that *the soul that sinneth shall die.* Can we be vindicated in killing our neighbors in Canada, because people on the high seas, or in England, injure and abuse us? Thousands among them are as ignorant of these things, and are no more accessary to them, than the inhabitants of Lapland, and many no doubt disapprove British aggressions as much as any among us. The declaration of war is against Great Britain and its *dependencies.* Were I travelling the streets of *Saba* in the West-Indies, or *Indostan* in the east, or *Demurara*, would it be a dictate of benevolence for me to kill as many as I should meet, under the cover or authority of the president's manifesto? Or exculpate myself by saying they all belong to one family, or government? It will be said, that it is according to the laws of nations to make no discrimination; but we have a statute of much higher authority, that informs, that there are things which are highly esteemed among men, that are abomination in the sight of God, Luke 16:15, that the fathers shall not be put to death for the children, neither shall the children be put to death for the fathers; every man shall be put to death for his *own* sin, Deut. 24:16.

Further: it is a species of dissimulation, when we justify that in ourselves, which we condemn in others. The rejection of what is called Mr. Erskine's treaty, by the British cabinet, has been a subject of great complaint, and attended with unhappy effects, which we all deprecated; and how much blame was attached to England in the affair, is out of my province to determine. Perhaps our objections and opposition, would have appeared with a better grace, and more consistent, and influential, had it not been preceded by conduct of a similar nature. Did not our late president reject the treaty signed by our ministers, at London, Dec. 31, 1806, without even submitting it to a decision of the Senate?

St. Paul's comment on the subject is in point, Rom. 2. Therefore thou art inexcusable, O man, whosoever thou art, that judgest? for wherein thou judgest another, thou condemnest thyself; for those that judgest doest the same things. Thou that sayest a man should not commit adultery, doest thou commit adultery. Thou that preachest a man should not steal, doest thou steal.

Again: that love bears the marks of dissimulation, that is partial in its obedience to laws, and does not respect all God's commandments, Ps. 119:6, especially, when matters of less importance are punctiliously regarded, and those of great magnitude are treated with contempt. It must excite the most painful sensations in every benevolent mind, to see with what indifference the command with respect to the sanctification of the sabbath is treated. Public and private property in abundance transported to harbors and to market on God's holy day, and no notice taken of it by authority, unless it be to forward them on their journey. Divorces granted to almost every applicant, upon no other pretence, than only they conceive that a new companion would be more agreeable to their lust, and render their lives more comfortable. In 1793, one thousand eight hundred divorces took place in Paris, in consequence of the French decree to abolish the ordinance of marriage. Where is the man to execute law on the sabbath-breaker—the debauchee—the swearer, etc. Is it for want of knowledge of these things? No. Should a man attempt to transport a loaf of bread, or a piece of meat to his suffering friend in Canada, a critical watch is kept both night and day, and a careful search made, lest he has something aboard prohibited by the law of the state. Should a man be found conveying a few quarts of salt across the line, to save and season his food, perhaps he is shot through the heart, with high pretences of regard to our country, and the laws of the state.—None will understand by these observations, that the speaker would encourage the violation of the embargo, and non-intercourse laws; he verily believes that they ought to be regarded, being sanctioned by authority, whether we see their utility or not; and he would be the last to transgress them. What I am anxious to inculcate, is the great absurdity of attending to such things, and neglecting the more weighty matters of the law: that it betrays the want of that love recommended in my text.

This sentiment is highly reprobated by the great law-giver, our Lord and Savior Jesus Christ, Matt. 23:23, 24, Woe unto you, scribes and pharisees, hypocrites! for ye pay tythes of mint, and anise, and cummin, and have omitted the *weightier* matters of the law, judgment, mercy, and faith: these ought ye to have done, and not to leave the other undone. Ye blind guides, which strain at a gnat, and swallow a camel.

When men pretend friendship to their country, to society, and to the church of God, and pursue such measures as tend to their destruction, they are destitute of that love that is without dissimulation. As peace and unanimity are essential to the well-being and happiness of society, the true

159

friend of God will use all proper means to restore harmony and friendship: knowing that a kingdom divided against itself cannot stand. He regards the divine maxim, As much as lyeth in you, live peaceable with all men. We are to mark and avoid such as cause divisions. It is not uncommon to see men boasting of their love to God and society, and at the same time are great incendiaries, doing all in their power to sow discord among brethren, opposing every proposal for accommodation. Perhaps on a candid inquiry, amidst the prevalence of party faction, we may find things among us that tend to irritate and increase our difficulties, rather than heal and compromise. Are not men often too lavish of their invectives on the present administration, and too hasty in judging and condemning without evidence? Doubtless there are many things wrong, and must be corrected; but is there not much said against men and measures, that are uncandid? Would not a more mild and dispassionate mode of conduct be more becoming, and have more influence? The wise king of Israel observes, Prov. 15:1, A soft answer turneth away wrath; but grievous words stir up anger. It is very probable that all parties are reprehensible in this particular. I believe that the sacred injunction is too little regarded, "Thou shalt not speak evil of the ruler of thy people." It is painful to inquire, whether foreign ambassadors, sent on negotiations of peace, have been treated with all that tenderness and respect as might promise success.—When Mr. Jackson, the British minister, was appointed for the purpose of accommodation, a flood of scandal was cast out against him, calculated to destroy his influence, and inflame the minds of those who sent him: he considered even his life in danger. Volumes were written to stigmatize and destroy his character. "*Copenhagen Jackson*" was in the mouth of every school-boy. Whether he was a good man, or otherwise, I know not; he was the one appointed by England to negotiate a treaty of peace: and I conclude it belongs to them, and not to us, to appoint their minister. Mr. Rose and others did not escape unfriendly remarks. These things greatly tended to impede an accommodation of our difficulties. I am far from charging this on our administration: but the propriety of the remark, with respect to the populace, none can deny. What can we think of a recent declaration on the floor of congress? "If they had a real desire for peace, they would have done so, and agreed to a cessation of hostilities. The attack on Canada was not to make peace, but to make war." (Mr. Quincy). Much is said of late to irritate the people against Great Britain, on account of their not meeting us on the ground proposed by our executive, which is to exclude each other's subjects from their vessels, and to put an end to searches. I think the proposal reasonable, and England ought to comply; and why don't the matter take place? Our cabinet well know the reason. The prerequisite required by the British government for a negotiation is, that we stop the war; and on our part, that they give up the right of search.

The committee, to whom was referred so much of the president's message of the 4th of Nov. last, as relates to our foreign affairs, say, "To appeal to arms in defence of a right, and to lay them down without procuring it, would be considered in no other light than relinquishing it. To attend to any negotiation afterward for the security of such rights, in expectation that any of the arguments which have been urged after the declaration of war, and been rejected, would have more weight after that experiment had been made in vain, would be an act of folly, which would not fail to expose us to the *scorn* and *derision* of the British nation, and the world." I believe there is scarcely a man in the civil department, that doubts but that such a negotiation would succeed to the adjustment of our difficulties; but alas! here is national honor, national *scorn*, and national *derision*. The question is serious and solemn as death!—Is this national pride worth an hundred thousand lives of our fellow-creatures, and the calamities attending five, six, or ten years' war? Is this the fruit of love without dissimulation?

We proceed further to observe, that man or society exhibit no evidence of love to their country, that endeavor to destroy that which is the greatest palladium of its support—I mean religion. That any government can exist any considerable time to advantage, without morality, is evident from the reason of things—from the word of God—and from long and recent experience. This sentiment we find inculcated in the dying legacy of our illustrious benefactor, whose auspicious birth we this day celebrate. His words cannot be too often repeated.

"Of all the dispositions and habits which lead to political prosperity, religion and morality are indispensable supports. In vain would that man claim the tribute of patriotism, who should labor to subvert these great pillars of human happiness, these firmest props of the duties of men and citizens. The mere politician, equally with the pious man, ought to respect and cherish them. A volume could not trace all their connections with private and public felicity. Let it simply be asked, where is the security for property, for reputation, for life, if the sense of religious obligations *desert* the oaths, which are the instruments of investigation in courts of justice? and let us with caution indulge the supposition, that morality can be maintained without religion. Whatever may be conceded to the influence of refined education on minds of peculiar structure, reason and experience both forbid us to expect, that national morality can prevail in exclusion of religious principles. 'Tis substantially true, that virtue or morality is a necessary spring of popular government. The rule indeed extends, with more or less force, to every species of free government. Who, that is a sincere friend to it, can look with indifference upon the attempts to shake the foundation of the fabric? Promote, then, as an object of primary importance, institutions for the general diffusion of knowledge—in proportion as the structure of a government gives force to public opinion, it is essential that public opinion should be enlightened. Can it be, that providence has not connected the permanent felicity of a nation with its virtue? The experiment at least is recommended by every sentiment that ennobles human nature. Alas! is it rendered impossible by its vices?"

We see by these observations, that 'tis hypocrisy for any to claim the Washingtonian name, who do not promote religion, and those divine institutions appointed in the word of God. The importance of religion, to give energy to military operation, and to establish empire, forced itself so much on the mind of the tyrant of Europe, as to cause him to issue his most insulting and hypocritical proclamation, when he went into Egypt, to enlist the clergy on his side. "Frenchmen, adore the Supreme Being," says he, "and honor the prophet Mahammed. The French are true mussulmen, disciples of Mahammed." To see people intoxicated with zeal for their country, foaming out their rage and spite, offering the last drop of their heart's blood, and at the same time neglect the duties of religion, break the sabbath, curse their neighbors, thirsting for the blood of their fellow creatures—despising the gospel, and those who are set for the defence of it, sacrificing their profession of religion to political frenzy, we pity their delusion, and pray that they may be brought to their right mind, and to serious reflection.—This has nothing of that love recommended in my text. In addition to what has already been observed, 'tis peculiarly important that if we would promote true republicanism, great care should be taken in our suffrages for office; much depends on this. The man that wishes well to the commonwealth will love his God—will love religion, and seek such men to guide public affairs, that have benevolence and virtue. The great inquiry will not be, who will fall in with my party, and appoint me to office, as a reward for my services to him; but who will promote the general good, and seek the peace and prosperity of the nation? Who has talents, knowledge and virtue, and has love without dissimulation? That man's honesty is greatly to be suspected, that will pretend great zeal for God, and the political prosperity of the nation, and at the same time give his vote for such men who he is fully persuaded are hostile to religion and morality. If there is a single point clearly illustrated and inculcated in the sacred volume, and established by experiment, it is, that those who rule over men should be just, ruling in the fear of God. That when the wicked bear rule the people mourn.—With what propriety any can say, that religion is not an *"essential qualification"* in a ruler, I cannot conceive. The man who regards the public good, will be ready to correct any mistake that he has made, although he may expose himself to the reproaches of uncandid men. His own private reputation will give way to public good, and with the utmost satisfaction re-trace every step he has taken, that tends to plunge his country in ruin.

The foregoing observations suggest the following conclusion, or remarks:

1. Nothing can be determined with certainty concerning the characters of persons and societies, by the style or name they appropriate. The words *love to our country, republicanism, federalism*, etc. are common among men. They are words not difficult to pronounce. Words go cheap at the present day. They are doubtless often used without any meaning. Washington is a beloved and honorable name: people are proud of it: but all must be brought to the test, is it love without dissimulation. Men make high pretences, at the present day. Officers, both civil and military, may pronounce our cause just, and call loud to arms! to arms!—if they are honest men and good men, yet they are not perfect: they may be deceived. There is counterfeit gold, and counterfeit silver, counterfeit bills, and counterfeit men. It can give no offence to count money after the best of men, and look for ourselves. These men are paid high wages for their pains—We are all selfish, and love filthy lucre. Some there are, that love it better than they do God, or their country.

2. True benevolence may meet with great opposition. 'Tis an affection that opposes the selfishness of men: in short, 'tis true religion, and is the very thing that the wicked hate. We need not think it strange to see the most virulent scandal and invective cast out against missionary and bible societies, and every institution appointed for benevolent purposes. This is a fruitful source of the opposition to the ministers of Christ. They are sent on the most benevolent errand that ever came from heaven. How suitable that cutting interrogation of the Savior of the world, Many good works have I shewed you from my Father, for which of those works do you stone me?

3. We see the impropriety of a popular sentiment abounding in the world, that we should not mix religion with politics. It is greatly to be suspected, as a design to enervate the obligation on civil rulers to attend to religion. If the idea is, that it is not the province of the civil law to appoint courts of inquisition, and propagate religion by fire and sword, and establish any form of theology among men, prohibiting from worshiping according to the dictates of conscience, then we fully concur with the opinion. We have already considered that civil authority ought not to control the consciences of men—But if this be what is meant, why need we hear so much about it in this land of liberty, where no man pretends to any such thing, and I hope never will? I am jealous there is great hypocrisy and dissimulation concealed under such pretences. Should not rulers be men of piety, and be under the influence of religion in all their conduct? Should the legislator, the judge, and every statesman or civil officer have his conversation, and all his deportment seasoned with grace, or mixed with religion, would it be unsuitable, improper, or inconsistent with their important station? They are to be ministers of God for good, and be a terror to evil doers, and a praise to them that do well—to guard, defend, and, under God, be the "*Bulwark* of religion." 'Tis said in the word of God, that in the happy state of the church, kings shall be its nursing fathers, and queens nursing mothers. They will then mix religion with politics, viz. it will be subservient thereto. Are we to deprecate the commencement of this happy era? If not to mix religion with politics will save a nation, I believe we have little to fear in our day. How often is that text perverted, with a design to establish the above sentiment, where Christ says, "My kingdom is not of this world." The end of this declaration was, to shew to Pilate, that it was not his business to set up a temporal, or civil kingdom, or be such a king on earth, according to the expectation of many: therefore it was perfectly congenial with his design not to contend for, or accept of an earthly crown. To suppose that Christ's meaning was, that civil magistrates and civil law should be destitute of religion, is absurd, and confronts every dictate of scripture, reason, and even common sense.

4. Another sentiment, prevalent at the present day, that is equally unscriptural, and absurd, is, that the ministers of the gospel ought not to meddle with politics. If the preceding observations be just, we see no propriety in the remark: at least, the expression is so vague and indefinite, that nothing can be determined by it. If the meaning is, that ministers of the gospel ought not to leave their people, and be members of Congress, be

judges of the bench, be civil or military officers, we fully agree with the idea: for they are to give themselves wholly to their work. Let it be inquired whether clergymen, whose opinion and preaching fall in with the party feelings of the day, are not often called to posts of profit and civil betrustment, and highly caressed by those who are constantly declaiming that ministers should not meddle with politics. Does this look like love without dissimulation? We highly disapprove of ministers of the gospel, or others, entering into warm party disputes, with men noisy and clamorous, intoxicated with passion, ignorance and conceit: it answers no valuable purpose, Matt. 7:6. But when in their view they see a nation going to destruction, is it their duty to be silent? Does such conduct comport with the solemn charge given them, by him to whom they are amenable for all they do, and before whose tribunal they may expect every moment to appear? Let us, my brethren, read with trembling, the declaration of the Almighty, Ezek. 33:6. "If the watchmen see the sword come, and blow not the trumpet, and the people be not warned; if the sword come and take any person from among them, he is taken away in iniquity; *but his blood will I require at the watchman's hands.*" Will it avail us any thing to say, we dare not preach politics? Or because the destruction was national, caused by political error; can we plead impunity, on account of its being *great,* involving a whole country in ruin? Was Nehemiah to blame for rebuking rulers for their oppression? Neh. 5:7. I rebuked the nobles, and the rulers, and said unto them, you exact usury every one of his brother. And I set a great assembly against them. Was Isaiah, the evangelical preacher, to blame for pronouncing the whole political head sick? Or Micah for preaching, that the prince asketh, and the judge asketh for a reward; and the great man he uttereth his mischievous desire, so they wrap it up. The best of them is as a brier, the most upright is sharper than a thorn hedge. When Rehoboam went out to war against Israel, Shemaiah, the man of God, was ordered to tell him not to fight against his brethren, I Kings 12:24. Abijah protested against Jereboam's war. II Chron. 13:12. O children of Israel, fight ye not against the Lord God of your fathers, for ye shall not prosper. Jeremiah bore a persevering testimony against the war in his day, for which his life was exposed, and he suffered great reproach. Jer. 38:4. The princes said unto the king, We beseech thee, let this man be put to death: for thus he weakeneth the hands of the men of war, that remain in the city, and the hands of all the people in speaking such words unto them: for this man seeketh not the welfare of this people, but the hurt.

165

If ministers obtain evidence that a war is unjust, can they see the youth and others engage in it and be silent; and not warn them? Should their hearers, for want of information, go into the field of battle, and take away the lives of others, and fall themselves, can they meet them before the bar of Christ, with coolness, without being guilty of the blood of their souls and bodies? I even shudder at the thought. Was not our blessed Lord a political preacher, when he reproved those in authority, Matt. 23. Do not ye after their works: for they say, and do not: for they bind heavy burdens, and grievous to be borne, and lay them on men's shoulders; but they themselves will not move them with one of their fingers. 'Tis not the design of these observations to cast any reflections, or to apply them where they ought not to apply; but to oppose that wicked and abominable sentiment, that it does not belong to Christ's ministers to oppose political or national iniquity. Unless they have zeal to sacrifice their salaries, their reputation, yea, their lives for the cause of God and their country, they are unworthy the sacred office. They must cry aloud, spare not, and lift up their voice like a trumpet, and shew people, of every name, party, or description, their transgressions, and their sins, as they would escape eternal damnation.

5. The subject furnisheth us with a pertinent answer to this question, Is it the duty of ministers and others, to pray for the success of the present war? The answer is at hand. If we obtain no evidence that it is a defensive just war, and that the power with which we contend have done nothing worthy of death, although they have been greatly to blame, and if, in prosecuting it, we should be called to point our arms against a section of our enemies, that have not been the aggressors; every one will at once see, that to pray that we may be successful in taking their lives, or shedding blood, would be daring dissimulation and hypocrisy, and an awful insult on the majesty of heaven. But there is a sense in which we may pray for our army, and ought to do, even if we should not obtain evidence of its rectitude. We may pray that all parties may be inclined to peace: that all nations may be disposed to do us justice, especially the one with whom we are at war: that the savages may be kept back from devastation and slaughter—our armies be delivered from pestilence, and that there be no further effusion of human blood: our civil and religious liberties secured: an honorable peace soon take place: our troops returned home to their occupations, in health and safety—that swords may be beat into ploughshares, and spears into pruning hooks, cannon and cannon balls run into cauldrons and andirons, and the nations learn war no more.

6. The subject teaches us the great excellency and utility of benevolent affections, or that love enjoined in the text, and how much those ought to be regarded that possess it. Such men are more precious than the gold of Ophir. That this was a distinguishing trait in the character of the illustrious personage whose birth we are this day called to celebrate, I think we have evidence. We do not idolize the creature; but, by bringing his virtues into view, it may excite gratitude to God for raising up such an instrument, and qualifying him for great usefulness to our country. That love without dissimulation directed him in the senate and in the field, we have reason to believe. He forewarned us against foreign influence, which he saw taking place. In a letter to the Hon. Charles Carrol, in 1798, he thus writes: "Although I highly approve the measures taken by our government to place this country in a posture of defence, and even wish they had been more energetic, and shall be ready to obey its call whenever it is made; yet I am not without hope, mad and intoxicated as the French are, that they will pause before they take the last step. That they have been deceived in their calculations on the division of the people, and the powerful support from *their party*, is reduced to a certainty; though it is somewhat equivocal still, whether *that party*, who have been the *curse of this country*, may not be able to continue their delusion." That he would have the sword unsheathed in a *defensive* war only, is evident from his dying injunction, when he gave his sword to his friend. His words are, "These swords are accompanied with an injunction, not to unsheath them for the purpose of shedding blood, except it be for *self-defence*, or in *defence* of their country and its rights." He was an enemy to slaveholding, and gave his dying testimony against it, by emancipating, and providing for those under his care. O that his jealous surviving neighbors would prove themselves to be his legitimate children, and go and do likewise! He refused a stipulated salary, demanding only his expenses; and the voluntary compensation made him, he appropriated to public and benevolent purposes. He was very careful of the lives of his soldiers, not willing to sacrifice them in hazardous attempts, merely to obtain a plaudit. He deprecated the horrors of war, and would sacrifice matters of some importance for the sake of peace. This appeared in his conduct with respect to the treaty, formed by Mr. Jay and others: Although it did not contain all that we could wish, and perhaps had a right to demand; yet, viewing it much preferable to war, in the face of the most violent opposition and abuse, he affixed his name to the instrument, and was, under God, the savior of his country for a season. But that which was the brightest diamond

in his crown was, his recommending religion and morality, as the basis and support of civil government, which has already been considered. May we not hail this happy day, that gave birth to our beloved Washington! and raise a tribute of thanks to heaven for so great a blessing!

The society this day convened have attached great responsibility, by the name they have assumed. If it is their design to destroy our political system—enervate the bands of government, and cut its cords asunder, and sow the seeds of discord and sedition among brethren, under specious names, 'tis such dissimulation as we hate and despise. But if it is your desire and intention, to defend and support our excellent constitution, and the wholesome laws of our country—to establish our independence, and perpetuate a truly republican form of government, and to take constitutional measures to purge and purify administration, whenever it shall become contaminated; and above all, to promote love, peace, and benevolence, then we wish you God's speed. 'Tis by fruits that societies are distinguished, more than by names. There are objects of charity on every side to illucidate your characters. The poor and the needy, the widow and the fatherless, are objects of your attention. There are religious institutions, I mean missionary and bible societies, that perhaps demand your patronage and assistance. The ministers of the gospel, although they do not solicit pecuniary aid, yet they need the encouragement of all the people of God, to whatever society they belong. They live in a day of peculiar trials. That a system of operation against the clergy is at work, will not admit a doubt. We have the most conclusive documents on the subject, that societies hostile to religion, and to the ministers of the gospel, have been formed in Europe and America. (Those who would wish to obtain satisfaction or evidence of the truth of this remark, are requested to read Dr. Robinson's proofs of a conspiracy, etc. or Abbe Barruel, a French Catholic. Also Rev. Mr. Smith's late dissertations on the prophecies.) A boast has lately been made, that these societies are *abundant*, and that within twenty years, not a gospel minister would be heard or supported in our nation, and that they would be pointed at as they walked the streets. The recent and violent attack made on the ministers of the gospel, commenced nearly at the same time, for some hundreds of miles around: of this I have sufficient evidence. This shews that it was a pre-concerted plan.—'Tis true it is concealed under the garb of patriotism, etc. and the agents are in a manner kept out of sight: but this is congenial with their articles, which are, "Bind the world with *invisible* hands.—*Hide* the hand that gives the blow." It appears, says a late writer, that many years ago there had been two millions of people murdered in France, since it called itself a republic; among them were twenty-four thousand priests, many of whom were protestates.

Perhaps 'tis not ostentatious in the speaker to observe, that in early life he devoted all for the sake of freedom and independence, and endured repeated campaigns, in their defence, and has never viewed the sacrifice too great. Should an attack be made, as formerly, on this sacred ark, the poor remains of his life would be devoted in its defence; and he is sure he speaks the language of his brethren in the ministry. 'Tis with him the evening of life: eternal realities are opening to his view, and it is in prospect of these solemn scenes that he has made the preceding observations, and is willing to leave them as his dying testimony. Being sensible that he is liable to error and deception, but has a confidence, at the same time, that it is not intentional, hoping for pardon through a mediator.

My friends, secret combinations are viewed with a jealous eye; they can do mischief in the dark. Whether your society deserves this epithet, is not for me to determine, as I am not a member of your body. Would you shew yourselves worthy of the affection in the text, and the high character you have taken, lay aside all malice, guile, sedition, evil speaking, and let us all cultivate the spirit of the gospel, which is pure, peaceable, easy to be entreated, without partiality, and without hypocrisy, and study those things which make for peace, and by which we may edify one another. Finally, brethren, whatsoever things are true—whatsoever things are honest—whatsoever things are just—whatsoever things are pure—whatsoever things are lovely—whatsoever things are of good report—If there be any virtue, and if there be any praise, think on these things. Amen.

Outline of a Sermon on Is. 5:4

In 1814 on his way to a meeting in Fairfield, Connecticut, Haynes stopped at New Haven where he preached in the Blue Church, formerly Dr. Edwards', on the northeast corner of the green. Timothy Dwight, the president of Yale, was present in the congregation, but Haynes was not overly impressed. "I learned long ago not to fear the face of clay," he said.

———

"What could have been done more to my vineyard that I have not done in it? wherefore, when I looked that it should bring forth grapes, brought it forth wild grapes."

Is. 5:4

Vineyards were very common in the eastern country, and composed a considerable part of field husbandry. They were made in very fruitful places, and required much care and cultivation—often expressive of that care which God takes of people in this world, especially of Israel. A vine is a weak, slender thing, that cannot support itself,—unless it bear fruit it is of no value, as illustrated in Ezekiel 15. Unprofitable to God—themselves—saints—sinners—devils.

A great naturalist tells us of one single grape-vine, planted by the Empress Livia, that produced one hundred and eight gallons of wine in a year.

In the words before us, we have God's care of his people. He even appeals to man's own judgment, that they would decide the controversy between him and his people. What could I have done more? etc. What is it possible to do more?—*Sept.*

We have the barrenness of men under Divine cultivation. They did not answer the reasonable expectations of the Almighty.

There are two or three important points that are worthy of our serious consideration.

I. *In some sense* God does all that he can for sinners.

II. God may most reasonably look that men should bring forth good fruit under Divine cultivations.

III. Men in general are very far from answering such an expectation.

When it is said in the doctrine that *God does all that he can*, we are not to suppose that God does all that it is in his natural power to do. A parent may offer all his estate to a rebellious child to reclaim him; or he may relinquish his authority. So God has a natural power to give up the reins of government into the hands of sinners. But this would be inconsistent with God's holiness, goodness, and truth.

It is as much impossible for the Deity to do that which it is inconsistent with his moral character to do, as if it were not in his natural power to do it. *God does all he can do that is consistent with the general good*: and, should he do more, it would avail nothing. God has adopted the best possible plan for the salvation of men.

1. God has been at as great expense to make an atonement as he could. All the perfections of the Godhead centre in Christ. More than if he had sacrificed worlds.

2. God could hold up no more powerful motives. Ps. 50:23. Stronger than Adam had before the fall. John 10:10.

3. God has given us as great evidence as possible of his willingness to save sinners, and that he is sincere in his offers of salvation. Has sworn, Ezek. 33:11; Heb. 6:18. Has actually saved some of the chief of sinners,—yea, all that would come. In his conduct on earth—in heaven.

4. God has been as earnest in his invitations as he could be. Read Is. 55:1; Matt. 11:28, 29; John 7:37; Rev. 3:20; 22:17; Ps. 24:7; Jer. 3:4; 31:18, 19, 20.

5. God has brought down the conditions as low as he could.

6. We have as clear evidence as God can give and we receive of the truth of religion.

How futile the Jews' arguments? Mother's name *Mary*?

7. God has promised as great a reward as he can. All he has. Luke 15:31.

8. God waits on sinners as long as is consistent with the general good. It would be injurious to others, and even to sinners themselves, should he wait longer,—viz., on the finally impenitent.

9. God sets before men as great threatenings as he can,—eternal death.

II. God may reasonably expect, etc.

I looked, stayed, or *waited.—Sept.* Not that the Almighty is disappointed. Things are just as God knew they would be. The idea is, that men's bringing forth fruit is most reasonable, in itself considered. Many things are reasonable that do not take place.

1. From a view of the great advantages they enjoy.

2. We may reasonably expect an event will take place, when such exertions are put forth to produce it as would effect it, unless counteracted by the most unreasonable conduct. II Kings 8:15.

3. From a consideration of their relation to God. Is. 1:2. We owe all to God—*my* vineyard.

4. From the ability God has given them. If we have hands, ears, and eyes, 'tis reasonable that we should use them—'tis accepted according to what a man hath. The service is most reasonable. Rom. 12:1.

5. From the great reward promised—even eternal life.

6. From a view of the faithfulness of inferior creatures.

7. From the dreadful consequences of barrenness, v. 5, 6, 7, 10.

III. Men in general are far from answering such an expectation. 'Tis the general complaint in Scripture. Compared to barren trees—unprofitable servants—Ephraim is an empty vine.—Hos. 10:1; Deut. 30:32.

God destroys whole nations for their barrenness, verses following the text. Ten acres only seven and a half gallons, v. 10.

Christians complain. Examine the conduct of men towards God—others—law—gospel—under means; judgments. How do they improve their time—talents—faculties of soul and body?

From the charge that will be brought in against men at the day of judgment, "Ye gave me no meat."

Improvement

1. 'Tis impossible for God to save more sinners than he does.

2. Yet 'tis possible for all to be saved.

3. A reason why sinners complain is because God does so much for them.

4. The wicked do much to oppose their salvation. What could they do more? They would do more if God would let them. Jer. 3:5.

5. God's character will appear glorious at the day of judgment. He will let it be known what he has done.

6. Sinners will likely be damned,—since God does all he can and they are not saved,—and they do all they can to be damned.

7. We should do all we can for the salvation of men.

8. All should examine their fruit—this is the way to know Christians.

9. Sinners should repent, and make it possible for God to save them.

The Sufferings, Support, and Reward of Faithful Ministers, Illustrated

Published in Bennington in 1820, this is Haynes' dramatic farewell sermon to the Rutland congregation he had served for thirty years.

For Haynes this was a moment of mixed emotions. Recalling 1,500 Sabbaths and 5,500 sermons led him to confess, "I did not realize my attachment to you before the parting time came." But embittered by what he felt was the congregation's persecution and slander led him later to say "he lived with the people in Rutland thirty years, and they were so sagacious that at the end of that time they found out he was *a nigger*, and so turned him away."

———

The Sufferings, Support, and Reward of Faithful Ministers, Illustrated. Being the Substance of Two Valedictory Discourses, delivered at Rutland, West Parish, May 24th, A.D. 1818.

"But none of these things move me, neither count I my life dear unto myself, so that I might finish my course with joy, and the ministry, which I have received of the Lord Jesus, to testify the gospel of the grace of God."

Acts 20:24

Long and painful experience evinces this truth, that the present world is a state of suffering: its influence is as extensive as the inhabited globe. The fall of man points out its commencement and duration. No age, country, or character can plead exemption. The gifts, grace and inspiration of the great apostle of the Gentiles could not deliver from this calamity. He could recapitulate scenes of distress as well as anticipate troubles yet to come. Ephesus was the metropolis of what is called the minor Asia; Paul visited them in the year 53; preached three years; but on account of dissentions and persecutions departed and went to Troas, from thence to Macedonia and Corinth: Proposing to embark for Syria at Cenchrea, which was about nine miles from Corinth, on its eastern boundary; but fearing the Jews, who understanding his course, and that he was carrying money to Jerusalem, that he had collected for the saints, they lay in wait to rob and kill him; he altered his course, and returned to Macedonia: visited many churches, and came to Miletus, several miles to the south: where he sent for the elders at Ephesus, that he might have an interview with them, to whom he gave the valedictory address contained in the chapter from whence my text is selected.—The people at Ephesus were acquainted with the peculiar trials of their former minister, which might excite sympathetic and distressing feelings: and perhaps tend to dishearten them in the cause of religion. To fortify their minds against such discouragements, the holy apostle gives them to understand, that he was not in the least intimidated, or turned aside from advocating that cause in which he had embarked: but was still adhering to those important truths that he had heretofore inculcated at Ephesus and elsewhere. This sentiment is expressed in the heroic and ecstatic language of the words before us: "But none of these things move me, neither count I my life dear unto myself, so that I might finish my course with joy, and the ministry which I have received of the Lord Jesus, to testify the gospel of the grace of God."

The method I propose in illustrating the subject before us is,

I. To show, that ministers of the gospel receive their commission from the Lord Jesus Christ.

II. That they will soon accomplish their work and finish their course.

III. That wherever they go they may expect to meet with trials and sufferings.

IV. That they ought not in the least to fear or be moved from the path of duty by their trials, but persevere in their work.

V. The faithful ministry of the servants of Christ will terminate, or issue in their great joy and satisfaction.

Paul says in my text, that he received it of the Lord Jesus Christ. The same apostle is very explicit on this subject, Gal. 1:11, 12. But I certify you brethren, that the gospel which was preached of me is not after man. For I neither received it of man, neither was I taught it, but by the revelation of Jesus Christ. Again, Rom. 10:15. How can they preach except they be *sent?* No man taketh this honour unto himself, but he that is *called of God*, as was Aaron, Heb. 5:4. In the early periods of time, preachers of righteousness were called and sent forth by the Almighty. In every succeeding age, God has been carrying on his work by the ministry of men, such are called prophets, apostles, etc. It was through the instrumentality of gospel ministers that the kingdom of the Redeemer was promulgated in the days of the Messiah, who gave them their commission, and sent them forth upon the important embassy, see Matt. 10:26, Luke 10:3. Although primitive bishops were many of them called in a miraculous and extraordinary manner; yet this by no means suggests the idea that ordinary ministers do not receive their commission from God, and are not equally sent by him.

The appropriate names belonging to the ambassadors of Christ, illustrates the sentiment before us. They are called *Stewards, Servants of the Most High, Angels' Ambassadors*, etc. These characters involve the idea of negotiating business for others, and of receiving commission from them. Plenipotentiaries are invested with full power to act by the court who sends them. Angels are sent from heaven to be ministering spirits on earth: and so in this sense bear a relation to the servants of Christ.

The faithful ministers of Christ are engaged in the cause of God: and it seems suitable that He should appoint them.—They are messengers sent on the King's errand, to transact business for him, and receive their commission from above.—They come to people in the name of the Lord. The motives by which the faithful ministers of Christ are influenced to enter upon their work, are not congenial with the natural and carnal dispositions of men; no wicked man, while in that state, was disposed to be a pious preacher of the gospel: so that when any are inclined, they are moved thereto by the Holy Ghost. When Paul engaged in this work, he had to contend with a fleshly and selfish heart: did not confer with flesh and blood, Gal. 1:16. All those natural, spiritual, and acquired abilities that ministers possess, are from God: He directs outward circumstances, by which a door is opened for their usefulness and improvement. When Paul came to Troas to preach, he observes that a door was opened unto him *of the Lord*, II Cor. 2:12. The gospel ministry was an ascension gift of Christ, Eph. 4:8.

Faithful ministers derive strength from Christ to preach, and discharge ministerial duties. They are taught to go to Him for help; and can exclaim in the language of a pious preacher, I can do all things through Christ who strengtheneth me, Phil. 4:13. Who could say the Lord stood with me, and strengthened me, II Tim. 4:17.

Ministers receive directions from Christ *how*, and *what* to preach. They are to preach the preaching that God bids them, Jonah 3:2. With *plainness*: The trumpet is to give a distinct, and certain sound. They are to deliver God's messages with *earnestness*, under a feeling sense of the importance of their work. Jonah was to *cry* against Nineveh. Isaiah was to cry aloud, and spare not; and lift up his voice like a trumpet, etc. Those awfully betray their trust, who deliver their discourses in a cold, formal, and lifeless manner, as though death, judgment and eternity, and the souls of men were things to be trifled with. Paul could tell the elders of Ephesus, that he had not shunned to declare unto them all the counsel of God, verse 27. That he had kept back nothing that was profitable unto them, verse 20.

The servants of Christ are directed by him how long to tarry with a people. The dispensations of Divine Providence dictated to Paul, that after a three years continuance at Ephesus, it was time to leave them. He that sent forth primitive evangelists, gives them this direction, Matt. 10:14, 15. And whosoever shall not receive you, nor hear your words, when ye depart out of that house or city, shake off the dust of your feet. Verily I say unto you, it shall be more tolerable for the land of Sodom and Gomorrah in the day of judgment than for that city—verse 23. But when they persecute you in this city, flee to another. Jeremiah was directed by God to terminate his ministry among his people, Jer. 7:17. Therefore pray not for this people, neither lift up cry nor prayer for them, neither make intercession to me: for I will not hear thee. There was a time when the ministry of Hosea with Israel was to cease. He is to *let them alone*, Hos. 4:17.

The usefulness of a minister among a people may appear to be at an end; this may be occasioned by the unfaithfulness of ministers, or of people, or both; there is criminality somewhere. It may be the case that people may make violent attacks on a minister's character, and do all they can to destroy his influence, and come forward with this hypocritical plea, "the man's usefulness is at an end:" and so cloke their wickedness and deceit under the garb of religion. The great clamour and hue & cry against the church and servants of Christ, is from high pretences to sanctity; and you will find that those who make the widest mouths in their vociferations, are the most destitute of virtue and religion.

II. It was proposed to show, that ministers will soon accomplish their work, and finish their course. Paul speaks in my text of finishing his course. We are all on a journey, travelling into another world. This is the case with ministers in common with other men. They are not suffered to continue by reason of death, Heb. 7:2. They *run, fly swiftly*, as the word Dromon signifies. They have an object in view, on which their attention should be fixed, even on the things that are ETERNAL, II Cor. 4:18.

The prophets, the apostles, and those eminent servants of Christ, who afford us daily instruction, where are they? Do they live forever? no; they ran their race, they have finished their course, and their work on earth, and among the people once committed to their care, is come to a final end. St. Paul pursued his work with diligence and rapidity, like one in a race. He visited many places and planted churches. Seven towns in Italy—in Greece, nine—in Syria, nine cities—in Asia minor, ten—in Asia, fifteen—in Egypt, three. He visited seventeen islands. 'Tis said that he was converted on the 25th day of January, and baptized the 28th. In nine years he had travelled 1928 miles. He had preached much in Arabia. In a second travel he went 1744 miles. His third was 2154.—His fourth was 3396 miles.

He travelled much more after this. St. Paul is supposed to be about 70 years of age when he died. He calls his life only a moment: that the time is short. The lives of ministers are often shortened by the trials they meet with; some times they are actually put to death for the sake of the gospel: they can say with this holy apostle, As dying, and behold we live! As chastened, and not killed; As sorrowing, yet always rejoicing. The memory of a Patrick, a Beveridge, a Manton, a Flavel, a Watts, a Doddridge, an Edwards, Hopkins, Bellamy, Spencer and Fuller is previous to us; but alas! we see them no more. No more in their studies; no more the visitants of their bereaved flock; no more in their chapels or sanctuaries on earth. They have run their race, finished their course, and are receiving their reward. Their successors in office are pursuing them with rapid speed: and will soon, very soon accomplish their work. The labours of faithful ministers are of that nature that subjects to pulmonic, and many diseases, incident to public speakers. Instruments there are on every side to hurry them to the bar of God, and put an end to their labours. That with propriety they may adopt the language of dying Peter, "I must shortly put off my tabernacle." Since

I came to this state, which is a little more than thirty years, twenty-seven ministers have died on this side of the Green-Mountain, and forty have been dismissed from their people; two lie dead in this burying yard. Paul lived nine or ten years after delivering his farewel discourse. Moses continued his ministry for eighty years. Noah for one hundred and twenty. Jeremiah thirty-two years; but how soon did they finish their course, and bid farewell to the world!

III. Wherever ministers go, they may expect to meet with trials and sufferings.

This was what was taught Paul by the Holy Ghost, as you will see in the two verses immediately preceding my text.—And now, behold I go bound in the spirit unto Jerusalem, not knowing the things that shall befal me there: save that the Holy Ghost witnesseth in every city, saying that *bonds* and *afflictions* abide me. We are taught by the same spirit, that 'tis through much tribulation we are to enter into the kingdom of God, Acts 14:22. Our blessed Lord, when he sent out his disciples to preach, he lets them know, that they went forth like sheep among wolves, Matt. 10:16. Ezekiel's hearers were to him as *briars* and *thorns*: as uncomfortable and tormenting as thorns and briars are that tear and wound the flesh; hedged up and armed that he could have no access to their minds, or influence among them. The wicked are compared to a hedge of thorns, Prov. 15:19. God says of people, Behold I will hedge up thy way with thorns, Hosea 2:6. It is the case with sinners that they are so prejudiced against the doctrines of the gospel and the servants of Christ, that it is dangerous to come near them. What a sore complaint was made against Jeremiah's hearers, Jer. 9:8. Their tongue is as an arrow shot out; it speaketh deceit: one speaketh peaceably to his neighbour with his mouth, but in his heart he layeth his wait.

If we trace the dispensations of Divine Providence, we obtain further evidence in proof, that the servants of Christ may expect to meet with trials wherever they go. Paul went to Arabia, the Jews sought to kill him. He went to Jerusalem, to Judea, to Syria, Celicia, and most of the countries of the minor Asia. His sufferings increased upon him. A minute catalogue of them we have in the sketches he gives of his life, I Cor. 4:10. [H]e observes, We are fools for Christ's sake.—Another time he is so cunning and crafty that there was no dealing with him, II Cor. 12:16. Paul suffered in his name or character. Defaming him by propagating falsehood and lies, was not uncommon. People had the impudence and boldness even to affirm, and slanderously report, that he and others said, Let us do evil that good may come, Rom. 3:8. In Acts 17:18. he is called a Babbler. "The *babbler*, is observed by the critics, to be a term of the utmost contempt: in allusion to a little worthless chattering bird, that used to pick up the seeds which were scattered in the market place." See Dr. Guyse on the place. They pretended he was a man who had picked up a few scraps of "learning, in different places, of which he wanted to make a show; and as one who was fond of hearing himself speak, even among those who had studied more than he had." Dr. Scott. "The tongue of a Tertullus is uncommonly eloquent, (though more gifted in lying, says one) when called to calumniate Paul before a Roman Tribunal. He begins, says Beza, by a diabolical rhetoric, and flattery, and ends with lies." Acts 24. For we have found this man a pestilent fellow, and a mover of sedition among all the Jews throughout the world, and a ringleader of the sect of the Nazarenes: Who also hath gone about to profane the temple; whom we took, and would have judged according to our law, etc.

Lying about the ministers of Christ has been a common thing. Being defamed, we entreat: we are made as the filth of the world, and are the off-scouring of all things unto this day, I Cor. 4:13. "We are become the purgation of the world. The learned observe, that the persons who were sacrificed to the Gods for averting their anger and for procuring deliverance from any public calamity, were called *purifiers*, and were commonly very mean worthless persons, and at the time of their being sacrificed were loaded with execrations: that all the misfortunes of the state might rest upon them.—The word signifies *expiation*. The apostle compares himself to those devoted persons, who were sacrificed for the purpose above mentioned. The filth of all things. The word signifies filth scoured off: to scour off all around. It is used most commonly to denote the sweeping of the streets, and stalls, which being nuisances are moved out of sight as quick as possible." (Dr. Macknight).

Dr. Scott observes, "They were held as the filth of the world, and refuse and scum of the earth. They were considered below contempt: or as worthy of execration as pestilence and nuisance: who ought to be purged, or extirpated out of society, as the common sewer carries away the filth and off-scouring of the city, to prevent infection and disease. Like human victims, peculiarly mean and vile, offered to the infernal Gods, with vehement expressions of abhorrence and execration."

Paul's enemies thought him to be the fruitful source of their calamities, and could they only be rid of him, their troubles would cease, their gods would be at peace with them. The united cry was, "Away with such a fellow from the earth; for it is not fit that he should live." Acts 22:22. It was a perilous event with this holy apostle when he was with false brethren, II Cor. 11:26. Hear a detail he gives us of sufferings: "In labours more abundant, in stripes above measure, in prisons more frequent, in deaths oft. Of the Jews five times received I forty stripes save one. Thrice was I beaten with rods, once was I stoned, thrice I suffered shipwreck, a night and a day I have been in the deep; in journeying often, in perils of waters, in perils of robbers, in perils by mine own countrymen, in perils by the heathen, in perils in the city, in perils in the wilderness, in perils in the sea, in perils among *false brethren*; in weariness and painfulness, in watchings often, in hunger and thirst, in fastings often, in cold and nakedness." It was not the least of his trials, that those who professed friendship to him and the cause of religion should turn traitors, and become his enemies. How painful was the reflection of the pious apostle to think, that many of the Galatians, who had given recent expressions of friendship to him, had so awfully departed from the truths of the gospel, and become inimical to him?—See his affectionate expostulations, Gal. 9. I am afraid of you, lest I have bestowed upon you labour in vain. Ye know how, through infirmity of the flesh, I have preached the gospel unto you at the first. And my temptation which was in my flesh ye despised not, nor rejected; but received me as an angel of God. Where is then the blessedness ye spake of? for I bear you record, that, if it had been possible, ye would have plucked out your own eyes, and have given them to me. And I therefore become your enemy, because I tell you the truth!—When vindicating the cause of God against opposers he complains, that *all* forsook him at first, II Tim. 4:16. When the professed friends of God forsake the ministers of Christ, it is attended with circumstances peculiarly aggravating. The sweet council and communion they have taken together, is now interrupted; mutual confidence destroyed, the parties exposed to peculiar temptations: which renders it difficult to retain that forgiving spirit, manifested by the holy apostle, when all men forsook him, "I pray God that it may not be laid to their charge."

David, the man after God's own heart, was tried in this particular, Ps. 55. For it was not an enemy that reproached me; then I could have borne it: neither was it he that hated me, that did magnify himself against me; then would I have hid myself from him; but it was thou, a man mine equal, my guide, and mine acquaintance. We took sweet counsel together, and walked unto the house of God in company. Above all, when the professors of religion take sides with the world against the servants of Christ, they then strengthen the hands of the wicked, and the Saviour is wounded in the house of his friends: which must excite painful sensations in the hearts of faithful ministers. The history of the preachers of the gospel in every age of the world, afford distressing evidence in proof of the point before us. The imprisonment of a Rutherford, a Baxter, the sufferings of a Manton, Flavel, Whitefield, and their contemporaries, evince this truth, that opposition to the servants of Christ is not an accidental thing; but that it is congenial with the corruption or depravity of the human heart.

Should our own experience, or the consciences of any present prompt them to declare in favour of the sentiment that has engaged our attention, such evidence will be admitted, without the imputation of perjury. To carry on their opposition against Paul, friendship to the gospel, or to the doctrines he preached was pretended; that it was not religion, or his preaching that excited their dissatisfaction; but the character of the man: and could they be rid of him, they would be advocates for the same sentiments. This attachment to the cause of Christ was the motive by which they professed to be influenced. They would therefore employ and hear men who preached Christ, with a design to carry their point against Paul, and render him contemptible. Phil. 1:15, 16. Some indeed preach Christ even of envy and strife; and some also of good will.—The one preach Christ of contention, not sincerely, supposing to add *affliction* to my bonds.

III. The wretched and dangerous state of unconverted sinners is another source of distress to the faithful servants of Christ: this caused great heaviness and continual sorrow in the heart of Paul, Rom. 9:2. The word is used to express the torments of hell, says Mr. Leigh in his *Critica Sacra*.—The history of Moses, of David, and the prophets, yea of the blessed Saviour of the world, afford painful demonstration in proof of the point under consideration.

All gospel ministers know experimentally, in some degree, the terror of the Lord, and are led to persuade men, II Cor. 5:11. That man that does not appreciate the worth of souls, and is not greatly affected with their dangerous situation, is not qualified for the sacred office. It was the saying of a pious minister, who would arise at midnight, and retire for prayer, "How can I rest, how can I sleep, when so many of my congregation are exposed every moment to drop into hell!"—The ambassadors of Christ have been called to sacrifice their property, ease, characters, yea their lives for the salvation of men's souls: like Paul suffer the loss of all things, not counting their lives dear unto them; being driven from town to town, and have no certain dwelling place, I Cor. 4:11. The requitals or returns made to the apostle for his benevolence to men, and his sacrifices for their good, was a bitter ingredient in the cup of affliction. He was cast among beasts at Ephesus, to be torn in pieces—carried the scars of the whip on his back: and the more faithful, the more hated and abused, and the less beloved, II Cor. 12:15.

The consequences that often attend a minister's leaving a people are distressing: God frequently gives them up to divisions and carnal dissipation, to heresy, and an awful contempt of divine institutions; or if the externals of religion are attended to, it is often to keep themselves in countenance, and support a character among men, and they often sink into a state of mere formality. Oh! how affecting to a pious minister, to see the flock, that was the delight and joy of his heart and once committed to his charge, become an easy prey to the enemy of their souls! How bitter was this reflection to our apostle? Acts 20:29, 30, For I know this that after my departing shall greivous wolves enter in among you, not sparing the flock. And of your own selves shall men arise, speaking perverse things, to draw away disciples after them.

The analogy between cause and effect, suggests the idea, that the servants of Christ may expect to meet with trials and opposition wherever they go. They will continue to preach the same soul-humbling doctrines, perhaps with greater and greater degrees of perspicuity and zeal: they will still testify the grace of God; they will have the same kind of hearers, whose hearts are enmity against God: and so may expect to meet with similar treatment. Paul preached the same gospel at Jerusalem, at Macedonia, Rome, etc.

In a word, there is no place in this world that either ministers or people can find a peaceful asylum; 'tis compared to the rolling sea:

> "No, 'tis in vain to seek for bliss:
> For bliss can ne'er be found,
> Till we arrive where Jesus is,
> And dwell on heavenly ground."

IV. In following the method proposed, I aim to show, that whatever trials the servants of Christ meet with in finishing their course, they ought not to fear or be moved out of the path of duty, but persevere in their work. None of these things move me: "I look on them as mere trifles, and make no account of them."

He did not account even his life dear unto him: He argues from the greater to the less. If the dearest thing, even life was of no value, compared with the cause of God, how diminutive those afflictions that were only for a moment: especially when we consider,

That they suffer in obedience to the commands of God, Ezekiel 2:6. And thou, son of man, be not afraid of them, neither be thou afraid of their words, though briars and thorns be with thee, and thou dost dwell among scorpions; nor be dismayed at their looks, though they be a rebellious house—Jer. 1:8. Be not afraid of their faces: for I am with thee, to deliver thee, saith the Lord. Acts 18:9. Then spake the Lord to Paul in the night by a vision, Be not afraid, but speak and hold not thy peace, verse 10; For I am with thee, and no man shall set on thee to hurt thee. Luke 12:4. And I say unto you, my friends, Be not afraid of them that kill the body, and after that have no more power that they can do. Obedience to the commands of God will as effectually secure his people from eventual harm, as the high and adamantine walls of the New Jerusalem, will the inhabitants of heaven.

The examples of him, that spake as never man spake, should be a powerful incentive to encourage his servants in their work, I Peter 4:1. With what persevering diligence did he prosecute his ministry in the face of earth and hell, until, in dying accents, he could exclaim, IT IS FINISHED! The *cause* in which ministers of Christ are engaged may well excite them to persevering faithfulness and fidelity in their work. 'Tis that dear interest for which all things were created, and the cause of the ever blessed God in three persons: for which the glorious Redeemer shed his precious blood, and is now pleading. A cause in which all the dispensations of divine providence are subservient, and in which all heaven are engaged. The character, oath, life, yea all the perfections of the Deity, are pledged for its defence: Lo I am with you always, even unto the end of the world. Amen, Matt. 28:20 is a promise that to all faithful ministers, at all times, even to the second coming of Christ, is as replete with encouragement and support, as can be given by the pen of inspiration.

By being steadfast and unmoved under trials, the servants of God can bear an honourable testimony in favor of religion: This is one way by which God has furnished the advocates of the gospel with peculiar arguments in defence of the truth; and has made them rejoice and glory in tribulation. It is not a stoical apathy that reconciles God's people to sufferings; not because that they are not susceptible of injuries, and ignorant of abuse; but God is glorified by their patiently enduring:—therefore it is that the language of the persecuted apostles was so appropriate. Acts 5:41, And they departed from the presence of the council, rejoicing that they were accounted worthy to suffer shame *for his name*. From hence it was that our blessed Lord says to his disciples, Matt. 5:11, 12. Blessed are ye when men shall revile you, and persecute you, and shall say all manner of evil against you falsely, for my sake. Rejoice, and be exceedingly glad: for great is your reward in heaven: for so persecuted they the prophets which were before you.

The ministers of Christ are frail imperfect creatures in common with other men; they need thorns in the flesh to humble and keep them low; and their afflictions tend, if patiently endured, to work for them an exceeding weight of glory, II Cor. 4:17. A reason of Paul's being so useful to the church of God, was on account of his being a vessel chosen and formed in the furnace of affliction. Perhaps a more accurate attention to order would have led me to an additional detail of the sufferings of God's people, under a former head, such as a body of death, which Paul so much complains of: this made him cry out, O wretched man that I am! I believe this is the greatest enemy that faithful ministers have to contend with, and excites the most painful sensations. Oh! the pride, the stupidity, the corrupt passions, the selfishness, that they often feel! tending to draw away their minds from God, and divert them from a close adherence to duty. These are trials that cleave unto us, go where we will. They are too apt to be intruders, even into our solemn acts of devotions, like Abraham's fowls, descend to mar the sacrifice, and 'tis hard to drive them away.

Ministers of the gospel need not be moved from the path of duty, nor be discouraged under suffering, because it is what they may reasonably expect: this was suggested by Christ to primitive preachers, to fortify against despondency, John 16. These things have I spoken unto you, that ye should not be offended: they shall put you out of the synagogues, yea, the time cometh, that whosoever killeth you will think that he doeth God's service, etc. But these things have I told you, that when the time shall come, ye may *remember that I told you of them*.

The ambassadors of Christ have sworn to be faithful, are all under oath; and for them to betray their trust is treason, and high handed perjury. Their profession is before many witnesses: In the sight of God, who quickeneth all things, and before Jesus Christ, etc. I Tim. 6:13. What is a life, yea ten thousand lives, when contrasted with that sacrifice that must be made by our deserting the cause of God? The great and sure reward promised to the faithful servants of Christ, for all their sufferings, should more than barely support them, amidst all the sorrows of life. Every pain, every tear, every insult they bear for Christ's sake, will secure them a great reward in heaven, Matt. 5:12. The wearisome and tiresome nights they spend here in running their race, and in finishing their course, will only prepare them for a more sweet repose and rest at their journey's end, when the morning shall break forth.

V. The faithful ministry of the servants of Christ will terminate, or issue in their great joy and satisfaction. "So that I might finish my course with *joy*."

1. They will have the approbation of their own consciences, II Cor. 1:12. For our rejoicing is this, the testimony of our conscience, that in simplicity and godly sincerity, not with fleshly wisdom, but by the grace of God we have had our conversation in the world, and more abundantly to you-ward. It arises to an holy triumph, says Guyse. Conscience will not be an idle or indifferent spectator at the day of judgment; it will have peculiar influence in accusing or excusing in the day when God shall judge the secrets of men, Rom. 2:15, 16. It will be a source of unspeakable torment to the wicked, a gnawing worm, that will never, never die; but where its dictates have been held sacred and not violated, peace, comfort, and holy rejoicing will be the attendants. The true friends of God amidst all the calumny cast upon them by men and devils, can say in the face of a frowning world, "we trust we have a good conscience."

2. When godly ministers have finished their course it will end all their imperfections and trials. They see so many defects in themselves, so much self-seeking, unfaithfulness and ignorance, that they often tremble lest after they have preached to others they may be cast away: that they shall fall short of that heaven they have so often recommended to others, and have their dwelling with the wicked; but these fears will subside, and to their surprise they will hear their Redeemer say, "Enter thou into the joy of thy Lord!"

All those sorrows, caused by the state of impenitent sinners, which has occasioned them many wearisome days and nights, will forever cease. No more slander, no more stripes or imprisonments: they will be out of the reach of men and devils, and obtain a complete and everlasting victory, and shout that ecstatic song, I have fought a good fight, I have finished my course! etc.

3. God will explain to them those things that now appear dark and intricate: Why so much distress, why they must be made the song of the

drunkard, why they must be driven from town to town, and have no certain dwelling place. The providences of God will all appear harmonious, calculated, through divine ordination, to promote the highest glory of the universe, and their personal good. Who shall not fear thee, O Lord, and glorify thy name? for thou only art holy: for thy judgments are made *manifest*, will be their song forever, Rev. 15:4.

4. It will afford peculiar joy to the people of God, especially to the ministers of Christ, when they have finished their course, in that God will publicly plead and espouse their cause, vindicate the doctrines they inculcate according to truth. The enemies of religion are often complaining that preachers are setters forth of strange things, too rigid, too pointed and *overbearing* in their preaching: tending to wound the delicate feelings of their hearers, like goads and nails, Eccles. 12:11.—There is no stopping the wide mouths of gainsayers; but so far as ministers have been faithful, God will own them, and vindicate their cause against the vile aspersions of wicked men. Their characters will be exonerated and cleared from those hard speeches which ungodly sinners have spoken against God and his people, Jude 15.

5. The sentence that will be pronounced and executed on the wicked will afford joy to the saints. In this world the ministers of Christ often tremble by anticipating the misery that is coming on sinners, and especially on their hearers that disregard their admonitions and reproofs, and like their divine Lord and master weep over them; but at the day of judgment, although pain and misery will in itself considered be undesirable, and an object of displacence; yet their holy and perfect attachment to the divine character, will render the displays of vindictive justice glorious, and excite praise and adoration, Rev. 18:20. Rejoice over her, thou heaven, and ye holy apostles and prophets: for God hath avenged you on her.

6. The great and unspeakable reward and honour that will be bestowed and conferred on the faithful servants of Christ will be matter of great joy: it will exhibit the condescending grace of God, and excite humility in them; they can scarcely believe that God could ever take notice and reward such poor services as they have done, and will cry out with wonder, love and praise, "Lord, when saw we thee and hungered and fed thee? or thirsty, and gave thee drink? When saw we thee a stranger, and took thee in? or naked, and clothed thee? or when saw we thee sick, or in prison, and came unto thee?" Matt. 25:37, 38, 39. As God's rewarding the saints will humble them, so it will tend to fit them for the world of everlasting adoration. One great

design of the day of judgment will be to exhibit the riches of divine grace: which will excite endless songs of joy to the saints.

> "The more thy glories strike mine eyes,
> The humbler I shall lie;
> Thus, while I sink, my joy shall rise
> Unmeasurably high."
>
> —Watts.

God will make it appear, that those who had trials of cruel mockings and scourgings, of bonds and imprisonments, that were stoned and sawn asunder, tempted, slain with the sword, who wandered about in sheep skins and goat skins, in deserts, and in mountains, and in dens and caves of the earth, being destitute, afflicted, tormented, etc. were men, after all, of whom the world was not worthy, Heb. 11.

The scars and signals of sufferings in the cause of God, that his people will carry with them, will procure more illustrious monuments than pillars of marble; they will possess that kingdom prepared for them, and be made kings and priests unto God. This was that dignity to which St. Paul was aspiring, the prize of the high calling: that for which he did not account his life dear, honourable unto him. [*The Greek word is* Timian, *honourable, precious.*]

FINALLY, It will enhance the joy and reward of the ministers of Christ to meet all their brethren and companions in tribulations. There will be so great a degree of similarity in the sufferings of the servants of God, and in the interpositions of divine providence towards them, as to excite a pleasing and holy fellow-feeling in their souls; the celestial spark will catch from breast to breast, while an harmonious flame of divine love and adoration will ascend as from one altar, to him that hath given them all the victory. Ministers will meet the pious part of their congregations with great rejoicings: those especially to whom they have been instrumental of saving good: Such will be their crown of rejoicing in the day of the Lord Jesus, II Cor. 1:14, I Thes. 2:19, 20, Heb. 13:17.

Paul will meet with his brethren that were at Corinth, Rome, etc. A more public and interesting rehearsal of their mutual and personal interviews will be attended to: What reciprocal joy will his meeting with Timothy and his son Onesimus afford! The parting of the apostle and his Ephesian brethren at Miletus, was painful and distressing; what weeping and sorrowing! but at their arrival at the haven of eternal rest, what a contrast! No fearing that they should see each others faces no more; nay, that once mournful parting, and Paul's valedictory sermon, is recognized with emotions of joy, as an event necessary to promote the further promulgation of the gospel, and accomplish the decrees of heaven.

Ministers and their people when they have finished their course, will remember those Bethel visits that they have enjoyed in the sanctuary, and around the table of the Lord, and the sweet counsel they have taken together; they will remember the seasonable reproofs given to each other, and whatever differences have taken place between them, will all be forgiven, and forever exterminated; they will see the wisdom and goodness of God in all these things. Thus, when the ministers of Christ have finished their course, it will finish and put an end to all their troubles: and so their ministry will end, or issue in their unspeakable joy and consolation.

Improvement

1. Since ministers receive their commission from Christ, none have any right to forbid them preaching. All courts of inquisitions, all prohibitory measures adopted by men to prevent their declaring the glad tidings of the gospel, or fulfilling the ministry they have received of the Lord Jesus, is an insult on the majesty of heaven, and discovers a spirit hostile to religion, and the rights of men: and ought to be treated with a holy contempt by all the servants of Christ. With what religious indignation were those presumptious measures treated that were used to stop the mouths of those recorded in Acts 4. And they called them, and commanded them not to speak at all, nor teach in the name of Jesus. But Peter and John answered and said unto them, Whether it be right in the sight of God to hearken unto you more than unto God, judge ye:—For we cannot but speak the things which we have seen and heard. Again, Chapter 13. When the Jews opposed Paul and Barnabas, they waxed *bold* in their work.

2. Since ministers receive their commission from heaven, we see the obligations that people are under to regard them, and pay attention to the sacred lessons they are to inculcate. To reject and despise the ambassadors of Christ is very dangerous: 'tis insulting the sacred Trinity, and accounted high treason in the court of heaven; it indicates the displeasure of the king when ambassadors are abused and recalled: that the treaty, or negotiation of peace is closing, II Chron. 36:16. But they mocked the messengers of God, and despised his words, and misused his prophets, until the wrath of the Lord

arose against his people, till there was no remedy. Let the enemies of God fear and tremble when they read the credentials of Christ's ministers, sanctioned with this capital label or inscription, Luke 10:16. He that heareth you, heareth me; and he that despiseth you, despiseth me; and he that despiseth me, despiseth him that sent me.

3. Since ministers must soon finish their course, the thought should excite them to the utmost faithfulness, constancy, and engagedness in their work, seeing their time is short. We can scarcely believe the senate, or legislative department, to be the place assigned to gospel ministers, who are to give themselves wholly to the work. Paul could remind his Ephesian brethren, that for the space of three years he ceased not to warn everyone night and day with tears. The same apostle exhorts Timothy to give attendance to reading, to exhortation, to doctrine, I Tim. 4:13.

How desirable that the servants of Christ receive such a decent support as to be able to devote all their service to the sanctuary, and the souls of their hearers. Every sermon should be a kind of farewell discourse. It is said of the pious Mr. Shepherd that he used to say, That he never preached a sermon but what he thought it might be the last. Oh! how does it become us to preach and act like dying men, that we may finish our course with joy!

4. It is no evidence that ministers are not the true servants of Christ because they meet with great opposition from the world, and even from the professors of religion: Yea it is from the high pretenders to sanctity that the Saviour of men suffered most severely. St. Paul observes concerning bishops, That they must be of good report of them that are without. Did the apostle mean by this to prove that himself was disqualified for the sacred office, being of bad report among the enemies of God? This above all others would disqualify Christ for the ministry. He observes to those whom he sent forth as preachers, Luke 6:22. Blessed are ye when men shall hate you, and when they shall separate you from their company, and shall reproach you, and cast out your name as evil, for the Son of man's sake. When men shall revile you, and persecute you, and shall say all manner of evil against you falsely for my sake, Matt. 5:11. That the ambassadors of Christ should so conduct as to give no just occasion to them that are without to reproach the cause of God is evident. Doctor Macknight has the following paraphrase on I Tim. 3:7. "Moreover, before his conversion he must have behaved in such a manner as even to have a good testimony from the heathen, that he may not be liable to reproach for the sins he committed before his conversion, and fall into the snare of the devil, who, by these reproaches, may tempt him to

renounce the gospel, knowing that he has little reputation to lose." That the heathen may more willingly receive him he being formerly a man of good reputation. Consult Henry and Scott on the place, whether the learned commentator has given the meaning of the text or not. We are assured that it was never designed to fix a reproach on the characters of the faithful servants of Christ, or sanction those invectives and slander so often cast on them by the enemies of God.

That the word of God is often wrested and perverted by him who is no stranger to the art, and introduced as an auxiliary to his evil machinations, is evident, even from the farce he attempted with the blessed Saviour of the world. He can say "It is *written,*" etc. It is far from being a singular case, to have people make and spread false and scandalous things concerning the ministers of the gospel, and even to offer rewards to such as will join in the game: then to accomplish their designs have the audacity and duplicity to say, "O! the man is of bad report! of them that are without." Was not the Saviour of men betrayed in this way?

Let not his faithful servants relinquish their work, or determine against their call to the sacred office, because they have so many trials and persecutions: for so persecuted they the prophets which were before you, Matt. 5:12.

5. Since ministers receive their commission from the Lord Jesus Christ, 'tis dangerous for them to go before they are sent. 'Tis suitable that they have some exterior evidence of their mission: Something more than their pretensions to inward sanctity. Primitive extraordinary ministers could exhibit miraculous testimonials of their being called to the sacred office: It seems equally necessary, that in all succeeding ages, the ambassadors of Christ have some kind of credentials of their being regularly called to the work: We therefore find that ordinary ministers not only appeared to be inwardly called by the Holy Ghost, or were in the judgment of charity good men, endowed with ministerial gifts and graces: but were recommended and set apart by those in office, and ordained by the laying on of the hands of the Presbytery. Those, therefore, that thrust themselves into the work without these pre-requisites, do not come in by the door appointed by the great head of the church, but climb up some other way, and ought not to be treated and encouraged as the true ministers of Christ.

6. Since all true ministers receive their commission from the court of heaven, there ought to be a cordial union among them: they should treat each other as brethren. Although they may have gifts differing, the strong

are not to despise the weak: they derive licence from the same authority, bearing the same signet; they are called by different names, such as Bishops, Overseers, Ministers, Elders, Angels, etc. But we do not conceive that they are expressive of superiority or diversity of grades in office, any more than various names among men imply different species. The soldiers of Jesus deriving their commission from the same king, and being engaged in the same cause, should as far as possible see eye to eye, and strengthen each others hands.

7. We infer the truth of the holy scriptures, that so accurately foretell the trials and sufferings of gospel ministers.—The benevolent embassy with which they are entrusted, and the authority with which they are invested, would indicate better treatment, were it not confronted by predictions in the sacred volume. While therefore the enemies of God slander and persecute the servants of Christ, they in a degree establish the truth of divine revelation.

8. The subject teaches how to account for that firmness and intrepidity discovered by the people of God, especially the ministers of Christ in every age. They will not give up the cause, come life, or come death. This rendered Luther, Melancton, Huss, Jerome, Polycarp, Wickliffe, and a thousand others invincible to all the flatteries and intrigues of wicked men and devils, and the menaces and terrors of an inquisition: they could say, none of these things move us, etc.

9. There will be a very solemn meeting of ministers and people at the day of judgment: Joy and terror will attend the transactions of that day. Ministers and people will meet as having special business with each other; their reciprocal conduct will be publicly investigated. How suitable that these things are now seriously examined, with candor before the commencement of that day.

As in the course of Divine Providence a dissolution of the pastoral and ministerial relation between me and this people has lately taken place, according to the declaration of an ecclesiastical council convened for that purpose. I have been requested to deliver a valedictory discourse. As I am still residing among you, the occasion is different from the one that took place between Paul and those he was then taking his leave of; he tells them, that he knew that those, among whom he had been preaching the kingdom of God, should see his face no more: this may or may not be the case of the speaker. I am willing to say some thing on the occasion, which I esteem solemn and interesting; hoping that I shall be enabled to address you with all that plainness and prudence which becomes one who expects to give an account. The apostle reminds the Ephesian brethren of some things that had transpired while he was with them.

My Brethren and Friends,

The church of Christ in this place was organized forty-two years ago the 20th day of October last, by the assistance of the Rev. Benajah Roots, my worthy predecessor.

It was thirty years ago, the 28th day of March last, since I took the pastoral care of this church and people; the church then consisted of forty-two members; since which time, there has been about three hundred and twelve added to it, about sixty have been removed by death, and about four hundred have died in this society, including those above mentioned.—There are only ten of the church now living in this place who were here when I first came among you; the greater part sleep in death. I have preached about five thousand five hundred discourses, four hundred of them have been funeral sermons. I have solemnized more than an hundred marriages.— During this period we have had two remarkable seasons of the out-pourings of the spirit, as well as some refreshings at other times, which many of us who are yet alive recognize with emotions of joy. Twice I have been brought, in my own apprehensions, to the borders of the grave; but God has spared me to see this day of trial, which I desire to meet with resignation to His will.

The flower of my life has been devoted to your service:—and while I lament a thousand imperfections which have attended my ministry; yet if I am not deceived, it has been my hearty desire to do something for the salvation of your souls. He that provided the motto of our discourse could say on his farewell, I have coveted no man's silver or gold, or apparel.—Yea, ye yourselves know, that these hands have ministered unto my necessity. The appropriation of such language is in a degree congenial with the testimony that many present could give, and might be admitted were it not for the danger of comparison. I have sometimes thought that, perhaps God designated that I should spend the few of my remaining days among you, and with a degree of satisfaction I have looked into the repository of the dead, adjoining this house, intending to sleep with them, claiming a sort of kindred dust, intending to rise with them; but the ways of God are mysterious, who often destroys the hope of man. In my solitary reflections, I cast a look towards this house, to bid it a final adieu; but in spite of all that fortitude, dictated by reason and religion, the sympathetic tear will betray the imbecility of human nature. Can we suppose that even a Paul was unmoved, when they all wept sore, and fell on his neck, sorrowing most of all that they should see his face no more, Acts 20:37, 38.

A three years ministry had excited such reciprocal endearments, that made the parting like tearing soul and body asunder. More than one thousand five hundred Sabbaths have I spent with you, the most of them in this house. More than one hundred and thirty seasons of communion have we enjoyed around the table of the Lord. Oh! how many sweet and comfortable days have I spent in this house with you that are alive, and those who are dead! We have taken sweet counsel together; I trust I have at times felt the powerful presence of Christ, while speaking from this desk; cannot we adopt the language of the Psalmist,

> " 'Tis with a mournful pleasure now,
> I think on ancient days:
> When to thy house did numbers go,
> And all our work was praise."

It appears in the course of Divine Providence that my labours among you have come to an end. We have done meeting in this house; I am called to give you the parting hand; but let us all remember that a very solemn meeting awaits us at that day suggested in my text, when we shall all have finished our course.

Our meeting at that day will greatly differ from what it has been in this house: I have often been here and found but few within these walls, some trifling excuse has detained you; but at that day, it will not be optional with people whether they attend or not, all will be there: the congregation will be full, not one in a town, state, or in the world, but what will appear. Some times you have manifested great stupidity, and I have witnessed drowsiness and carelessness while I have been speaking; but at that day you will be awake, and be all attention. You will believe, realize, and feel interested in the things exhibited. Often through the depravity of the human heart, and the prejudice that sinners have to the truth, and to the servants of Christ, they will turn their backs on divine worship, and leave the house of God: But when ministers and people meet before the tribunal of Christ, there will be no deserting or quitting the assembly, there they must hear, however disagreeable their preaching will be, and tormenting to their consciences. In this house our meeting has been promiscuous, or indiscriminate; saints and sinners sit on the same seat; around the same table, we cannot certainly say who has, and who has not on the wedding garment; but at the day of judgment there will be an exact separation, Christ will separate the sheep from the goats.

In this house we have *often* met, not less than four thousand times; we go and we come: Although we see no fruit of our labour, we do not wholly despair, we hope God may yet bless his word; but when ministers and people meet before the bar of God, it will be the last interview, none to follow it: The case of sinners will then be forever hopeless, and helpless.

One great design of our meeting together in this world is to offer salvation to sinners, to entreat and to beseech them to be reconciled to God; but at the day of judgment an irreversible sentence will be pronounced on the righteous and on the wicked; the saints will be rewarded, and sinners condemned, and sent to endless perdition.

When the ambassadors of Christ have finished their course, and meet their people a critical examination will take place: I must give an account concerning the motives which influenced me to come among you, and how I have conducted during my thirty years residence in this place: the doctrines I have inculcated: whether I have designedly kept back any thing that might be profitable to you, or have, through fear of man, or any other criminal cause, shunned to declare the whole counsel of God. Also, as to the *manner* of my preaching, whether I have delivered my discourses in a cold, formal manner, and of my external deportment. You, who have been the people of my charge, must give an account, what improvement you have made of my ministry: whether you have attended as you ought: whether your excuses for withdrawing from public worship at any time, were sufficient. God will attend to them, and they will be weighed in a just balance: not a single neglect will escape divine notice. We have a thousand excuses, when put in the scale of the sanctuary, will be lighter than a feather.

You must give a strict account as to the *manner* of your attending in this house: whether you have received the word with joy, and obeyed its precepts. Parents must render an account, whether they have taught their children, by precept and example, to reverence the word of God, and respect the servants of Christ. Whether they have endeavoured to maintain or support the influence of their minister among the youth or rising generation, and so been workers together with him. Whether the servants of Christ do not fall into contempt in a measure through their instrumentality. People will be examined whether they have contributed to the temporal support of the ministers of Christ; it will not be left with men how much they ought to impart; but God will be the judge how much was suitable, and whether it was agreeable to the word of God, and the exigencies of the preacher.

On the separation of a minister from his people there are often very criminal causes existing, either on the part of the minister, or people, or both. There may be *pretended* reasons while the truth may be kept out of sight, to escape censure.—Ecclesiastical, partial councils may think it inexpedient to make any inquiry into the matter; but they will have a plain, candid and thorough investigation before the tribunal of Christ. No deception, no hypocrisy will be concealed under religious pretences; but it will all be detected and exposed before the assembled universe, and the hearts of all men be revealed.

> "Nothing but truth before his throne,
> With honour can appear:
> The painted hypocrites are known
> Through the disguise they wear."

The accusations brought before the ministers of Christ will be examined. Ministers will fare no better for the name they sustain; their wickedness will be exposed; they condemned, or exonerated, not according to popular noise and clamour, but coincident to truth and equity. These are scenes, my brethren, that are just opening before us, and to which we are hastening with the utmost rapidity. These are things that should move us, and call up our attention. It is a small, very small thing to be judged of man's judgment. Oh! let us labour to be found of God in peace. This day to me in some respects is very solemn and interesting, on which I am called to give you the parting hand: but its importance is eclipsed when contrasted with that awful period when we are to meet before him, who is to judge the quick and the dead.

There you and I must shortly appear. Much has been said on the subject of my dismission: that it has been in consequence of my request. I think I have been sufficiently explicit on the matter; but I am willing to repeat it in this public manner, that had the people been united, wholesome discipline properly exercised, a firm and unshaken attachment to the cause of God manifested among all the professors of religion, I should have chosen to have continued with you, at the expense of temporal emolument; but considering the divisions existing, and the uncommon stupidity prevalent, I have been fully satisfied that it was my duty to be dismissed, and have requested my friends not to oppose it. I am persuaded that it will appear another day, that unfaithfulness in the minister did not originate the event, to the exclusion of criminal causes in this society; but this matter is laid over to the day of final decision. I trust I feel in a degree reconciled: knowing that God's way is in the sea, and in the deep waters, and his footsteps are unknown.

I find my strength in a degree inadequate to itinerant labours, and that I am shortly to put off this my tabernacle; but I purpose, so long as life and health continues, to preach the same gospel that I have been publishing to you for more than thirty years, and on which, I humbly hope, I have ventured my eternal salvation. O that I may be enabled to discharge the duty with greater zeal and fidelity! And now I am called to go, not to Jerusalem, but from place to place, not knowing the things that shall befall me, saving what the Holy Ghost, and the providence of God witnesseth in every city, that trials await me; but I hope I can in some small degree say, But none of these things move me, neither count I my life dear unto myself, so that I might finish my course with joy, and the ministry which I have received of the Lord Jesus, to testify the gospel of the grace of God.

My dear brethren and friends, I did not realize my attachment to you before the parting time came. Many disagreeable things have taken place; but still I feel my heart going out toward this people. How many pleasant days have I spent with you in this house? How many hours under your roofs, and delightful visits in your families? I will not except a single door that has not been hospitably opened for my reception. Many kindnesses have I received from you, both in sickness and in health. You will accept my warmest gratitude for the many instances of kindness shown me. I hope, my dear brethren and sisters in the Lord, that you will still remember me at the throne of grace; that God would support me under every trial, and that he would render the evening of my life useful to the church of God: that utterance may be given unto me, that I may open my mouth boldly to make known the mystery of the gospel.

May the great head of the church send you a pastor after his own heart, vastly superior in gifts and grace to him who is giving you his farewell address. 'Tis a distressing thought to think that I am about to leave any of you in an unconverted state: that my labour among you will prove to your heavier condemnation. Particularly let me call on you that are young: this house, and your own consciences, are witnesses that I have repeatedly called on you to attend to the important concerns of your never, never dying souls, and I fear too many of you in vain. Have you not turned a deaf ear to the calls and invitations of the gospel? and to the solemn warnings of God in his providence? I fear you are going down to eternal destruction, under the intolerable weight of aggravated sins. I will now, perhaps for the last time, invite you to Jesus, the God-man Mediator. Some of your parents on a death bed have charged me with their dying breath, to be faithful to you; should it appear at our meeting at the day of judgment, that I have in any good measure answered their request, must I re-echo to the tremendous sentence of the judge, depart, Amen! Amen! Oh! how dreadful! how heart-rending the anticipation! Must this be the case? Nothing but a speedy and thorough repentance and turning unto God can prevent it.—Dear youth, your souls were once committed to me, I would now commit them to him, who is able to keep you from falling, and present you faultless before the presence of his glory, with exceeding joy.

In general you have treated me with respect; I do not remember of ever receiving an insult from a single youth.—Many of your parents sleep in dust, where I must shortly be; should I be so happy as to sit down with them in the kingdom of heaven, and should you arrive to those blissful regions, Oh! what a blessed interview! With what ecstatic joy and congratulation should we present the offering before the throne of God, with the humble, grateful, and astonishing exclamation, Here Lord we are, and the natural and spiritual children thou hast graciously given us!

You will shortly hear of the death of the speaker: whether his grave will be here or elsewhere, is to us uncertain; O remember that those icy fingers were once employed in writing sermons for you, those lips, that are now chained in gloomy silence, were once speaking to you in accents that were sounding from Sabbath to Sabbath, and from year to year within the walls of this house: that his soul has taken its flight to yonder tribunal, where a rehearsal of those discourses, that you have heard from him, will be made in your ears, and before the assembled universe. Ministers, who have finished their course, may be useful to people after they are dead: this is an idea suggested by a dying apostle, II Peter 1:15. Moreover, I will endeavour that you may be able after my decease to have these things always in remembrance. How far, consistent with truth, and christian modesty, I may adopt the language of the holy apostle, verse 26, will be better known hereafter, Wherefore I take you to record this day, that I am pure from the blood of all men: for I have not shunned to declare unto you the whole counsel of God.

It was for your sake principally that your fathers called me here, they sat under my ministry but a short time, their memory is still precious, and though dead still speak. O! for their sake, and for your soul's sake, and above all for the sake of him that created you, hearken to the things that concern your eternal interest. Could you consider your former minister worthy of any respect, I beseech you to manifest it by preparing to meet him, and be a crown of his rejoicing in the day of the Lord Jesus. You that are young will be those who will compose this society within a short time: we who are advanced in life must soon leave you.

Let me warn you against Sabbath breaking, against neglecting the public worship of God. Willingly and promptly contribute to the support of the gospel ministry, as you would prosper in this world, and meet your judge in peace. Beware of carnal dissipation, a sin which I have often warned you against. Beware of slander and detraction, those banes of society; the influence of which, even among us, you cannot be strangers to. According to scripture testimony, they have their origin in hell, James 3:6. and are incorporated with characters not very ornamental to human nature, nor do they stand fair candidates for the kingdom of heaven, I Cor. 6:9, 10. Know ye not that the unrighteous shall not inherit the kingdom of God? be not deceived; neither fornicators, nor idolators, nor adulterers, nor effeminate, nor abusers of themselves with mankind; nor thieves, nor covetous, nor drunkards, nor REVILERS, nor extortioners, shall inherit the kingdom of God.

Suffer me to warn you against false doctrines, such as are pleasing to the carnal heart. The inventions of men are skilful in exciting prejudices to the plain truths of the gospel:—hence it is, that faithful ministers are accused with being too pointed and unpolite in their discourses. Beware of false teachers, and of being led astray by the errors of the present day. Remember these are damnable *heresies* as well as damnable *practises*. Paul predicted this danger, verse 29: For I know this that after my departing shall grevious wolves enter in among you, not sparing the flock. But, beloved, I would hope better things of you, things that accompany salvation, though I thus speak. Dear children, and lambs of the flock, you have in a sense for a time been committed to my care; with the tenderest affection I would, in the arms of faith, bear you to that divine Saviour, who has said, suffer little children to come unto me, and forbid them not: for of such is the kingdom of God.

May your cheerful hosannahs fill this house, when your fathers and mothers, shall sleep in dust.

My friends in general,

Whatever we have seen amiss in each other, it becomes us to exercise forgiveness, as we hope God, for Christ's sake hath forgiven us, and as we would find mercy in that day. How often have our united prayers ascended up in this house; may we not forget each other for time to come. Live in peace and may the God of peace be with you. May my family have a share in your affections, and intercessions, who have been brought up among you; they will doubtless soon be left without parents. May the wife of my youth, who has been my companion in tribulation, whose health and strength, and domestic ease have been sacrificed and devoted to your service; should she survive me, not be forgotten. As I still continue to reside among you, should you at any time be destitute of a minister on a sick bed, be ready to send for me; it will be the rejoicing of my heart to do all I can to comfort you in the hour of distress, and to facilitate the groans and terrors of a dying moment; I request the same from you, as there is opportunity.

And now brethren, I commend you to God, and to the word of his grace, which is able to build you up, and to give you an inheritance among all them which are sanctified. AMEN.

Mystery Developed

The sensational trial of the Boorn brothers for the alleged murder of Russell Colvin led to the issuing of a three-part pamphlet published in two editions in Hartford in 1820. It consisted of "A Narrative of the Whole Transaction" by Haynes, his sermon "upon the development of the mystery" entitled "The Prisoner Released," and a sketch of the case by S. Putnam Waldo, Esq.

The Boorn case became an important example in American jurisprudence of the dangers of circumstantial evidence. Using its "dead-alive" theme, Wilkie Collins used the case as the basis of his short story "John Jago's Ghost." William H. Robinson says Haynes' narrative, despite its intent of reporting events, can be called the first short story by an Afro-American.

———

Mystery Developed; or, Russel Colvin, (Supposed to be Murdered,) in Full Life: and Stephen and Jesse Boorn, (His Convicted Murderers,) Rescued from Ignominious Death by Wonderful Discoveries.

Narrative

The wonderful occurrence that has lately been exhibited at Manchester, in relation to the supposed murder, may be ranked among those rare events that seldom, if ever take place. The public mind has been uncommonly agitated. Reports have been circulated, tending to create prejudices, and lead astray. That many things without any foundation in truth, should be spread abroad in a matter so astonishing and interesting, could hardly have been expected. The writer of this narrative believes that there are many things in relation to the event, that may be useful and entertaining, and calculated to throw some light upon this mysterious subject.

Mr. Barna Boorn and his wife, the parents of Stephen and Jesse Boorn, are advanced in age, have been residents of Manchester for about 40 years, and are persons of respectability: they have three sons and two daughters; they all have families. Sally Boorn was married to Russel Colvin eighteen years ago. They have children: their eldest son's name is Lewis; another is Rufus. Of the latter his father was very fond, and used often to carry him from place to place on his back. Colvin had been in a state of mental derangement for a long time, by which he was incapacitated to attend to the concerns of his family, who were dispersed among the connections. Colvin's parents formerly resided in Manchester; but are both dead. He has a brother supposed to live in the western country. He has a sister named Clarissa, who is mentioned in Mr. Chadwick's letter. The sudden departure of Colvin, which was seven years ago the 7th day of May last, excited some inquiry about what had become of him; but as he had frequently absented, (at one time he was gone nine or ten months, and was heard of at Rhode-Island.) it was expected he would return as usual. There were, however, some surmises that possibly he had been murdered. Many observations were made by Stephen and Jesse Boorn that excited jealousies that they were guilty.

With respect to *dreaming*, about which so much has been said and published, it may be remarked, that there has been much said about the murder, and conjectures where it was committed; and where the body might be deposited. By this the mind was prepared to receive similar impressions when asleep; and there was nothing miraculous in the matter, about which so many strange things have been circulated. The dream is here related for the sole purpose of correcting those fabulous reports, of which the human mind is too susceptible.—A Mr. Boorn (Uncle to the aforesaid Stephen and Jesse, and a gentleman of respectability, whose character is unimpeachable.) dreamed that Russel Colvin came to his bed side, and told him that he had been murdered, and he must follow him, and he would lead him to the spot where he was buried: this was repeated three times. The deposit was the place talked of previous to the dream, which was where an house had formerly stood, under which was a hole about four feet square, which was made for the purpose of burying potatoes and now filled up. This pit was opened, and nothing discovered but a large knife, a penknife, and a button. Mrs. Colvin, anterior to their being presented to her described them accurately, and on seeing them said they belonged to her husband, except the small knife.

An impression made on the mind by previous circumstances, may dictate a dream, which is commonly the case, and nothing strange, should it have influence in the present affair, in *searching* after truth; but that any decision was predicated in the least on such nocturnal fancies, we have no evidence. They were not mentioned on occasions of enquiry, before court or jury. Perhaps the court had never heard of them. It is certainly to be regretted that such seeds of delusion should be disseminated among mankind, and that truth and propriety do not receive more attention previous to such publications. Much has been said about skulls and bones being found of the human kind. I think we are without sufficient evidence that anything of this nature has been discovered. A circumstance took place that excited much attention. A lad walking from Mr. Barna Boorn's at a small distance with his dog, a hollow stump standing near the path engaged the notice of the spaniel, which ran to the place and back again several times, lifting up his feet on the boy, with whining notes, as though to draw the attention of his little master to the place; which had the effect. A cluster of bones were drawn from the roots of the stump by the dog's paws. Further examination was made, and in the cavity of the stump were found two toe nails, to appearance belonging to a human foot; others were discovered in a crumbled state, which to appearance, had passed through the fire. It was now concluded by many that some fragments of the body of Colvin were found. The cluster of bones were brought before the court of inquiry. They were examined by a number of physicians, who thought them to be human; one of the profession, however, thought otherwise. A Mr. Salisbury, about four years ago, had his leg amputated, which was buried at the distance of four or five miles. The limb was dug up, and, by comparing, it was universally determined that the bones were not human. However, it was clear that the nails were human, and so appeared to all beholders. The bones were in a degree pulverised, but some pieces were in a tolerable state of preservation. Suspicions were excited that the body was burnt, and some part not consumed, cast into the stump and other bones put among them for deception. Sometime after the departure of Colvin, a barn belonging to Mr. Barna Boorn was consumed by fire accidentally: it was conjectured that the body was taken up and concealed under the floor of the barn and mostly consumed. About that time a log-heap was burnt by the Boorns near the place where the body was supposed to be deposited: it was thought by some that it was consumed there.

Some indeed looked upon the manner of the discovery as a kind of prodigy; others with more propriety that there was nothing marvellous in the affair; that the dog was allured to the spot by scent or game, which was common to the species. The attention of people was greatly excited; they had strong prepossessions that murder had been committed; by which some were prepared to look even on common things as supernatural. But still, as has before been observed, none of these things were introduced or even mentioned in any part of the examination or trial. The strange disappearance of Colvin, his not being heard of, together with some things that took place on the day he was missing, could not fail to create strong suspicions that he had been murdered. Evidence was adduced, that on the day of his departure, a quarrel commenced between him and his brethren, which led to believe he had fallen a victim. But, after all, the evidence was circumstantial, though the general evidence was that the prisoners were guilty. Some thought that it was best to dismiss Jesse from any further examination, which had commenced on Tuesday the 27th day of April. He was, however, still kept in custody. Search was made on Tuesday, Wednesday, Thursday and Friday, for the body, during which time those discoveries were made above alluded to. Jesse was on the eve of being set at liberty, but on Saturday, about ten o'clock, he with a trembling voice observed, that the first time he had an idea his brother Stephen had murdered Colvin was when he was here last winter: he then stated that he and Russel were hoeing in the Glazier lot, that there was a quarrel between them, and Colvin attempted to run away; that he struck him with a club or stone, on the back part of his neck or head, and had fractured his skull and supposed he was dead. He observed that he could not tell what had become of the body. He mentioned many places where perhaps it might be found. Search was accordingly made, but to no purpose.

The authority issued a warrant to apprehend Stephen, who about two years before had removed to Denmark, Lewis County, State of New-York, 198 miles. Capt. Truman Hill, grand juryman for the town of Manchester, Esquire Raymond, and Mr. R. Anderson, set out for Denmark, and arrived there in three days. They called on Mr. Eleazer S. Sylvester, inn-keeper, who in the night, together with a Mr. Orange Clark, and Mr. Hooper, belonging to the town, accompanied them to the house of the supposed criminal. Mr. Clark went in first and began some conversation about temporal concerns; the others surrounded the house, and he was easily taken. The surprise and distress of Mrs. Boorn on this occasion is not easily described: it excited the compassion of those who had come to take away her husband, and they made her some presents. The prisoner was put in irons, and was brought to Manchester on the 15th day of May. He peremptorily asserted innocence, and declared he knew nothing about the murder of his brother-in-law. The prisoners were kept apart for a time, and assigned to separate cells. Nothing material transpired, and they were afterwards confined in one room. Stephen denied the evidence brought against him by Jesse, and treated him with severity. Both the prisoners were repeatedly admonished to pay the strictest regard to truth. Many days were taken up in public examinations of the reputed criminals. Evidence was brought forward which was much against them. Lewis, son of Colvin, testified that he saw his uncle Stephen knock down his father, was frightened and ran home. This witness is before the public. Jesse Boorn, after an interview with his brother, denied that Stephen ever told him that he killed Colvin, and that what he had reported about him was false. Evidence appeared so strong against the prisoners that they were bound over to await their trial at the sitting of the Supreme Court, to be holden at Manchester, the third Tuesday of September.

During the interval, the writer frequently visited them in his official capacity, but did not discover any symptoms of compunction; but they persisted in declaring their innocence, with appeals to Heaven. Stephen, in particular, at times, appeared absorbed in passion and impatience. One day I introduced the example of Christ under sufferings as a pattern worthy of his imitation: he exclaimed, "I am as innocent as Jesus Christ!" for which extravagant expression I reproved him: he replied, "I don't mean that I am guiltless as he was, I know I am a great sinner; but I am as innocent of killing Colvin as he was." The Court sat in September; a judicious and impressive charge was given to the grand jury by his Honor Judge Doolittle, and a bill of indictment was presented against Stephen and Jesse Boorn, but as it was not a full court, the trial could not commence, according to a late act of the legislature of this state.

The Court was accordingly adjourned to the 26th of October, 1819. It was with much difficulty that a jury was obtained; but few could be found who had not expressed their opinion against the prisoners. The Hon. Judge Skinner and Mr. L. Sergeant were counsel for the prisoners. Mr. C. Sheldon, late state's attorney, was employed in behalf of the state. The counsel on both sides discovered much zeal and ability. The trial commenced on Tuesday the 27th day of October, and continued until Saturday night following.

An indictment was presented, containing a charge against Stephen and Jesse Boorn, for the murder of Russel Colvin, to which they pled NOT GUILTY. The occasion excited uncommon attention. Six hundred people attended each day during the trial. Much evidence was introduced which was rejected by the Court as being irrelevant. The case was given to the jury, after a short, judicious and impressive charge by his Honor Judge Doolittle, which was followed by a lengthy and appropriate one, by the Hon. Judge Chase. The jury retired, and within about one hour returned; and in compliance with a request of Mr. Skinner, they were severally enquired of whether they had agreed upon a verdict, and each agreed that they had found both of the prisoners guilty of the murder charged against them. The verdict was then publicly read by the clerk. After a short recess, his Honor Judge Chase, with the most tender and sympathetic emotion, which he was unable to suppress, pronounced the awful sentence, "that the criminals be remanded back to prison, and that on the 28th day of January next, between the hours of ten and two o'clock, they be hanged by the neck until each of them be dead! and may the Lord have mercy on their souls."

None can express the confusion and anguish into which the prisoners were cast on hearing their doom. They requested by their counsel liberty to speak, which was granted. In sighs and broken accents, they asserted their innocence. The convulsion of nature attending Stephen at last, was so great as to render him unable to walk; but was supported by others, and carried to prison. The compassion of some was excited, especially towards Jesse, which inclined them immediately to send a petition to the legislature, then sitting at Montpelier, praying that the punishment of the criminals might be commuted for that of imprisonment for life. But few, however, signed the petition in favor of Stephen. The assembly spent several days on the subject, and finally granted the request of Jesse, yeas 104, nays 31. The request of Stephen was negatived in the house, yeas 42, nays 97. The decision of the Assembly was brought to Manchester by His Excellency Gov. Galusha, and immediately communicated to the prisoners. Jesse received the news with peculiar satisfaction; while Stephen was greatly depressed, being wholly left without hope. Jesse lamented that his brother could not share in the same comparative blessing with him, and that they could not be fellow-prisoners together. Little did these brothers think that the fate of Stephen would terminate more favorable than that of Jesse, and be the cause of a more speedy deliverance. 'Tis often the case, that the darkest dispensations of divine providence are presages of the rising morning. This should teach us always to trust in the Lord, and consider that although clouds and darkness are round about him, yet justice and judgment are the habitation of his throne.

On the 29th day of October, Jesse took a final farewell of his brother, of his friends, and family at Manchester, and was carried to the State-prison at Windsor, expecting to spend the remainder of his life there. None can express the melancholy situation of Stephen, the poor prisoner: separated from his wife and children, parents and friends, under sentence of death, without hope. I visited him frequently with sympathy and grief, and endeavoured to turn his mind on the things of another world; telling him that as all human means failed, he must look to God, as the only way of deliverance. I advised him to read the holy scriptures, to which he consented, if he could be allowed a candle, as his cell was dark; this request was granted; and I often found him reading. He was at times calm; and again impatient. The interview I had with him a few days before the news came that it was likely that Colvin was alive, was very affecting. He says to me, "Mr. Haynes, I see no way but I must die: every thing works against me; but I am an innocent man: this you will know after I am dead." He burst into a flood of tears, and said, "What will become of my poor wife and children; they are in needy circumstances, and I love them better than life itself." I told him God would take care of them. He replied, "I don't want to die. I wish they would let me live even in this situation, some longer: perhaps something will take place that may convince people that I am innocent." I was about to leave the prison, when he said, "Will you pray with me?" He arose with his heavy chains on his hands and legs, being also chained down to the floor, and stood on his feet during prayer, with deep and bitter sighings. A Mr. Taber Chadwick, of Shrewsbury, Monmouth County, New-Jersey, brother-in-law of Mr. Wm. Polhamus, in Dover, N.J. where Colvin had lived ever since April, 1813, seeing the account of the trial of the Boorns at Manchester, he wrote the letter that has been so often published. (Mr. Chadwick and Mr. Polhamus live distant from each other about 40 miles.) When the letter came to town, every one was struck with consternation. A few partly believed; but the main doubted. "It cannot be that Colvin is alive," was the general cry. Mr. Chadwick's letter was carried to the prisoner, and read to Stephen; the news was so overwhelming that, to use his own language, nature could scarcely sustain the shock; but as there was some doubt as to the truth of the report, it tended to prevent an immediate dissolution. He observed to me, "that he believed that had Colvin then made his appearance, it would have caused immediate death. Even now, a faintness was created that was painful to endure." Soon a letter was sent to Manchester, informing that there was a probability that the man supposed to be murdered, was yet alive, and that Mr. Whelply, of New-York, formerly of Manchester, and who was intimately acquainted with Colvin, had actually gone to New-Jersey in quest of him. Thus there was increasing evidence in confirmation of the letter. As soon as Mr. Whelply had returned to New-

York, he immediately wrote, "that he had Colvin with him." A Mr. Rempton, a former acquaintance of Russel's, wrote to his friend here, "that while writing, Russel Colvin is before me." A New-York paper announced his arrival also, and that he would soon set out for Vermont. Notwithstanding all this, many gave no credit to the report, but considered it a mere deception. Large bets were made. On the 22nd of December, Colvin arrived in the stage with Mr. Whelply at Bennington. The County Court being then in session, all were filled with astonishment and surprise. The Court suspended business for some hours, to gaze upon one who in a sense had been dead, and is alive again. Many who formerly knew him, now saw that there could be no deception: Russel could call many of them by name. Toward evening, the same day, he came to Manchester; notice being given that he was near at hand, a cry was heard, "Colvin has come!" The stage was driven swiftly, and a signal extended: it was all bustle and confusion. The stage stopped at Capt. Black's Inn. The village was all alive; all were running to obtain sight of the man, who they had no doubt was dead, and had come as a kind of Saviour to one who was devoted to the gibbet. Some, like Thomas, in another case, would not believe without tangible evidence. People gathered around him with such eagerness, as to render it impossible to press through the crowd, or obtain a sight of him. Almost all his old acquaintance he could recognize, and call them by name. Several guns were discharged for joy; people ran to different parts of the town to give notice. The prison door was unbolted, the news proclaimed to Stephen, that Colvin had come! The welcome reception given it by the joyful prisoner, need not be mentioned. The chains on his arms were taken off, while those on his legs remained: being impatient of an interview with him who had come to bring salvation, they met. Colvin gazed upon the chains and asked, "What is that for?" Stephen answers, "Because they say I murdered you." Russel replied, "You never hurt me." His wife and friends and people from every part of the town were collected—Joy and gladness sat on every countenance. Many shouts of rejoicing were heard, together with the discharge of cannon. The news having been spread, that Colvin had come to Manchester, the next day there was a large collection from the neighbouring towns, who met to behold the returned exile, and to express their high satisfaction on the occasion. I think I can say, that I scarcely ever saw more exultation and tender sympathy, on any occasion. Not less than fifty cannon were discharged, and at a seasonable hour they returned to their places of abode. Mrs. Colvin came to see her husband, but he took but little notice of her, intimating that she did not belong to him. Some of his children came to see him, of whom he appeared somewhat fond. He wondered how they came here, as he said, "he left them in New-Jersey, and must take them back.["] He fancies that he is the owner of the farm belonging to Mr. Polhamus, in Dover; talks much about his property there. It is observed by those who formerly knew him, that his mental derangement is much greater than it was when he left Manchester. Many things that took place years ago he can recollect with accuracy, and describes with a degree of propriety. He discovers a placid and harmless disposition. The family where he resided in New-Jersey, are fond of him, wish him to return, and spend his days with them, of which he seems very desirous: accordingly, on the 29th day of December, he set out from Manchester, with Mr. Whelply, for New-York, who engaged to convey him from thence to his former habitation, in New-Jersey: having received remuneration from this town for that purpose. There it is probable Colvin will end his days. Stephen is not in a state of confinement, but lives with his family. Jesse is still in State's prison, has heard the news, and has wrote to his attorney to use means for his release. It is probable that the honourable court will provide some way by which they may obtain a legal dismission at their session, which is at Bennington on the 3d Tuesday of January inst.

The writer would observe, that publishing the above narrative, was the effect of friendly importunity. It may be expected that imputations of an unwarranted nature, on the town of Manchester, and on the civil authority of Vermont, will be made; but I am fully of the opinion, was the matter well understood, that the judicious and candid would be satisfied.

It must be acknowledged, that it is one of the most mysterious events recorded in the annals of time. There are circumstances attending it which are still inveloped in obscurity, that human sagacity cannot explore.—Has there murder been committed at Manchester? is a question often suggested by people abroad. We are ready to answer, that evidence, to prove such an event, does not appear. One thing we are sure of, that Russel Colvin has not been murdered; and that the prisoners condemned are, and ought to be exonerated.

LEMUEL HAYNES

Manchester, VT. 1820

ADDITION.—About four years after Colvin was missing, some children of Mr. Johnson's near the place where it was supposed that the murder had been committed, found a hat; they carried it home: all agreed that it was Colvin's hat: it was in such an injured state that it was pulled in pieces and thrown away.—Colvin was unwilling to return to Vermont with Mr. Whelply, who was obliged to have recourse to stratagem. A young woman of Russel's acquaintance agreed to accompany him, pretending that they only designed a visit to New-York. While there she was missing, which excited some uneasiness in the mind of the returning exile. While staying a few days at New-York, to prevent his returning, Mr. Whelply told him there were British men of war laying in the harbor, and unless he kept within doors, he would be kidnapped. This had the desired effect. Colvin when he set out for Manchester, concluded that he was on his way home to New-Jersey, and never perceived the deception until he came to Bennington, and saw many people with whom he had formerly been acquainted, and he was filled with surprise.

The Prisoner Released

It is likely Haynes' sermon on the Boorn case was also issued as a separate pamphlet, but no copies are known.

The Prisoner Released. A Sermon, Delivered at Manchester, Vermont, Lord's Day, Jan. 9th, 1820. On the Remarkable Interposition of Divine Providence in the Deliverance of Stephen and Jesse Boorn, Who Had Been under Sentence of Death, for the Supposed Murder of Russel Colvin. To which are Added, Some Particulars Relating Thereto.

"That thou mayest say to the prisoners, go forth; to them that are in darkness, shew yourselves."

Is. 49:9

Hieroglyphical illustrations were very common among the eastern nations; which shews the propriety of their being so much used in the sacred volume. The wretched and forlorn state of mankind, is set forth by metaphors the most apt and appropriate. The character and work of the ever blessed Redeemer, is designated in terms calculated to meet the exigencies of fallen creatures. Are men said to be *blind*, Jesus is exhibited as the light of the world; as one who has eye-salve and can open the eyes.—Are men said to be *poor*, Christ is compared to gold who can make them rich.—Are they *naked*, he has white raiment to clothe them, that the shame of their nakedness need not appear. Are men *starving*, Jesus is the bread of life. Are we in *bondage* or in *prison*, Christ is anointed to proclaim liberty to the captives, and the opening of the prison to them that are bound—Is. 61:1.—He says to the prisoners, go forth; to them that are in darkness, shew yourselves!

Prisons are of ancient date—they have their origin in human depravity. They are places where criminals are confined to restrain them from acts of

213

violence, and to secure the safety of the commonwealth. There is doubtless reference had in my text to the emancipation of the Jews from a long and distressing captivity, which is emblematical of the conversion of sinners, that are in spiritual thraldom: but yet, prisoners of hope, could the late wonderful providence of God in delivering our fellow mortals, be improved for the emancipation of precious souls from the prison of death and hell, O! with what thanksgiving, with what ecstacies of joy should we hail such an event! To improve it to this purpose is my main design on this occasion, and I am persuaded, my brethren, that you will this day bid me God speed, and not withhold your assistance in a matter so solemn and important.

Wherein there *is*, and *is not* a similarity in the matters before us, is order proposed.

1. Prisoners are in a state of *confinement* by an act of the civil authority, and are condemned by law: the murderer for shedding blood: so the wicked are arrested by an act of the court of Heaven, and are condemned already—John 3:18. The indictment against the wicked is very high: God makes inquisition for blood, Ps. 9:12. Is it not more than probable that the blood of a husband, a wife, a brother, a sister, a child, is crying from a repository of the dead against you, with accents not less severe and significant than the blood of a murdered Abel! Yea, perhaps from the prison of eternal despair, to which place your unfaithfulness has consigned them.—You are indicted for suicide, for destroying yourselves—Hos. 13:9. Neither does the charge stop here:—You stand convicted before the court of Heaven for shedding the precious blood of the Son of God, or making a violent attempt on the life of the God-Man Mediator; for piercing the Saviour—Zech. 12:10. For crucifying the son of God afresh, and for putting him to open shame—Heb. 6:6. Does not a groaning creation, adverse Providences, and a guilty conscience, bear a coincident testimony against you?

2. Prisoners are cut off in a great measure from human society as unfit for their communion and fellowship. So it is with the wicked—they separate themselves. Saints and sinners are prone to keep at a distance from each other.—The prisoner converses principally with his fellows in Jail, while those abroad are not fond of their place of abode, nor of their company. While constrained to stay with them, they are prone to exclaim in the language of David, 'Woe is me that I sojourn in Mesech, that I dwell in the tents of Kedar.' Ps. 120:5. Men naturally are deprived of the blessing of society, and the privileges of the children of God.

3. Another distressing circumstance that attends prisoners is, they are in a state of *darkness*, as mentioned in the text.—The light of the sun does not shine upon them. The wicked are said to *sit* in darkness, to *walk* in darkness, to *love* darkness, etc. They are blind to their own characters and the character of God—to their own danger, and to the only way of escape. Wicked men behold nothing of the divine glory in his word, or in his works. Their eyes are blinded and they cannot see. Like prisoners confined in a dungeon, no cheering ray can penetrate the impenetrable wall, or illuminate the solitary mansion.

4. A prison is a place of distress and trouble. What a wretched state was Jeremiah in when cast into the dungeon, where was no water, and his feet sunk down into the mire! Eastern monarchs, when they had cast their wretched captives into a dungeon, never gave themselves the trouble of enquiring about them; but let them lie a long time in that miserable condition, wholly destitute of relief, and disregarded, says Bishop Lowth.—Prisoners among the Romans were fettered and confined in a singular manner. One end of the chain, which was of a commodious length, was fixed about the right arm of the prisoner, and the other about the left arm of a soldier. Imprisonment, says Dr. Doddridge is a much greater punishment in the eastern part of the world than here. State criminals, especially when condemned to it, are not only forced to submit to a very mean and scanty allowance, but are frequently loaded with clogs and yokes of heavy wood, in which they cannot either lie or sit at ease; and by frequent scourgings, and sometimes by rackings, are quickly brought to an untimely end. These instances are introduced to illustrate the propriety of the appropriate allusion in my text. The wicked are represented as being under the bonds of iniquity—as perishing with hunger—as travailing in pain all their days, and like the troubled sea that cannot rest.

5. The prisoner assigned to an impregnable castle, is in a state of confinement; he cannot extricate himself. His case is in a sense hopeless and helpless, without an interposition of divine power, as in the case of Daniel and Silas and Peter. Sinners in scriptural bondage, cannot deliver themselves, being bound with the cords of their sins, and are morally unable to burst their bands asunder, scale or break through the adamantine walls of their iniquities.

6. Imprisonment is a state of *degradation*. Such are despised and treated with contempt. So the wicked are considered as out-casts, forlorn, vile and despicable, in the sight of God. They are said to be clothed with shame, like

prisoners having on them filthy garments—like wretched captives covered with vermin, loathed and abhorred by the Almighty, and will be treated with infinite contempt, at the day of judgment.

7. Criminals have a time appointed by authority for their execution, when they must be brought forth, and in a public manner experience a shameful death. So the sentence is pronounced by the judge of quick and dead, against all the finally impenitent, and in the council of God, the day of their death is appointed by an unalterable decree of Heaven.—The wicked is reserved to the day of destruction—they shall be brought forth to the day of wrath.—Job 21:30.

8. The poor prisoner in jail is an object of pity and commiseration. They excite the tender sympathy of the humane and benevolent. Their friends mourn their sorrowful state, and tremble at the approach of the day of their execution. Who can describe the distresses of a parent, a brother or sister, on the reflection of the state of a child, a brother, doomed to an untimely, and ignominious death! They bedew their pillow with tears, and wearisome days and nights are appointed to them. This, my friends, is but an imperfect picture of those agonies and pains that God's people sometimes experience, by reflecting on the state of sinners doomed to the first and second death. Paul travailed in pain for the souls of men; was in great heaviness and sorrow of heart. "O that my head were waters, and my eyelids a fountain of tears! Rivers of water run down mine eyes," were the exclamations of holy David, on account of those who were under the condemnatory sentence of God's holy law, and every moment exposed to its awful infliction!

2dly. But it may be useful to draw a contrast between the two cases before us.

1. Prisoners committed to jail among us are assigned there by *men*, or human tribunals, and not always sanctioned by the Almighty. But the wicked are doomed to punishment by an act issued from the Court of Heaven. "Jesus, who is appointed Judge, pronounces the awful sentence, 'Let him be taken from among men, from the prison on earth, and delivered to the tormentors, to suffer eternal death!' " The denunciation is from the majesty of Heaven, and fills the trembling criminal with terror and dismay. He shudders! he sinks! like an affrighted Belshazzar. His countenance is changed; the joints of his limbs are loosed, and his knees smite one against another! Prisoners condemned by earthly judiciaries, may entertain hopes that they may possibly escape the hands of men, or have the sentence reversed, or the punishment commuted; but when it is denounced by the Lord Jesus Christ,

the incorrigible sinner can have no hope in his present state. He cannot flee from the hands of the Almighty, nor support himself amidst his inflexible wrath.—God will not meet him as a man, but will take vengeance,—Is. 47:3. His hands cannot be strong, nor his heart endure, when God shall deal with him.

2. When the sentence is passed on criminals, they can sometimes appeal to higher authority, and obtain favour: have a new trial, plead an error of court, or a commutation of punishment; but there is no appeal from the Court of Heaven; no mitigation of sentence; but amidst all the schemes and inventions of men, the council of the Lord that shall stand.

3. Criminals among men are allowed council to plead for them; and their cause is often ably defended by gentlemen of the bar. But this will not be admitted before the tribunal of Christ. None will even dare to undertake for them, before the assembled universe: to none of the saints can they turn; their cause will appear so unreasonable and hopeless, that no man or angel will dare to say a word in their behalf.

4. Those confined in prison for crimes, bear a small proportion to the world in general. The rapid increase of late of men of this character, is an alarming consideration, and calls all classes of men, especially rulers, to vigilance, humiliation and prayer. But blessed be God, humanity and philanthropy are still distinguishing characteristics of our land in general; and there is a laudable disposition, prevalent among our citizens, to apprehend and detect those, who by their enormous crimes, forfeit their liberties and their lives, into the hands of civil justice. Murderers in our land and on the high seas, cannot elude the band of the pursuer. Although they flee to foreign countries, they are detected and remanded to our shores, to receive the punishment due to their crimes. But have we not reason to fear that the number of those who are in a state of spiritual bondage and imprisonment, is very great, vastly exceeding those who have been made free by the son of God; and still have a dreadful verdict laying against them in the Supreme Court above. Not to mention heathen lands, whose dreary regions have never been illuminated by the exhilarating beams of the Sun of Righteousness. How few comparatively, even under the light of the gospel, who are called upon to go forth from their wretched confinement, and shew themselves, and obey the heavenly mandate!

5. The imperfections incident to all men and all courts of judicature, renders them liable to wrong verdicts. The most prudent and experienced cannot plead exemption. The innocent may be condemned, and the guilty go

with impunity. But the great searcher of hearts cannot be deceived. Every decision is dictated by infinite wisdom and infinite goodness: he can by no means clear the guilty or condemn the innocent. God will judge the people with perfect equity, and justice and judgment are the habitation of his throne.—Ps. 89:14.

II. Let us attend to the other illustration in the text, which implies deliverance, "Go forth—shew yourselves."—The author of it is the Lord Jesus Christ. That THOU mayest say, viz. the person designated or appointed by the Father, see verse 8th, thus saith the Lord, in an acceptable time have I heard thee, and in a day of salvation have I helped thee: and I will preserve thee, and give thee for a covenant of the people, to establish the earth, to cause to inherit the desolate heritages.

This deliverance of sinners is consistent with the law of God, and dignity of divine government. It is by the blood of the covenant that prisoners are sent out of the pit wherein there is no water, Zech. 9:11. It cannot be admitted in any other way, as intimated in the text, "That thou *mayest;*" suggesting the idea that the thing may not take place on any other condition. The Lord Jesus Christ brings about the deliverance of his elect, through the instrumentality of means; not that they are efficacious; for after all, God gives the increase. God is said to save men by the foolishness of preaching—I Cor. 1:21. In the late instance among us, it was God who wrought the salvation; but it was brought about by means, and very unexpected. There were a series of events that might be traced; but they were all directed by the invisible hand of him, who worketh all things after the counsel of his own will—Eph. 1:11. In delivering men from the bondage of sin and death, God defers it to an extreme hour, that his power and grace may clearly appear to which men are apt to be exceedingly blind. The sentiment suggested may derive a degree of illustration by the late providence of God, with which we are all acquainted. Measures were used in vain to deliver from punishment. Court and jury were unanimously against the prisoners. The public voice pronounced the verdict just; and were not altogether satisfied with the commutation of the punishment of death for that of imprisonment for life, granted to one of them by legislative authority. With respect to Mr. Stephen Boorn, there was ninety-seven against forty-two members in the house who were opposed to affording him any relief, so that he "was left to suffer death agreeable to sentence." Able counsel was employed—No hope of escaping out of custody; being cast into the inner prison, bound in triple chains, and carefully guarded. The object of going in search of the exile, supposed to be murdered, was pretty much relinquished. The advertisement published at the request of the criminals, was not a means of the information that Colvin was yet alive; as Mr. Chadwick's letter was anterior to his having seen that publication. The time of execution was drawing nigh, and not a gleam of hope from any quarter. Until, behold from a far country, the Lord raised up an instrument of deliverance, a stranger to us all. It was *great, seasonable, satisfactory* and *sure*.

It may be worthy of remark, and tend to illustrate divine interposition, that Mr. Chadwick was not in the habit of taking the Evening Post, which contained the trial at Manchester, and which inclined him to write the letter, by which information was obtained that the man supposed to be murdered was yet alive; but had the paper put into his hand by what we are wont to call mere accident.

> "Just in the last distressing hour,
> The Lord displays delivering power:
> The mount of danger is the place
> Where we shall see surprising grace."

When God says to prisoners, Go forth! shew yourselves! What power in the word! Their chains are taken off, the bars of the prison house broken. With joy they leave the solitary dungeon! They are quickened and made to stand on their feet, and walk at large, and are restored to the arms of their friends, and to the liberties and immunities of God's people. The poor prisoner leaps for joy—comes to the light—shews himself—is beheld with raptures of transport—appears in a different point of light to all beholders—shews himself as one exonerated, and to whom there is no condemnation, is a fellow citizen with the saints. To open the blind eyes, to bring out the prisoners from the prison, and them that sit in darkness, out of the prison-house. Sing unto the Lord a new song; and his praise from the end of the earth, ye that go down to the sea, and all that is therein; the isles, and the inhabitants thereof. Let the wilderness and the cities thereof lift up their voice, the villages that Kedar doth inhabit: let the inhabitants of the rock sing, let them shout from the top of the mountains. Let them give glory unto the Lord, and declare his praise in the islands—Is. 42. And the ransomed of the Lord shall return, and come to Zion with songs, and everlasting joy upon their heads; they shall obtain joy and gladness, and sorrow and sighing shall flee away—Is. 35:10.

There is certainly a degree of likeness in the two cases before us, or the deliverance of men out of common jails, and the sentence denounced against them, and the freeing the wicked from the bondage of sin and condemnation.—To draw a striking contrast may be useful on the present occasion.

1. In the case of the former their trial is before earthly courts—their sentence denounced by them; but the deliverance of the wicked from the power and dominion of sin, is the special and immediate work of God, or the mighty agency of the Holy Spirit. The people of God may work; ministers may preach, and say to prisoners, come forth! but it will be foolishness; it will be ineffectual, until the arm of the Lord be revealed. Then, and not till then, will the foundation of the prison be shaken, and all the doors opened, and the bands loosed.

2. Sinners confined in the prison of their sins, are unwilling to leave it—they love prison fare and company—love their chains—love darkness; and although the door is thrown wide open, and liberty proclaimed to the captives; yet they will not come forth, nor shew themselves; but exert their power and faculties to close the door, and deeper drive the massy bolts, and shut out every ray of divine light: it being painful to them. But men confined in earthly dungeons, when they hear the news of their emancipation, How do they leap to lose their chains, and bid adieu to their gloomy abode! O how welcome the invitation! Go forth out of darkness!—shew yourself! When a poor prisoner reflects on the many painful days spent in the melancholy cell, separated from dear connexions and friends, in expectation of a horrible death, O! how welcome the reversion of the doom! none but the experienced can form a conception.

3. 'Tis sometimes the case that criminals are acquitted on the principle of distributive justice; they are not found guilty of the crime alleged, or for which they were committed; but the wicked can never be acquitted in this way. They are fully guilty of the every crime with which they are charged. There can be no error in the testimony and decision to oppose or commute the punishment. No irrelevant witness can be admitted for or against the prisoner. 'Tis pardoning grace through a mediator that frees the penitent from the sanctions of the law.

4. The emancipation granted by human courts is only a reprieve of the body for a few years, months or days, perhaps hours or moments. Death may be inflicted by the hand of God before the time specified in the sentence

of civil authority. But the act of the Almighty frees the *soul* from the terrors of the first and second death.

When God delivers sinners from the slavery and bondage of their sins, and the sentence thereto annexed, he confers great blessing upon them; bestows many valuable gifts by which they are made rich.—Ps. 68:18. Thou hast ascended on high, thou hast led captivity captive; thou hast received GIFTS for men, yea, for the rebellious also. When men are liberated from prisons, people may be disposed to make them some remuneration; but it is only temporal good at best they can impart, which can only relieve them and family from bodily wants.

5. Persons exonerated by earthly judiciaries, are liable to arrests for new offences. Many have been acquitted from jails or state-prisons, but again commit crimes and are sentenced to death, and in a few months executed. Such instances of late have been within our observations. But those whom the Lord acquits will never again be arraigned before the court of Heaven and condemned. None can or dare lay any thing to their charge, so as to sentence them to death; for there is no condemnation to them: Rom. 8:1. There is an immutable and an eternal act of absolution issued for all past and future crimes.

The late remarkable occurrence or dispensations of divine providence among us, in relation to the prisoners condemned, and their wonderful deliverance, will form an epoch in the annals of history that will be transmitted to generations yet unborn. Reflections of a serious and interesting nature are suggested.

1. The imperfection of human nature, under peculiar advantages is clearly exhibited. Perhaps in no case were circumstantial evidence more clear and conclusive, or greater unanimity in court and jury, or coincidence in the public mind. But few who did hesitate to bring in their verdict of GUILTY. The wisdom, candor and integrity of the board of trial cannot be questioned. Neither are we disposed to impeach the witnesses in general. Even the prisoner himself had confessed the crime, and after all we are assured that they are innocent. It may prove a caution to us to look as favorable as possible on the side of innocency, and to the exercise of that charity that "hopeth all things," and not be too hasty in taking up a reproach against our neighbour—Ps. 15:3. Courts of judicature are hereby taught to proceed with the utmost deliberation and carefulness, especially in cases of life and death, and not decide without very clear and conclusive evidence.

(These remarks are not designed as the least reflection on the honourable Court who attended at Manchester. I have often observed, that during the trial, there appeared to be a favorable leaning in behalf of the criminals, and a very candid indulgence. Evidence not directly in point was not admitted. Mr. S. Boorn has repeatedly told me and others, that he did not blame the authority for deciding against him, considering the evidence adduced. This he has observed to me since the sitting of the Supreme Court.)

How far the opinion of our first commentaries on law ought to be regarded, is out of the preacher's province to determine; but a point to be discussed by gentlemen of the bar. "All presumptive evidence of felony should be admitted cautiously, (says Blackstone.) for the law holds that it is better that ten guilty persons escape, than that one innocent suffer: and Sir Matthew Hale in particular, lays down two rules, most prudent and necessary to be observed. "1. Never to convict a man for stealing the goods of a person unknown, merely because he will give no account how he came by them, unless an actual felony be proved of such goods. 2dly. Never to convict any person of murder or manslaughter, till at least the body be found dead; on account of two instances he mentions, where persons were executed for the murder of others who were then alive, but missing."

2. The final issue and termination of the event, so plainly in favor of the reputed criminals, should by no means be improved as a discouragement to search after iniquity, and use all proper measures to detect transgressors, and bring them to condign punishment. In apprehending criminals there are two objects proposed. viz. to find out the guilty, or clear the innocent. These ideas are inseparably involved. When the latter is effected, character is retrieved, the man honoured and restored to society, and the dignity and safety of the state secured. A more important point is obtained, even to the public, than if criminality were discovered.

If positive evidence in the minds of all must be obtained of offence, anterior to public process, it would render investigation in almost all cases unnecessary. That there were grounds for suspicion that murder had been committed at Manchester, none acquainted with all the circumstances will deny; and that it became an imperious duty to enquire into the matter, will not be disputed by the candid. Whether there has been too much, or too little attention paid to the matter, and whether every thing has been attended to in the best manner, would be to contend with the doctrine of human imperfection. The result is favorable, and we rejoice.

3. We are clearly taught, that there is a superintending providence, that directs all events; that the works of God are great and marvelous, and past finding out. The goodness of the Almighty is plainly illustrated. While he is one that will by no means clear the guilty; yet he will deliver the innocent in his own time and way.—"God will execute judgment for the oppressed—give food to the hungry: the Lord looseth the prisoners: He heareth the groaning of prisoners, to loose those who are appointed to death." If the Lord is so ready in such a wonderful way to rescue the bodies and lives of men from death, may we not argue from the less to the greater, and infer the infinite benignity of the Saviour, who delivers the souls of men from endless perdition. Verily the Lord is good, and ready to forgive.

4. We are evidently taught by reflecting on the late dispensation of the Almighty, the vast importance of paying a strict attention to truth and veracity, and that at all times, and under every trying circumstance. How pertinent that injunction of the apostle, Eph. 4:15—Speaking the truth in love. Those who have been the subjects of so much distress, cannot but see that the want of adhering properly to this important lesson, has been a fruitful source of their calamity and trouble, and how much pains and cost it has been the occasion of. Let parents inculcate this important duty on the minds of their children; and let every instance of vexation and sorrow to which a contrary conduct subjects us, teach us to pay the most sincere regard to truth and uprightness, as we would have the approbation of our Judge, and the testimony of a good conscience.

5. The subject is peculiarly interesting to those among us who have lately been remarkably emancipated from bondage, slavery and death. Was there ever a clearer display of divine interposition? and can they be blind to that Almighty hand that hath wrought deliverance? God has said to you that were prisoners, Go forth!—to you who were in darkness, shew yourselves! Human means were used in vain, especially for him who continued under sentence of death. Application to legislative authority only tended to render his case more desperate; as it diminished the power of the Governor and council to grant a reprieve. Nothing scarcely but the appearance of the supposed murdered exile, would satisfy the public mind, or reverse the sentence of death, and it was little to be expected. But amidst all these gloomy apprehensions, the arm of the Lord was revealed in your behalf, and has given incontestable evidence of your innocence. The prisoners released, especially the one present, will recognize those melancholy days and nights he has spent in the dreary dungeon; shut out from society, from your family,

and friends. I can never forget those many solitary hours I have spent with you, amidst that dismal habitation. I have in some sense been a kind of companion with you in tribulation. I have been an eye and an ear witness to your tears, agonies and groans, under the awful anticipations of an ignominious death, and of a speedy separation from the dear companion of your youth, and helpless children, whom you declared unto me were dearer to you than life itself. Had the event taken place who could relate the pitiful story to fatherless children! Could a broken hearted mother lead them to some obscure spot, and say, there, dear children, lies the remains of an unfortunate parent, who wished to be your support in life; the fondness of whose arms were wont to embrace you with parental affection! Could she point them to the gibbet, on which a father was suspended, and relate the melancholy disaster!—To conceal it would be improbable, and to relate it almost impossible. You ought to consider, that although you are restored to your family, yet God must be their support. That Almighty arm that has taken care of you and been your preserver, must also be their protector. Your anxious desire to be restored to your family, is granted and effected by him whose tender mercies are over all his works. You cannot but feel the obligations you are under of gratitude to Him, who has almost miraculously interposed in your behalf. Can you think on this without the most sincere emotions of praise and thanksgiving? Can you refrain from having an altar of praise erected in your house, to Him who has done such great things for you? Shall not the morning and evening sacrifice ascend like holy incense from your habitation?

This display of divine goodness should lead you to repentance—Rom. 2:4—Although you are found innocent of the charge alledged by an human court; yet with respect to other sins in common with your fellow sinners, you cannot plead exemption. 'Tis for our sins we are punished by the hand of God. 'Tis for our sins that others are suffered to afflict us. You cannot but see that some of your conduct during your imprisonment has had influence in the decision against you. By improper and wrong concessions, you have been led to self-crimination. I hope you will review your past conduct, and will be led to amendment of life. You have ingenuously confessed to me, that you have too much indulged yourself in imprudent and profane language, which has greatly been improved against you in your late trial. You have been sensible of this, and to your credit I mention it, you have promised to reform. The apostle James in relation to the tongue, says, 'Behold what a great matter a little fire kindleth!' The goodness of God in sparing you, is a sure pledge that he is willing to pardon and restore you to his favor. Oh! reflect on the wretched state that twenty days more would have introduced you, had you died in your sins. A more awful prison awaits the ungodly, where hope never comes. The sentence pronounced against you will doubtless soon be reversed; yet should you be found impenitent, the court of heaven still holds you a prisoner condemned, and the more awful execution may take place before the 28th of January. This day may form a kind of anniversary in your life: you will always remember it; and oh! may it during your abode on earth, be a day of thanksgiving to God for the signal display of his mercy towards you!

In this remarkable providence you can see judgment and mercy, chastisement and benignity. Affliction in subjecting you for months to a dark and gloomy prison in chains—in being reputed a murderer—cut off from society, your family, and lying under the sentence of death. But here is divine wisdom and goodness displayed, in reversing the sentence, retrieving your character, etc. Had you been exonerated by the court: or if the process had never commenced, 'tis probable that Colvin would never have been discovered, and a stigma might be fixed on you and unborn posterity. But God has effectually wiped away the reproach. The prisoners released will be under peculiar temptations to indulge a hard and bitter spirit towards some who have appeared in evidence against them. That a perfect adherence to propriety in all things, amidst such a series of events, could not be expected. If you have in any instance been injured, it is God's prerogative to avenge the wrong, and not yours, as it is written, 'To me belongeth vengeance and recompense. Dearly beloved, avenge not yourselves, but rather give place unto wrath: for it is written vengeance is mine; I will repay saith the Lord'—Deut. 32:35—Rom. 12:19. You see by what has taken place in your late trials, that God can conduct matters best even for you. Commit all to him. Be of a peaceable forgiving temper. Suppress every unruly passion, and all evil speaking. Let God's goodness so wonderfully displayed, excite you to be merciful, as our Father who is in Heaven is merciful. The general and unusual joy manifested by this and the neighbouring towns, on the return of your deserted brother in law, will I think, incline you to believe that they were not hostile to your life, and did not thirst for human blood. Every countenance expressed gladness, and every tongue hailed the auspicious day. Shouts and rejoicing resounded from house to house, and from town to town. All seemed anxious to drink deep with you in the cup of your deliverance.

However great you prize your escape from prison, how much more ought you to value and seek acquittance and freedom from the fatal bondage of sin and death! This would excite singing of a more sublime and exotic nature. All Heaven would exult in songs that would never, never end!—Luke 15:10. Since the Lord has in so wonderful a manner spared your lives, oh! what obligations are you under to devote the remainder to God. You cannot expect another call so powerful and alarming: and should this be misimproved, may you not consider it an awful presage of inevitable ruin—Prov. 29:1. He that being often reproved, hardeneth his neck, shall suddenly be destroyed, and that without remedy.

The aged parents, who have for months been groaning under the heavy hand of the Almighty, may greatly rejoice.—You have been mourning children devoted to a shameful and untimely death. Had it taken place, perhaps it would have brought down your gray hairs with sorrow to the grave. The miseries that come upon our children should lead us to examine, whether our unfaithfulness to the concerns of their souls has not had influence in the calamities to which they are incident. Every day, especially the shadows of evening did not fail to waft your imaginations to the doleful mansion, that contained your unhappy children, while horrible and frightful scenes of a disgraceful death, disturbed your nightly repose. Every enjoyment of life was embittered, and every walk became solitary. The yearning of the bowels of tender parents over their children, bound in chains, doomed to the gibbet, is taught only by experience. Could you not say with the broken hearted Jacob, "All these things are against me."

The dwellings of a brother and sister becomes a Bochim, and their responsive cries entered the walls of distress. At home, abroad, in the house of God, grief lies heavy on their souls; while every tender feeling of the heart swells the tide of anguish and distress. Could an affectionate sister hear of the fatal destiny of two brothers, and not sink beneath the heart-rending tidings! (Mrs. Richardson, sister of the prisoners, being on a visit to a neighbouring house, on hearing that the sentence of death was pronounced against her brothers, fell prostrate on the floor.) Oh the bitter reflections, the painful sensations among friends, whose mingled sorrows absorb all the pleasures of life!

But why should I harrow up the soul by too minute a detail, or dwell too long on those days of tribulation? They are passed and gone. God has turned your mourning into dancing. Although weeping endured for a long and wearisome night, yet joy came in the morning. Let Jehovah-jirah, the Lord will see and provide, be written on the posts of your door, and on the fleshly tables of your hearts. Let this motto be inscribed in legible and indelible characters, on all your deportment, that he may run that readeth—*The Lord hath done great things for us, whereof we are glad.*

I trust this and the neighbouring towns have, in a degree, by their conduct exemplified that inspired injunction, "Rejoice with them that do rejoice, and weep with them that weep." Their readiness to afford pecuniary relief to the distressed family, is a practical demonstration. It has for months past been a time of peculiar mourning and distress, to see our fellow creatures in wretched confinement, awaiting an awful execution. I trust our prayers have been ascended to Heaven for divine interposition, and the Lord in a mysterious way has granted us deliverance. Through the faithfulness and vigilance of our fellow-citizens, (under God,) the town of Manchester is delivered from the public censure of *Blood-guiltiness*; which otherwise would have clave to them to the latest posterity. All who read and hear this mysterious event, even generations yet to come, will be constrained to exclaim, "Verily there is a God, whose judgments are unsearchable, and his ways past finding out."

I can scarcely persuade myself to quit the subject, altho' it will be a kind of repetition, without advertising to that ecstacy and delight, with which we beheld the devoted man quit his direful abode. He was waiting between hope and fear, until the glad tidings were proclaimed—the prison-door opened, the chains unriveted, and he welcomed to the light. May it not reprove such who are under the sentence of God's law; prisoners of hope, and will not come out. O! that I could with success proclaim in your ears this day the expostulatory declaration of the great deliverer, Is. 61. The spirit of the Lord God is upon me; because the Lord hath anointed me to preach good tidings unto the meek: he hath sent me to bind up the broken hearted; to proclaim liberty to the captives, and the opening of the prison to them that are bound. Let me say to the prisoners, Go forth! To you that are in darkness, Shew yourselves. The door is thrown wide open—Jesus is ready to break your bonds asunder. Angels invite—yea, all Heaven stands ready to shout your deliverance through the streets of New-Jerusalem. The nature of our inability can be inferred by seeing the prisoner escape when the door is unlocked, that it is of the moral kind, being bound only with the cords of our sins, unwilling to depart. We are not convened this day to witness the awful death of a fellow mortal, suspended between the Heavens and the earth—Nor to hear the bitter sighs, or behold the distorted image of a devoted malefactor; but to hear the jubilee trumpet proclaiming salvation. Turn ye to the strong hold, ye prisoners of hope. May the arm of the Lord be revealed. Amen.

Sinners, Make Haste

The manuscript of this sermon, in Haynes' hand, is held by a private collector. Dated October 9, 1829, it has not been previously published. A few silent corrections have been made in Haynes' spelling and punctuation.

———

Sinners, Make Haste

Luke 19:5. And when Jesus came to the place he looked up and saw him and said Zaccheus make haste and come down: for today I must abide at thine house.

Among the many instances of sovereign grace recorded in the sacred volume that of the conversion of Zaccheus the publican is worthy of our serious attention. Let us dwell upon the subject of divine mercy before us, upon the conduct of the Saviour toward him, and the blessed effect produced.

His name was Zaccheus which shows that he was a Jew. Probably this was a common name among the Jews says Dr. Hugh Doddridge and Scott. [Zaccheus was] descended from them. Ex. 2:9. God often has the names of his chosen ones recorded that they may be had in everlasting remembrance. Ps. 112:6.

We have his occupation or employment. He was a publican or tax gatherer of the Roman Emperor or a receiver general. This rendered him odious in the sight of the Jews.

We have his character. He extorted from others more than was his due. This he virtually confesses. He had taken by false usurpation and in this way became rich.

He had a mind to see Jesus, only out of curiosity tis likely.

He labored under some inability. He was small in stature and could not on account of the crowd that followed the Saviour have access to him.

Doubtless he was so odious and contemptible in the eyes of the throng that they would wish to have him stand back.

We have the method he took to overcome the difficulty. Tis said he ran before which showed his engagedness and climbed up into a sycamore tree. In Egypt they are called Egyptian fig-trees; they grow as large and plenty as our oak.

A question may now be asked: Is it best for sinners to seek a sight of Christ with the temper of Zaccheus? Answer: Tis best to seek according to God's appointment. There is no holiness in it and no promise annexed to such seeking. Yet there is more encouragement as God blesses means. Some think Zaccheus' climbing up on this tree is an intimation of the soaring imagination of sinners who would exalt themselves above God.

Secondly, we may attend to the conduct of the Saviour. Christ knew all the affair. It was not by chance [Greek phrase]. He knew him by name. Perhaps he had never had an interview with him before but being infinite in knowledge as God, knew his name. He knew him to be his sheep long sought. He looked up. It was a look of condescention for Jesus to take any notice of him or stop under the tree. The multitude would not. [It was not] a look of pity or a compassionate look as he did on Peter. [It was] a look of reproof. Why dost thou stay on the tree since thou hast got a sight of me? He speaks to him, calls him by name, Zaccheus. It is a great thing to hear Christ's voice as directed to us in particular: John, Mary, etc., I call on thee.

> "Ephriam, what shall I do he cries
> To bring you back to me?
> Trust so with pity in his eyes
> He speaks my soul to *thee*."

It was a powerful efficatious look. He says make haste and come down. Jesus speaks as one [having] authority. Matt. 7:29. A reason is given or a motive assigned why he should come down. Zaccheus might tremble through fear: he is about to expose all my wickedness before the multitude and execute vengeance on me for all my wickedness, and is about to sink me from this tree into a pit of endless burning. But Oh! astonishing grace, It is today I must abide at thine house. Come down and accompany me to your apartment. Open your door that I may impart grace to your unconverted children. I must spend the whole day with you. Make haste.

Thirdly, the effect is worthy of notice. Ver. 6. And he made haste and came down and received him joyfully. He was obedient. He came down and that in haste. His obedience was not a mere local one to come down with the body through the laws of gravitation but voluntarily a motion of the whole soul which longed to be at the feet of Jesus.

The propriety of such immediate obedience will appear by considering:

1. Christ's call says make haste. This shows its importance.

2. We are as able as ever we shall be except the Lord appears. He is as ready now to assist us if we are willing as he will ever be. By delay we are more unable.

3. Haste is required as Christ is under a kind of necessity of saving him or house and household as *oikos* often signifies. I *must* abide. Zaccheus was his sheep. Christ had stipulated with the Father to save him and house and it must be done.

4. Religion requires haste in that there is no case of equal importance that can be named in the natural world whether in sickness, exposedness to death or enemies, etc. We are exposed to an infinite loss. Christ might soon go on and Zaccheus would lose his soul. Tis often now or never.

> "Infinite joy or endless woe
> Depend on every breath
> And yet how unconcerned we go
> Upon the brink of death."
> —Watts

5. We have the examples of holy beings. See David, 119 Ps. 60 verse. Ez. 10:6 and Gal. 1:16. Above all Jesus Christ. He came leaping over the mountain, skipping over the hills.

> "With pitying eyes the prince of grace
> Beheld our helpless grief.
> He saw and O amazing love
> He *ran* to our relief."

6. Our families' dying state calls on us to make haste. This was the case of the publican. Our children are struck with death. They need salvation today. None can heal them but the Lord Jesus Christ.

Another effect produced in the mind of Zaccheus was: He received him joyfully. Take notice of the object received. It was *Him* viz. John 1-12. Many will receive God's mercies, the gifts, but turn the giver out of doors.

Are there not many among us of this character? He received him with his heart. Into his house. Received him in his glorious character. Called him Lord, ver. 8. As his Lord and King and Saviour, I Peter, etc. [illegible]. Zaccheus was not ashamed to own Christ before men and take Christ home with him before the multitude, although they despised him.

Another effect of the work of grace on the heart of the publican was: he was willing to confess his sin as in verse 8 and was willing to make ample satisfaction. A benevolent spirit is communicated to him. The half of my goods I give to thee. Probably the half that was left after he had made restitution.

Improvement

1. We are glad to see sinners go where Christ is passing by like Zaccheus and like blind [illegible] though we have no right to direct them to go wrong.

2. Christ is found of them that do not seek him as they ought. Isaiah 6:1. Those who absent from the places where Christ is wont to be are more likely to be damned than those who do attend.

3. One evidence that God is at work among a people is when they attend meetings or public worship.

4. Let professors hear the voice of God who calls on you: Make haste. Christ calls you: Will you not open your hearts and houses? Is he not now passing by? Feel the necessity as John did. Let sinners make haste. [It is] Christ who calls you by name as it were: Come down. Tis a case of life and death. Satan is making haste to destroy you. Death makes haste. Tis [illegible] before you. Sinners awake [illegible]. Be wise.

Outline of a Sermon
on Acts 26:22

Haynes preached this sermon on the occasion of his last visit to Granville, Massachusetts, where he had preached forty years earlier. Now nearly eighty years old, Haynes was clearly conscious of his own mortality, and chose, as usual, a particularly appropriate text.

———

"Having therefore obtained help of God, I continue unto this day."

Acts 26:22

All creatures are effects which declare a first cause. All finite existence, whether natural or moral, is the product of omnipotent power. The great wheels of Divine providence are turned round by the hand of God. The motions of our souls and bodies are alike directed by the agency of him who rolls the stars along. For 'tis a sentiment acknowledged even by heathen,—by Homer, Hesiod, and especially by Aratus, that "we are the offspring of God." (" του γαρ και γενοσ εσμεν Hemistic or half verse."—Guise). With how much propriety, therefore, might St. Paul adopt the sentiment in the text!

The points before us are these:—

I. Our continuance in this world is wholly owing to the help of God.

1. Keeping people alive is ascribed to God. Deut. 32:39: "I kill, and I make alive." Ps. 68:20: "Unto God the Lord belong the issues from death."

2. We cannot keep ourselves alive any more than we can begin to live.

3. Others cannot—physicians cannot—Asa's could not.

4. None of the springs of nature commence without God. Every pulse, every breath the effect of Divine agency.

5. God cannot communicate independent power to men.

6. 'Tis not owing to what some call *fortune, luck,* or *chance.* Such things have no power, nor even existence.

7. That it is by God's help we continue is evident from the many dangers to which we are exposed.

II. We ought to be deeply sensible of this.

1. This is an important trait in the character of God's people,—Paul, Jacob, Caleb, David.

2. 'Tis God's due. Not to acknowledge it is robbing him.

3. Not to acknowledge God is practical atheism.

4. God has given us the requisite faculties—eyes, ears, reason—and is calling us to take notice.

Improvement

1. We should often take a review of past acts of God's goodness.

2. We should not place our ultimate dependence on second causes.

3. God must help for time to come, or we must die. "Boast not of *to-morrow.*"

4. How vile to take that help which God is giving us, and consume it on our lusts.

5. We cannot expect God to help us much longer.

6. Comfort in trials—God's help is sufficient.

7. People live just as long as God chooses—then die.

8. Goodness of God that has helped us to live so long.

Outline of a Sermon on II Cor. 1:9

At the conclusion of his visit to Granville, Haynes preached this sermon on death. He had just visited the cemetery where he had buried many of his early friends and parishioners, and he was contemplating his own end.

———

"But we had the sentence of death in ourselves, that we should not trust in ourselves, but in God which raiseth the dead."

II Cor. 1:9

Some think that the apostle has relation to his fighting with wild beasts at Ephesus, I Cor. 15:32. Others suppose that he refers to the uproar at Lydia or Asia Minor; but that it was an habitual temper of mind for the apostle to feel that he was a *dying man*, is evident from what he observes, I Cor. 15:31: "I die daily." Life and death are terms of the most solemn import. Some suppose life is of more importance than death, as it is that which can render death a blessing or a curse. Suitable reflection on death greatly tends to our right improvement of life. This is the sentiment in the text; and the inspired apostle speaks of it, as belonging not only to himself, but to others. *We* had the sentence of death in *ourselves*.

That we have all reason to view ourselves in this point of light, with the advantages arising therefrom, is the order proposed.

1. God has pronounced the sentence of death on us, and why should not we on ourselves? Gen. 3:19.

2. We may with propriety have the sentence in ourselves by viewing the providences of God. How many are dying around us! Is there any thing to

secure us from death which they had not? Are we young? so were they. Old, middle aged, full of worldly schemes?—was not this the case with them?

3. Weak state of our bodies.

4. Pains we feel from day to day.

5. Many instruments stand ready to destroy us. In the case of Paul, wild beasts—wicked men and devils—perils from sea and land.

> "We stand as in a battle, throngs on throngs
> Are falling round us, wounded oft ourselves."

6. We cannot resist or ward off the stroke, I Cor. 4:9: "For I think that God hath set forth us the apostles last as it were appointed unto death." This is thought to be an allusion to the Roman theatrical sports; for, from a passage in Seneca's epistles, quoted by Dr. Whitby, it appears, that in the morning those prisoners to whom they gave a chance of escaping with their lives fought with the wild beasts armed; but, in the afternoon, the gladiators fought unarmed.

7. By our sins we expose ourselves to the sentence of death. Justice, and abused patience, and mercy, cry, "Cut them down!"

8. All need carry the sentence of death in themselves. All have sinned—old and young—rich and poor—saints and sinners.

9. At *all times* and on all occasions—at home or abroad—awake or asleep.

> "Whate'er we do, where'er we be,
> We're travelling to the grave."

Finally, it has been the case with the people of God—pilgrims and strangers on the earth. Even Jesus Christ, though innocent, for our sake carried the sentence of death in himself.

Advantages

1. 'Tis acting rationally—correspondent to truth and divine exhibition.

2. To have the sentence of death in ourselves is complying with the word of God. Christ said repeatedly, "Watch."

3. It tends to wean us from the world. Did we hear the sentence of death sounding in our ears, should we be elated with worldly prospects?

4. Having the sentence of death in ourselves tends to make us diligent in the things of religion. Keeping death at a distance is the fruitful source of the sin of procrastination.

5. This is the way to obtain the victory over death. The reason why death is so terrible to many is, that they think so little of it, and are deaf to the sound and sentence of it.

6. Having the sentence of death in us leads to the use of means necessary to salvation. We see men, when death in their apprehension is approaching, wishing prayers and visits from ministers.

7. It supports under sufferings, II Cor. 4:17.

8. It will influence to self-examination. When the midnight cry is made, it is time to see whether our lamps are trimmed and burning.

Improvement

1. We see that there is evidently a controversy between God and mankind in general, in relation to the subject that has been discussed. God has pronounced the sentence of death on men, but they practically deny it, and pronounce the sentence of life.

2. There is the same propriety in treating our fellow-creatures as dying men, as there is when actually dying. Some that are now well may die before them.

3. Thoughtlessness about death is a source of great evil to men. 'Tis so in respect to families—closets—house of God—visits—death-beds.

4. We have reason to fear that the unconverted will never be saved. They are dying, yet neglect salvation.

5. Sinners are in a dreadful state. Under sentence of death, temporal, spiritual, and eternal.

Outline of a Sermon on Zech. 11:13

Haynes' biographer Timothy Mather Cooley used this sermon outline to demonstrate Haynes' ingenuity in the organization of his sermons. "Although he followed the method of the old divines," Cooley wrote, "in the multiplicity of his divisions, yet he never said 8thly or 9thly without a thought which richly rewarded the attention of the hearer."

———

"A goodly price that I was prized at of them."

Zech. 11:13

There are people to be found who sell the Lord Jesus, and are wicked enough to think they make a good bargain.

I. Who are those that sell the Lord Jesus Christ.

II. Whence it appears that they think they have sold him for a "goodly price," or traded well.

III. Expose the folly and criminality of their conduct.

Improvement

1. Were Christ personally here, he would fare no better than he did in the days of his flesh.

2. No wonder God has controversy with us;—*we have sold Christ.*

3. When God converts a sinner, he disannuls the soul-destroying bargain.

4. When he damns the sinner, he ratifies the bargain which he has made.

5. 'Tis more dangerous selling Christ than formerly. Truth of Christianity is more confirmed.

6. This conduct of men should be a town-talk. The reason why it is not is, that so many are in the trade.

7. All should do what they can to break up such bargains.

8. Examine—Have you sold Christ? Is it not written on your conduct—on the doors of your houses—your closets—your pew-doors—"CHRIST SOLD HERE?"

On Baptism

A fair copy of this manuscript, not in Haynes' hand, is held by the Schomburg Center for Research in Black Culture, The New York Public Library. The provenance is unknown, but it was most likely acquired by Arthur A. Schomburg himself. It was edited, titled, and first published by Richard Newman in the *Bulletin of Research in the Humanities* for 1986-1987.

———

In searching the scriptures of truth, I find on sacred record six several [i.e., separate or different] sorts of baptism.

Firstly, the Levitical baptism, Heb. 9.

Secondly, the baptism of fear or repentance, as Matt. 3 to 6, also in Luke 7:37, etc.

Thirdly, the baptism of affliction or martyrdom as our blessed saviour himself expresseth it in Luke 12 and in Matt. 20:22-23.

Fourthly, the baptism of the Holy Ghost, Acts 1:5, as on the day of Pentecost when the apostles received the gift of the Holy Ghost.

Fifth, the baptism of Christian faith or doctrine knowledge, Acts 18:25-26.

Also, there is the sacrament of baptism which we are now to speak of, as in Matt. 28:19, Mark 16:16, also Romans 6:3-4.

Baptism is commonly taken to be twofold—external and internal, viz., of water and of the spirit. The outward part is only the washing [of] the body with water and the minister's using the words of institution: Father, Son, and Holy Ghost. But the internal part is by the operation of the Holy Ghost applying the blood of Christ to the soul for justification in the sight of God, or the washing away [of] the filth of sin as sanctification by the spirit of Christ in the work of regeneration or new birth, John 3:3 and Rev. 1, the last clause of the fifth verse.

[In] Matt. 3:2 we find John the Baptist calls us to repentance. [He does so] again in verse 8, and directs us to confess our sins. In order [to prepare] for baptism so likewise doth Peter in Acts 2:38, etc. We also find that Philip directs the eunuch to believe with all his heart. And he answered and said, I believe that Jesus Christ is the Son of God, Acts 8:36, etc. Paul saith, For without faith it is impossible to please God. And James saith in his epistle that faith is dead being alone, as in James 2:17 and 26; and let us see what he saith in the 10th and 14th verses.

We also find in the centurion's conversion that the Holy Ghost was poured out on them [i.e., those] of the gentiles before they received the sacrament of baptism, and that they spake with tongues and magnified God. Then answered Peter and said, Can any man forbid water, that these should not be baptized[?], Acts 10:44 to the end. Our saviour saith to the Jews that believed on him, If ye continue in my word, then ye are my disciples, John 8:31. Here we find that we must continue in his word and do whatsoever he commands us or we cannot be his disciples.

Here then let us inquire what he commands us in his word to do. In the first place, he commands us to fear God and keep his commandments. In the second place, he commands us to repent and believe, and saith, Believe in God, believe also in me, for in my father's house are many mansions. Believe that I am the way, the truth, and the life, and that no man can come to the father but by me, for there is no other name given under heaven among men whereby we can be saved. He also saith, Bring forth works, meet [i.e., fit] for repentance. And be baptized in my name for the remission of sins.

Well, then, if we continue in his word we find that it is necessary that we bring forth works, and how can we bring forth works of repentance without confessing and forsaking all known sins, whether sins of omission or commission? And doing justice, loving mercy, and walking humbly with our God? Or how can it be said that we continue in his word or walk with God if we do not whatsoever he commands us by giving ourselves to him who first gave himself for us, and attending on all his ordinances?

Again, God saith in Proverbs, My son, give me thy heart, which implies that we must devote ourselves to him by keeping his commandments. If our hearts are given to God in baptism, as surely they must be when we take on ourselves the baptism covenant, surely we devote ourselves to him, to be for him and not for another. Then if we have devoted ourselves to God and accepted of Christ as he is exhibited to us in the gospel, surely we must keep his commandments. If we neglect to obey his dying command, saying, Do this in remembrance of me, or when we live in [illegible] of known duty, how can we suppose that we love God and Christ if we continue to disobey their commands? For God saith in his word, To obey is better than sacrifice, and to hearken than the fat of rams. Christ saith, Why call ye me Lord, Lord, and do not the things which I say? Luke 6:46.

Whenever a person takes on him the baptism covenant and is baptized into the all-adorable Trinity, he solemnly gives himself to God and accepts of Christ as prophet, priest, and king, and thereby professeth that he is as willing to be ruled by his laws as to be saved by his merit. Then surely all such as have devoted themselves to God by owning the baptism covenant and do not attend on all the ordinances which God hath appointed in his word do in effect mock God by calling Christ their Lord when they thus publically own his authority over them, profess to believe in him, expect salvation by him—and yet live in neglect of doing the things which he as Lord saith to them and requires of them.

Again, every person that professeth Christianity and consents personally to the baptism covenant is thereby externally marked for Christ's. He should be wholly for him and not for any other, and does, as it were, say before God, angels, and men that God is his father, creator, and preserver, and that he will live to him and magnify his name by showing forth to the world that Jesus is the Christ and redeemer of men and that he expects salvation by him from sin by what he has done and suffered for him in his stead, not only to be saved from sin but to be completely happy after death through the merit of Christ who ever lives to make intercession at God's right hand for him. And that God the Holy Ghost is his for sanctification by applying the purchase or merit of Christ's blood to his soul for justification before God. Thus every true Christian believes in God, and thus every nominal Christian professeth to believe.

Well, then, if a Christian does profess in such a manner as we have heard, certainly he has a right to all the ordinances which God hath appointed in his word. And if he does not attend on all the ordinances, the sin of omission lieth at his door, for God saith in his word to every believer, I have espoused unto you one husband, even unto Christ, and whatsoever God hath joined together, let no man put asunder.

Once more then, if we are baptized persons and have taken on ourselves the baptism vow, we do renounce the world, the flesh, and the devil, with all their carnal profits and gratifications whereby God is dishonored, religion wounded, or the spirit of grace resisted. We will take the holy scriptures for our rule of faith and life. We do engage to keep close to Christ's precepts, love and obey him with thankfulness for what he hath done for the salvation of our souls as he shall enable us by his spirit, by living in the constant expectation of death, judgment, and eternity. This is the nature and purport of our engagements when professing Christianity, and this is the substance of all our religion.

If after this solemn profession of faith and promising obedience to him, we live in sin by neglecting known duty and thereby cast his laws and ordinances behind our backs, don't we mock Christ with them in Matt. 27:29-30? Or don't we in practice say as the Jews did of old that we will not have this man to rule over us? Well, then, if in practice we deny what in words we profess, don't we mock God? And if we say we repent and believe and yet live in sin of omission, can anyone suppose that our repentance is sincere? And don't a church that consents to let persons who profess Christianity live in total neglect of duty, does not such a church trifle with the ordinances of God that are enjoined upon them? Don't they suffer sin to be upon themselves and their brother likewise?

Selected Bibliography

Adams, Doug. *Humor in the American Pulpit from George Whitefield through Henry Ward Beecher*. Austin: The Sharing Co., 1975.

Ashley, Robert. "Wilkie Collins and a Vermont Murder Trial." *The New England Quarterly* 21 (September 1948), 368-73.

Bogin, Ruth. "Notes and Documents. 'Liberty Further Extended': A 1776 Antislavery Manuscript by Lemuel Haynes." *The William and Mary Quarterly* 40 (January 1983), 85-105.

Bogin, Ruth. "Notes and Documents. 'The Battle of Lexington': A Patriotic Ballad by Lemuel Haynes." *The William and Mary Quarterly* 42 (October 1985), 499-506.

Brown, Richard D. " 'Not Only Extreme Poverty, but the Worst Kind of Orphanage': Lemuel Haynes and the Boundaries of Racial Tolerance on the Yankee Frontier, 1770-1820." *The New England Quarterly* 61:4 (December 1988), 502-18.

Burnham, Roderick H. *Genealogical Records of Henry and Ulalia Burt, the Emigrants, Who Early Settled in Springfield, Mass., and Their Descendants through Nine Generations, from 1640 to 1891*. Warwick: Elizabeth Burt, 1892.

Carvalho, Joseph. *Black Families in Hamden County, Massachusetts, 1650-1855*. Boston: New England Historic Genealogical Society and Institute for Massachusetts Studies, Westfield State College, 1984.

Cooley, Timothy Mather. *Sketches of the Life and Character of The Rev. Lemuel Haynes, A.M., for Many Years Pastor of a Church in Rutland, Vt., and Late in Granville, New-York. . . .* New York: Harper and Brothers, 1837. Reprinted 1969.

Coughlin, Ellen K. "A Black Preacher Decries Slavery." *The Chronicle of Higher Education* 26:6 (April 6, 1983), 27.

[Hileman, Gregor]. "The Remarkable Life of a 'Poor Hell-Deserving Sinner.' " *Middlebury College News Letter* 47 (Spring 1973), 4-11.

Kaplan, Sidney, and Emma Nogrady Kaplan. *The Black Presence in the Era of the American Revolution, 1770-1800*. Revised edition. Amherst: University of Massachusetts Press, 1989.

245

MacLam, Helen M. "Black Puritan on the Northern Frontier: The Vermont Ministry of Lemuel Haynes." *In* David W. Wills and Richard Newman, eds., *Black Apostles at Home and Abroad: Afro-Americans and the Christian Mission from the Revolution to Reconstruction.* Boston: G. K. Hall, 1982, pp. 3-20.

MacLam, Helen M. "The Search for Lemuel Haynes." *Dartmouth College Library Bulletin* 17 (November 1976), 21-26.

⟜ Mitchell, Robert W. "Lemuel Haynes: The Search for History." *Vermont Sunday Magazine* (July 1, 1984), 4-5, 12-13.

Newman, Richard. *Lemuel Haynes: A Bio-Bibliography.* Foreword by James M. Washington. New York: Lambeth Press, 1984.

Newman, Richard. "Lemuel Haynes on Baptism: An Unpublished Manuscript from the Schomburg Center for Research in Black Culture." *Bulletin of Research in the Humanities* 87:4 (1986-1987; i.e., 1989), 509-14.

⟜ Newman, Richard. " 'The Presence of the Lord': An Unpublished Sermon by Lemuel Haynes." *Bulletin of the Congregational Library* 32:1 (Fall 1980), 4-12.

Tuttle, Charles E., Jr. *Vermont and the Anti-Slavery Movement.* Unpublished B.A. honors thesis, Harvard University, March 1, 1937.

About the Contributors

Richard Newman, head of publications at The New York Public Library, is the author or editor of a dozen books in African-American studies. The most recent are *Black Power and Black Religion* (1987) and *Words Like Freedom: Afro-American Books and Manuscripts in the Berg Collection* (1989). He is currently writing a biography of Florence Mills.

Mechal Sobel is Associate Professor of History at the University of Haifa and the author of *The World They Made Together: Black and White Values in Eighteenth-Century Virginia* (1987).

Helen MacLam is Social Science editor at *Choice* magazine and the author of several articles on Lemuel Haynes.

Index